Virginia B Treadwell

A HANDBOOK OF POPULAR ANTIQUES

A HANDBOOK OF
Popular Antiques

Katharine Morrison McClinton

Published by **RANDOM HOUSE** *New York*

CONTENTS

ILLUSTRATIONS

vii

viii

FOREWORD

A HUNDRED years from now someone will be collecting ration books, cigarette cases, comic strips, face-powder compacts, amateur kodachromes. These and many other convenient gadgets that are commonplaces to us today will be more than curiosities to the collector of the future. They will be, in their small way, a part of human history. They will be the tangible record of various aspects of everyday living which we now take for granted—little customs and habits and passing vogues which seem so unimportant that they will never get into the history books, but which are nevertheless a quite essential part of life in America in the 1940's.

Today people are collecting the same sort of little everyday articles of a hundred years ago and more—such things as snuff boxes, paperweights, buttons, silhouette portraits and even shaving mugs. These objects are not exceedingly old, as antiques go. Many of them are not particularly beautiful, according to generally accepted aesthetic standards. Many are not rare. And most of them are not expensive today, nor were they when they were new. But they are worth collecting for historical reasons. While it may sound pompous to say it, they reveal a facet of the civilization of the past, for they can tell a great deal about the people who made them and those who first owned and enjoyed them. In that respect, they are comparable to the gold earrings and the tear bottles from the tombs of Egypt which we see in our museums.

Such things are popular antiques, not in the sense that Donald Duck is popular, but in the sense that they are closely related to people. They were made for personal or home use and adornment, and they belonged to the many rather than to the few. As intimate and eloquent souvenirs of a closed era, they deserve to be popular among collectors today.

Foreword

Collecting is fun, and that is the best reason for collecting. There is no need to make it a ponderous business. But I have noticed that the collectors who get the most fun from their collecting are those who have a certain seriousness of purpose. They really study their antiques and learn all they can about how and when and where and why they were made. They see them in relation to their period, as part of the surroundings of once-living people, not as objects in a curio cabinet. In other words, through their antiques they bring the past to life. In doing that they enlarge immeasurably their own capacity for enjoying their collecting.

That, I believe, is why Mrs. McClinton has written this book. It is not a book to lure you into sentimentalizing over the quaint old bibelots of yesteryear, or into indiscriminately accumulating worthless objects—as I collected horse chestnuts when I was a child. It is a book to give you serious information about many things—which in themselves are not very serious—so that you may get more fun out of collecting these popular antiques. If, besides, it makes the very collecting of antiques an even more popular pursuit than it is already, so much the better.

Alice Winchester

Editor, *The Magazine* ANTIQUES

INTRODUCTION

THE collecting of antiques has greatly changed since the days when the collector exclaimed over the "charm" and "lure" of his hobby. Even if he collects only the less-expensive objects, he now wants to know exactly what to expect and what to look for. He wants to know the scarcity of the objects, their comparative values and their identifying marks.

The purpose of this book is to satisfy these specific needs of the collector. The subjects have been chosen with particular reference to what is available in the shops today. From this stock, objects have been selected which will appeal to a variety of tastes, to beginning as well as to advanced collectors, to the small as well as to the large bank account.

I have treated some subjects not fully covered in other volumes, and, I hope, have added new and useful data. Throughout the book I have endeavored to point out the intrinsic qualities which make a collection worth while and which should make it appreciate in value as the years go by. As Homer Eaton Keyes once said, "The difference between a collector and an accumulator is largely determined by relative sensitiveness to the quality of contours and proportions in objects of artistic import and to the propriety of their decorative treatment." In present-day collecting there is not enough attention given to these qualities, for the reason that few collectors have sufficient understanding of design or color or historical background.

I want to thank all those who have assisted in the preparation of this book for their numerous courtesies, especially the following:

The New York Historical Society: Miss Dorothy C. Barck, Librarian, Miss Carolyn Scoon, Registrar, Donald A. Shelley, Curator of Paintings and Arthur Carlson, Print Department; Metropolitan Museum

xi

Introduction

of Art: especially Miss C. Louise Avery, the Library Staff, Miss Jessie Matson, Library Cataloguer, and Miss Elisabeth Narramore; The Museum of the City of New York: Miss Grace Mayer, Print Department, and Miss Isabell Miller; Museum Staff of Cooper Union; Miss Elizabeth Hall of the New York Botanical Gardens Library; The New York Horticultural Society; Ruth Sterling Benjamin, Curator of "Home, Sweet Home," East Hampton, Long Island; Gregor Norman-Wilcox, Curator of Decorative Arts, Los Angeles County Museum, Los Angeles, California; Mrs. Hazel Webster; Mr. Albert Shannon, Lord & Taylor; Douglas Carson of Steuben Glass, Inc.; M. M. Lourens of The Netherlands Information Bureau; Earl L. Poole, Director of the Reading Museum and Art Gallery, Reading, Pennsylvania; The Pennsylvania Museum of Art, Philadelphia, Pennsylvania; Mr. J. E. Treleaven of Needham's Antiques; Robert Abels, W. Porter Ware, Laura Tanner of *House Beautiful;* Harry MacNeill Bland; Charles Woolsey Lyon; The Old Button Shop; and the following collectors whose collections I have studied: Charles W. Green, M.D.; S. Weldon O'Brien; A. H. Merritt, D.D.S.; Warren F. Kaynor; Mr. and Mrs. A. E. Coddington; Samson Selig; Earl Robacher; Mrs. Douglas Sutherland; Marguerite Maples; Philip Medicus and Raymond Riling. Mr. William Sherman and Robert Emlen of Copeland & Thompson; Mr. John Goddard, President, and Maddock & Miller, New York representatives of Geo. L. Ashworth & Bros. Ltd., Hanley, Stoke-on-Trent.

Chapter 1

IRONSTONE CHINA

IRONSTONE china is a neglected field for the collector and it is still obtainable. However, while there is a great deal of late dark-transfer ironstone and also plain white ironstone on the market, the really fine hand-decorated pieces, which compare favorably with old Worcester and other old English wares, are harder to find.

Ironstone china is a hard porcelain-like earthenware. Although it has the hardness and fine surface of porcelain, it is opaque, while porcelain is transparent when held to the light.

The invention of ironstone is attributed to Josiah Spode, II, who first made it in 1805. However, prior to that date, Miles Mason of Lane Delph was experimenting with a china formula that reproduced the appearance of Chinese porcelain, and in 1813, when Mason's son, Charles James Mason, took out the patent, it was listed as an "improvement on ironstone china." Both Spode's and Mason's ironstone are desirable, and old pieces from either factory are the finest examples of ironstone that the collector can find. Although complete dinner sets were made, plates are the most available items today, and the information in this chapter refers to plates, which, incidentally, are the best way to study china patterns. Spode's stone china closely resembles porcelain but, like Mason's, it is an earthenware. Its blue-white color was made in imitation of Chinese ware and the patterns were also copied from the Chinese. Many Chinese plates have their exact prototypes in Spode stone china.

The first use to which Spode's stone ware was put was in the copying of so-called Lowestoft patterns. The English nobility at this time had their armorial or initialed table ware made in China, but replacements were so slow that English potters were finally called upon to make these replacements. The old pattern books of the Spode factory contain many so-called Lowestoft patterns. In fact, many pieces in old Lowestoft sets were made as replacements at the Spode factory. While such pieces are usually unmarked they have been found with "Spode" impressed in small letters. These patterns include crests and coats of arms and initials in shields with borders of small floral or leaf patterns or delicate ribbons.

A well-known pattern on Spode's Lowestoft is Willis #2147, called Tree of Life by antique dealers. It is a design of the *famille rose* type, with center and rim motifs of peonies and other flowers, and a butterfly. It is painted in blue, green, yellow, brown and pink. The mark is printed in black with the name "Spode" set on a rectangle of fretwork.

Patterns on Spode's Lowestoft also include *Queen Charlotte's* pattern which was selected on Her Majesty's visit to the Spode factory in 1817. It is decorated in blue and has a butterfly border and a Chinese landscape center and is a version of the old willow pattern. This design was first made by Minton in 1783 and was also used on earthenware.

While many designs from the Spode factory and especially those on stone were copied from Chinese sources, others were adapted, the Spode adaptation usually being more elaborate than the simple Chinese original. Two types of old Chinese porcelain influenced Spode. First, the old blue-and-white Nankin designs with pagoda and landscape center and the well-known blue butterfly border; second, the *famille rose* porcelain designs of the Yung Cheng period of 1734. These latter patterns were in polychrome with gold and had floral and bird motifs. These Chinese designs had also been employed on the earlier output of the Spode factory including both earthenware and bone china. In fact, the presence of a design on stone does not mean that it was exclusively used on stone.

The pattern numbers on early Spode china are marked in red on the backs of pieces in addition to the other factory mark, but a certain number on a plate does not necessarily mean that the plate was made of stone

4

or bone china or that the pattern was first used on that particular plate. However, the low numbers do indicate an early date, and enough definite information concerning the relation between date and marks and pattern numbers has been found to allow us to place a piece within certain years even if the exact date cannot be ascertained.

There are many patterns of early Spode stone which are available to the collector today. One of the earliest is an unidentified pattern, #2054, the number placing it between 1800 and 1810. The plate has a floral Chinese design in a circle in the center and three large sprays of flowers between the center and border, and a narrow edge of fretwork. This is marked "Spode New Japan," a rare mark. Chinese Crackle or Marble has large hand-colored prunus flowers on a crackle ground. This is an early pattern and is marked "Spode's New Stone," impressed.

Cabbage, #2061, is a pattern with a large leaf and flowers. It is printed in blue and filled in by hand in blue, gold, rose and Chinese red. The mark is "Spode Stone China," printed in blue, and the pattern number is painted in red. Peacock, #2118, dated 1814 by Jewitt, is also one of the earliest and most popular patterns even today. The design is of birds and peonies in gold and colors in the *famille rose* style, and it has an earlier border known as India edge. The oldest Peacock pieces are marked "Spode's New Stone," impressed, and the pattern, #2118, painted in red. This is an early and rare mark. Bude, #2232, has the printed fretwork mark. The design is of Chinese peonies, bamboo and birds, printed in blue, and painted in dull yellow and faun. It has a brown painted edge which is found on many old patterns, but is also still used on patterns of present-day Spode china. Pattern #2283 is early; however, it shows a definite Japanese Imari influence. The center has a formal oriental basket of flowers and medallions; fan motifs and large flowers are placed amid leaves on the remainder of the plate's surface. The design is completely hand-colored in Chinese red, blue and gold. The reverse of the plate has two flower sprays and a blue-printed fretwork mark, and the pattern number painted in red.

Landscape, #2857, is printed in blue with a Chinese diaper pattern on the rim and Chinese figures in blue and gold in the border, while the center landscape scene of water and buildings is painted in colors. The plate is marked with a blue-printed fretwork mark. Bang-up pattern, although found with various numbers and in several colorings, was first made in polychrome. It is a pattern of Chinese flowers with an English adaptation. The mark on the polychrome #2886 is the Spode printed fretwork mark in blue. Other Bang-up patterns have variations in the borders or coloring, and do not have the bracket border around the center flower group.

Bang-up, #3504, is printed in blue and has an impressed mark, "Spode's New Stone." The design is painted in blue, Chinese red and gold. Bang-up, #3769, is printed in blue with gold outlines and has a star border. It has an impressed mark, "Spode's New Stone."

Ship and Star, #3067, has the Spode printed fretwork mark. It is a charming pattern of a ship, buildings and figures set in a center cartouche and has a star border printed in brown. Ship and Star, #3134, is printed in blue. Both plates have the colors filled in by hand. The printed mark usually matches the color used in the printing of the design and is brown on the brown-printed plate and blue on the blue-printed plate. The brown printing is found on the earlier plate.

Kings Regiment, a design of vases of flowers and a border of Chinese scrollwork, is painted in blue, Chinese red and green outlined in gold.

George IV, #3248, was first made for the Coronation of George IV on July 19, 1821. The center of the plate has a design of Chinese still-life motifs with flowers and vases and it has a heavy ornate border. The colors are blue, Chinese red and gold. It is marked "Spode's Stone China" in blue and carries the inscription and date of the Coronation. The service is still in Windsor Castle. This pattern gives us an exact date from which to date other pieces, and from this date Jewitt's placing of Peacock, #2118, in 1814 seems correct. 100 Antiques, #4155, is another interesting pattern. It is printed in blue on white and has hand-painted decorations in Chinese red and gold. The center design has a Chinese seal and still-life groups of vases, scrolls, etc., and the border is Firbob. The mark is impressed "Spode's New Stone." A set of this china was made for the British Second West Indian Regiment and some of the plates are printed in blue with this inscription. The number dates the plates in the late 1820's.

Grasshopper is an old Chinese design used on stone china. It is printed in blue on white and usually has the blue-printed mark.

Bow-pot was made on stone china in the early nineteenth century. The outline was printed under the glaze and the enameling done over the glaze. The pattern shows Chinese vases with flowers and fruit, two in the foreground and one on a low table. The border is of four sprays of flowers, two single flowers and two butterflies. This pattern is also found on bone china and plain earthenware.

Flower-Vase has one vase of flowers set within a landscape. The border is of flowers and scrolls. It is printed in brown, and the colors are filled in by hand. It is a much later pattern, but some Chinese influence is still seen.

The story of Mason's ironstone china is no less interesting than that of Spode. Miles Mason, the father of Charles Mason, the patentee of Mason's ironstone china, owned a china shop in Fenchurch Street, London, where he sold East Indian china. Finding that his customers were not inclined to wait for breakage replacements from the East, and also because of the heavy duties, Miles Mason decided to manufacture china "upon the principle of the Indian and Seve china." He opened works at Lane Delph near Newcastle-under-Lyme in about 1780, and sought to manufacture china superior to Indian Nankin china. He also proposed "to renew or match the impaired or broken services of the nobility or gentry. The articles are stamped on the bottom of the large pieces to prevent imposition." An invoice of 1797 lists blue dessert ware sets, each consisting of "1 centerpiece, 4 shells, 2 hearts, 2 cucum. tureens,

7

dishes and stands, and 24 dessert shapes; melon shapes, squares, oval and round baking dishes, oval and square salad dishes, Nankeen spitting pots, etc." Mason was so successful that in 1805 he moved to a larger factory.

Miles Mason's marks were "Miles Mason," "M. Mason," or "Miles Mason" with a small square Chinese seal. The marks were impressed. Pieces with these marks are very rare. These are before the ironstone patent and are not ironstone proper. One such early piece is a porcelain plate with a flower and ribbon decoration associated with Lowestoft. It is in the Victoria and Albert Museum. It is marked, "Mason," impressed. A pale-blue willow design is also of this period, but the china has much of the quality of the later ironstone. Much of the coloring on the old pieces is blue and Chinese red. The designs are printed in one color, and gold and other colors are painted in by hand.

From 1800 to 1805, the mark was "C. J. Mason & Co. Lane Delph" in a cartouche printed on the ware. In 1805, "Fenton Stone Works" was the printed mark and was used until 1813, when the impressed mark, "Mason's Ironstone China" and the printed mark, "Mason's Patent Ironstone China" on a scroll with a crown above, came into use. On plates with a willow pattern the name of the pattern, such as "Mason's Cambrian Argil," was printed.

It was Charles James Mason who made the enormous vases, about three feet high, of oriental pattern. He also made chimney pieces of ironstone china with medallions of oriental designs, which are still in existence. These are usually impressed "Mason's Ironstone China."

Patterns on Mason's ironstone china are oriental in character. Blue and vermilion red are the predominating colors, but polychrome designs of the *famille rose* type, including rose, green, yellow and blue were also used, as were heavy Imari patterns with bold coloring. The first design made in Mason's ironstone and which is still being used, shows a peacock or pheasant on a branch with peonies and an oriental tree. The border is of several sprays of flowers with a lacy conventional printed edge.

Ironstone China

Another old pattern was the Bible or Mercia, as it is now called, which shows an open book in the foreground with Chinese peonies and other flowers, and has a border of floral sprays in the oriental manner. Variations of an oriental flavor using such detail as large peonies, leaves, vases with feathers, and trees within fences of Chinese fretwork, as well as medallions with scenes of Chinese gardens with figures, are typical subject matter on the earlier Mason's ironstone. Motifs of Chinese vase forms, both tall and round vases with flowers or feathers, are used again and again on Mason's ironstone. Borders are either in flower sprays or a design of Chinese fretwork or scrolls, or clouds with small all-over patterns. Many patterns also drew inspiration from bold Japanese Imari designs.

Old Mason's ironstone patterns were not named, but were known by their number or shape such as Nankin Shape, Bedford Shape or Ningpo Shape. Jugs were Hydra Shape and Mason Shape. Indian Vases have Chinese forms and often have red and green dragon or lizard handles, and other Chinese animals are used as finials on the tops of the lids. Mugs and ewers have dragon handles also. These ewers or pitchers were made in as many as ten different sizes and have a squatty, octagonal, angular form known as Hydra Shape. Typical colors on jugs are red and blue, red and gray, and green and white.

In the catalogue of the London Exposition of 1851, some of the items listed on exhibition by Charles Mason were: "Jars with raised enamel mandarin figures and sea-dragon handles. Large jars and covers

9

of Anglo-Indian pattern. Jars, covered; dragon handles of Anglo-Indian and Anglo-Japanese patterns. Ewers and basins with oriental figures and a rose border. Jars, the old India crackle with India red grounds. Jugs showing various patterns in Bandanna Ware. Table ware of a Japanese pattern in blue, red and gold. White patent Ironstone."

When Morely & Co. took over Mason's patent, molds and designs in 1851, they often changed the mark to "Real Ironstone China," impressed upon the ware. In 1860, the patent changed hands and George Ashworth & Bros. bought the firm and usually added the name "Ashworth's" below the old mark of the crown and banner.

Although the old patterns with Chinese influence continued to be made and are still being made from the old molds, new designs were also introduced from time to time. Two designs which relate to the changing styles of later years are the English Fruit Basket and Vista. Both are Victorian in character; Vista includes a scene of men and women on a terrace and English castles in the background, framed by an archway of trees. The border is of begonia leaves and delicate flowers. Black Mansard, another design of buildings and trees printed in black, is also a later type, as is the well-known American Marine, which was made both by Morely and Ashworth. This design is usually printed in brown and has panels of ships outlined in rope. The marks are a two-masted vessel with a scarf below, with "American Marine" and the initials of the potter, "F.M. & Co." for Morely; or "G.L.A. & Bros.," "G.L.A. & T." or "Ashworth" for Geo. Ashworth & Bros. The firm continues under the name of Ashworth today and the old patterns and molds are still in use, so that a knowledge of the marks is necessary in order to date a piece.

Ironstone reached its greatest popularity from 1820 to late in that century and became one of the most important branches of china manu-

Ironstone China

facture. It was made at many factories, but none, with the exception of Davenport, made as good ironstone as the early wares of Spode and Mason. The majority of the pieces of ironstone are marked with the maker's name and the word Ironstone, Granite ware, Opaque porcelain or some similar name. The two most common types of later ironstone are the white undecorated pieces with molded knobs in the shapes of fruit or flowers on the tops of tureens, tea pots and coffee pots, and the brown-black printed scenes which show remnants of Chinese influence. These decorative chinoiserie or pastoral or garden scenes have such names as Doric, Oriental, Medici, Scinde, etc.

Among the well-known manufacturers who made some variety of ironstone were John and Richard Riley of Burslem, who worked before 1827. Their china of the stone type is marked "Riley's Semi China," on an oval belt with buckle.

James Edwards and Son of Burslem also made stone china of a good, semi-transparent quality. Among their patterns are Scroll, Tulip, Rope, Barley, Bishop and Medieval. The mark of the firm in 1842 was the royal arms and "Stone China, James Edwards & Sons, Dale Hall." Sometimes a dolphin and anchor trade mark is added and often the mark is "J. E. & S." in script, surrounded by a garter bearing the words "Ironstone China" or the name "J. Edwards & Son, Dale Hall," surrounded by a garter with "Ironstone China." These were printed marks.

J. W. Ridgway (1814–30) were well-known makers of ironstone. Their printed mark has the royal coat of arms, a belted oval with "Stoneware J. R." or "J. W. R.," and the name of the pattern, "Victoria," or "Bentick." Another mark is "Opaque China J. W. R. Oriental Birds," within a wreath of leaves and flowers. The pattern India Temple is marked with a printed shield containing the name "India Temple" and the letters "J. W. R."

Davenport made fine stone china at Longport. The marks are a printed "Davenport" and "Stone China" on a circular garter, and an impressed mark with an archway and columns and an anchor within, and "Davenport" above and "Stone China" below. Chinese red and blue and gold used in large floral designs are the most typical Davenport ironstone patterns. A brown oriental scenery pattern is marked "Cypress Ironstone Davenport."

J. & G. Meakin operated three potteries, one in Hanley, one in Cobridge and one at Burslem. The mark on their ironstone is stamped in black, with the royal coat-of-arms and "Ironstone China, J. & G. Meakin."

Another well-known firm that made ironstone was W. Adams and Son. Printed patterns were made earliest and marked "W. Adams & Sons," "Adams," "W. Adams and Sons Stroke-on-Trent," all printed marks. The firm's name for stone was enameled ironstone. After 1840, they made plain white ironstone and the mark was an eagle with the trade mark in a circle and a ribbon with "Estab. Wm. Adams & Co., 1657." Dover was a raised pattern made by Adams.

Josiah Wedgwood experimented with ironstone, but did not use it except for cameos, medallions and plinths of vases. However, ironstone was made after 1850 by E. Wedgwood and Co. of Tunstall. One of their patterns is Asiatic Pheasants and the marks are impressed "E. Wedgwood & Co., Stone China," or "Imperial Ironstone China, Wedgwood & Co.," within a circle. A Chinese floral design with hand painting is stamped in black "Wedgwood's Stone China."

E. & C. Challinor of Fenton also made ironstone after 1850. The marks are "E. & C. Challinor Ironstone China," and a Staffordshire knot impressed, or a printed mark with a royal coat of arms and a ribbon with "Ironstone China, Challinor, Fenton." Often the pattern name is printed as "Australia," "Gothic," or "Portland" and the initials, "E. & C. C." These patterns were made with various borders. Embossed iron-stone patterns by Challinor are Ceres, Garland and Vine-Leaf. A plate with a brown oriental scene and a green conventional printed border is marked "Ironstone," with an eagle, the name of the pattern, "Sciro" on a ribbon, and "E. Challinor," printed in black, as well as the impressed

Ironstone China

Staffordshire knot. White china sprigged wih blue or purple flowers and leaves in relief is often marked, "E. Wood, Burslem, Ironstone China" and a printed eagle. This pattern copies the old Chelsea pattern.

An oriental scene with a pavilion and trees printed in black is marked, "Corean, P.W. & Co.," with a stamped eagle. This is a mark of Podmore, Walker, who had two factories at Tunstall in 1842 and operated until 1862.

Joseph Meigh and his son, Charles Meigh, operated a factory at Hanley from 1770 to 1861. They made many kinds of china, including stone china, which is marked with their name within a rectangle: "J. Meigh, Hanley and Improved Stone China." Another mark is a crown and a belted circle with "J. M. & S. Indian Tree" or "Indian Stone China" in a circle; "Opaque Porcelain"; or the late mark after 1861, "Indian Stone China O.H.E.C.L.," for Old Hall Earthenware Company, Limited. A blue transfer plate with primroses and peacock feathers is impressed "Improved Felspar C. Meigh & Son."

Manufacturers of ironstone china after 1850 are almost too numerous to mention. They include Anthony Shaw of Burslem, who used a printed mark with the royal arms, "Stone China" and his name; Thomas Hughes, who stamped his ware, "Ironstone China"; William Brownfield & Sons, of Cobridge, who imitated some of the old Mason patterns on their ironstone and marked them: "W. & B.," "W.B.," or "W.B. & S." in addition to the name of the pattern, and Furnival & Sons of Cobridge, who made granite ware with Chinese patterns. Their mark is "Furnival" impressed in the ware. Holland & Green of Longton exported a great deal or ironstone to America. Their mark is the name "Ironstone" and the royal arms, and the name or initials of the firm. T. & R. Boote of Burslem marked their ironstone with a black-printed mark with royal arms, "Royal Patent Ironstone" or "Royal Premium Ironstone" and "T. & R. Boote" and the impressed initials "T. & R. B." After 1857, this firm manufactured only granite ware for the American market, having discontinued their other types of china.

13

A Handbook of Popular Antiques

On Minton china the words "Improved Stone China, Newstone" or "Semi-stone," and "Minton" (impressed) and "B. B. Newstone," (impressed) are used from 1845 to 1861. Amherst Japan is a pattern of Minton's stone china, and the pieces are usually marked with the pattern name and "Stone China."

Scottish makers of ironstone include Bell & Co. and R. Cochran & Co. Bell & Co. marks are an eagle holding a roll on which is inscribed the name of the pattern and underneath the initials of the firm, "J. & M. P. B. & Co."; a vase and the name on a scroll, "J. & M. P. Bell & Co."; and later a garter bearing the initials of the firm and enclosing a bell. These are all printed marks, while an impressed bell with the initials "J. B." is also found.

The R. Cochran & Co. mark is the royal arms and "Warranted Stone China R. Cochran & Co. Glasgow," printed in black, or "Royal Ironstone China, Cochran and Fleming Glasgow" and the royal arms. A raised pattern of wheat called Ceres is from this factory.

Ironstone was also made at the Anchor Pottery, Trenton, New Jersey, as late as 1894. It is marked with an anchor in a circle and the words "Anchor Pottery," "A. P." and two lions or "Ironstone China Warranted," the name of the pattern, such as "Berlin," and also "Anchor Pottery, J. E. N."

BIBLIOGRAPHY

Ceramic Art of Great Britain, Llewellynn Jewitt, Virtue & Co., Ltd., London.

Marks and Monograms on Pottery and Porcelain, Chaffers, Reeves & Turner, 1912.

Spode and His Successors, Arthur Hayden, Cassell & Company, Ltd., London.

14

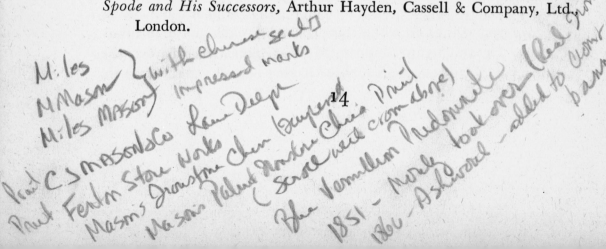

Chapter 2

GAUDY DUTCH AND WELSH,
SPATTER AND ROSEWARE

THE bright color and bold, crude designs of the china manufactured in Staffordshire for the Pennsylvania Dutch market appeal to many collectors. This china is decorative and seems to fit in with all types of English and American furnishings. The field is small and the patterns few, so that with good luck, patience and a fat pocketbook, one may be able to assemble a comprehensive collection. These wares are scarce and expensive because disregard and rough handling in the past have reduced the number of pieces available.

The demand for all types of this china is far beyond the supply. The best hunting ground is still Pennsylvania or one of the big antique shows, and, for really fine pieces, the auction rooms. Within the last few years three big collections have been auctioned in New York.

Gaudy Dutch is the oldest of the English china made for the Pennsylvania Dutch market. It is characterized by bold designs of flowers, leaves and line borders which show an oriental influence. This influence, however, was indirect, since the Staffordshire potters sought to copy the more expensive Worcester which was influenced by similar designs that derived from Japanese Imari ware. Delft must also be mentioned. The usual colors of Gaudy Dutch are deep rust-red, a pinkish, grayed intensity of the same hue, cobalt blue, apple green and lemon yellow. Often a red-brown rim is used on the edge of plates and saucers. The background is a soft white china, light in weight, and frail in appearance. The designs are handpainted with a free-hand stroke over the glaze, and all of the designs resemble each other in their vigorous growth,

15

the type of large overgrown blossoms, and lush foliage. A Chinese peony is certainly the original inspiration for several and a comparison with Chinese paintings will reveal the same large flowers and the same shape leaves. However, for some strange reason, these patterns have been called Carnation and Grape. War Bonnet, Dove or Lord Bird, Sunflower, Dahlia, Oyster, Urn, Primrose, Zinnia and Butterfly are other patterns, some of them named with no connection between the design and the name. However, a brief description may aid the collector in placing the various designs. The easiest pattern to distinguish is the Urn or Vase design.

The typical vase is deep blue with a crisscross inset of apricot. From the vase springs a crude, bold flower and two large peony-type leaves and other small leaves. The vase is set on a foreground of apricot or blue. The border is made up of flowers and leaves broken into panels by bands of blue set vertically or diagonally and daubed with yellow. This pattern has been found marked 'Riley.' Other patterns found with the impressed "Riley" mark include the No-name pattern, Zinnia pattern and Strawflower pattern.

John and Richard R. Riley were considered excellent potters, according to Simeon Shaw, a Staffordshire authority. They worked in Burslem between 1802 and 1827, the latter date marking the death of both brothers. Their works are listed as the Nile Street Pottery in 1802, and in the Directory of 1818 as the Hill Works, while their home, Portland House, was one of the showplaces of Burslem. Few pieces of Gaudy Dutch are marked, but the discovery of the name Riley places Gaudy Dutch earlier than the old blue printed ware. However, the fact that some pieces of Gaudy Dutch have been found with blue transfer printed borders shows that they were also made at the same time as the beginnings of early blue in about 1818.

An Urn pattern with a vine border has been found marked "E. Wood & Sons, Burslem." Enoch Wood worked at the Hill Works prior to 1814 when the Rileys took over but was working elsewhere before 1800.

The pattern War Bonnet is one of the most popular and most interesting designs. It shows a bowl with crisscross, holding a flower and leaves, and four blue feathers and mosses below. The floral border is divided into sections by blue bands. This pattern is often marked 2/1037 in script. Cups, saucers, plates of various sizes, and creamers, pitchers and hot-water jugs and bowls indicate that this pattern was made in complete tea sets.

The Oyster pattern is also rare. It takes its name from an outline of an oyster, but the design is dominated by a large rose-like flower. This pattern is found on a lemon yellow and apricot ground, and with the blue panel floral border, and also with rare blue transfer borders, one with a scroll and rose border, and another with a wild-rose border in blue transfer. On the back of plates with the borders in a blue transfer is the inscription, "Lady of the Lake," similar to the mark of T. & J. Carey of Lane End. One of the loveliest patterns from the standpoint of design is the Carnation. A large blossom springs from the foreground and rests on a triform leaf, and the remainder of the space is filled in with smaller blossoms and leaves. It has a decorative vine border within a rim of deep blue with yellow dots. It is often confused with the Double Rose pattern which has the large rose to the side amid smaller leaves and flowers and two circles with a band of triangle shapes set in the foreground. The prices and articles found are about the same as those of the Carnation pattern. The Single Rose pattern is similar, except that the rose is single, the foreground reminiscent of Chinese groundwork and the border wider than that on the Double Rose. The border is sometimes light and sometimes dark, and often has an inside vine border. Carnation has been found on a coffee pot, creamer, cup and saucer, round dish, cup plate, hot-water jug, bowl, teapot, sugar bowl and various sizes of plates.

The Grape pattern springs from a light salmon ground. Three blue grape leaves and a double flower that resembles a bunch of grapes dominate the design. The border is deep blue with lines of yellow. The various articles of a tea and coffee service are found in addition to a rare platter. The Grape pattern is often marked "2/1036," plus the artist's initials in script. The variations in the pattern are thus traced to different workmen. A similar serial number appears on War Bonnet, and both patterns were thus made at the same factory. Although the name of the factory is not known, we do know that they were made near the great pottery center of Burslem.

The Dahlia pattern is easily recognized. The flower is more naturalistic than the other Gaudy Dutch flowers, and looks like a dahlia. It has one full blossom and several buds and leaves. A delicate wavy line border is bound by a blue band with teeth. It is a rare pattern but one of the most popular. The No-name pattern has a symmetrical design of branches springing from double foreground hillocks and a blossom in the center above. It, too, has a delicate wavy border bounded by a blue band with yellow daubs. "Riley" impressed in a straight line has been found on variations of this pattern of a tree with three blossoms and leaves filling the center of the plate and a semicircle of blue ground at the top and bottom and a narrow blue border. The Sunflower has one full face flower, and one in profile, and a trifold leaf above. It springs from a blue foreground and has a wavy line border, or a vine border held in by a blue band. From the standpoint of design, these patterns with double borders are more decorative and distinctive than those with panel borders or patterns with line borders such as the Dove. The Dove pattern, however, is rare. It has a peculiar flower which springs from a crest of leaves set on a foreground with scattered blossoms. The leaves suggest the wings of a dove. The Butterfly pattern with its rusty-red butterfly set to the lower right is one of the rarest patterns. It shows the Worcester-oriental influence more than some of the other patterns. There are very few pieces of this pattern on the market. It is found with a plain or wavy line, and a vine border. Other patterns of Gaudy Dutch include the rare

Gaudy Dutch——Spatterware

Zinnia with apricot and lavender flowers and a vine border on a blue ground. This pattern is usually marked "Riley." The Strawflower pattern is also very rare and is usually marked "Riley." Another maker's name which has been found on Gaudy Dutch is an impressed "Rogers." Rogers had a factory at Longport in the Burslem District from 1815 to 1842. "Davenport" has also been found impressed on Gaudy Dutch ware. This factory was also located at Longport.

The rarest Gaudy Dutch form is the platter. Coffee pots, especially with the Butterfly pattern, teapots, and other hollow ware are also very rare.

The value of Gaudy Dutch depends upon condition rather than pattern. Proof pieces with no cracks, chips, or discolorations are rare, since the hand painting chips easily. Although I have listed markings, marked pieces are very rare and probably not on the present-day market. However, the markings used by each firm identified are early marks and definitely place Gaudy Dutch as a late eighteenth-century or early nineteenth-century product.

The most popular patterns are the War Bonnet, Urn and Butterfly. However, all pieces are sought after and are equally hard to find. From the artistic standpoint, patterns with a dark-blue border and a vine border are more desirable than those with a panel border. Also, patterns with good spotting of design such as the Carnation, Single Rose and Primrose are more desirable than the Urn or War Bonnet which have more open spaces.

Roseware is more delicate than Gaudy Dutch and has a feminine character. It is light in color and less bold in design. It is found in three patterns. The King's Rose design is red, yellow and green, with pink shading. It has one recognizable rose and several round flower forms and a border of delicate leaves and lines, a solid pink border, a sectional border, or no border at all. The Queen's Rose pattern is similar, but the dominant rose is pink. The shapes of the King's and Queen's Rose are delicate and similar shapes and designs are found in old New Hall.

Many cups have flutings and scalloped edges, and sugar bowls, creamers and coffee pots have fluted shell ends and fluted tops. A King's Rose with a blue-scroll border identical with the border on the Oyster pattern has been found, and in the collection of the New York Historical Society is an Oyster pattern on Roseware with a solid pink border, thus linking the Oyster pattern and Roseware to the same factory. The Adams Rose pattern has a border of red roses and leaves. The mark "Adams" is impressed.

Gaudy Welsh has not had the same popularity with collectors as the other so-called Pennsylvania Dutch wares; however, it is deserving of more attention. In design it is cruder than Gaudy Dutch, but the coloring is similar, particularly the use of a certain yellow-green. The weight and texture of the china are more related to Spatterware. Most of the Gaudy Welsh was made in the middle of the nineteenth century. The shapes are crude and heavy and often an impressed border is found with the design painted over as though it were an afterthought, as, for example, the design on Niagara by E. Walley. The decoration includes large flowers and leaves freely painted in blue, vermilion and green, with gold lustre. The border is dark blue with scallops.

The most decorative design of Gaudy Welsh is the one with tulips and vines and triangles of deep purple-blue. This design comes with and without a center flower and is unmarked. It is found in tea sets. The cups are usually straight-sided without handles; the plates are irregular in shape, and the hollow pieces have short feet.

Another Gaudy Welsh pattern has bands of blue dividing the plate into a wheel pattern and the color is embellished with gold lustre. This pattern is unmarked. Other Gaudy Welsh patterns show Chinese influence similar to that of Gaudy Dutch, but Gaudy Welsh usually has gold lustre added to the design.

The spatter process, which was done by putting on color with cut sponges, was an old one. John Niglett painted a heron and other birds with spatter trees on Bristol Delft and his style must have had some influence on the Staffordshire potters. John Niglett worked at Brislington and Bristol during the years between 1714 and 1754. He was the most original and daring of all the decorators of English Delft. His designs were bold caricatures of scenes, men and animals. He worked in red, green, blue, yellow, manganese purple, blue and sage green and many of his designs combined spatter borders, trees and backgrounds with line designs. He made a farmyard series which included cocks, peacocks,

cottages and windmills, and this series could well have been the source of spatter made a century later at Lane Delph, the center of the Spatterware district. In the Staffordshire directory of 1802, Lane Delph is also spelled Lane Delf, and it is more than a coincidence that Thomas Heath made Delft pottery there.

Simeon Shaw describes a plate by Thomas Heath of Lane Delph, 1710: "In the landscape mere lines or strokes form the edifice; the clouds seem formed by the finger's end and a soft rag or sponge." This is Staffordshire Delft, the designs similar to those of Niglett. Painted peacocks and trees with spatter foliage were also made at Leeds and by Wedgwood and are earlier than the common type of spatter. The Wedgwood peacock has a spotted tail, spatter leaves and the dishes have a scalloped blue rim and are marked with an impressed "Wedgwood."

Spatterware proper was a later product and the spatter, once a means of incidental decoration, is the chief theme of the pottery with both design and border in some cases in spatter work, as seen in the Schoolhouse pattern. Spatterware for the American market, the type which we associate with the Pennsylvania Dutch, was made in the Tunstall District of Staffordshire in the middle of the nineteenth century. The date for this type of spatter is given by William Turner in his book, *William Adams, an Old English Potter*. He says that plain printed ware and sponged and painted goods were made for the East. "Also in gaudy colors and in dark blue for the West Coast of Africa and North and South America. Much of it was done by means of cut sponges and was first made in Staffordshire by William Adams at his Greenfield Pottery in 1845–50." In order to introduce it he procured persons from Scotland who understood the process.

Llewellynn Jewitt in *Ceramic Art in Great Britain* gives the output of several factories making spatterware and common earthenware for the American market, namely, the Fenton Pottery operated by W. Baker & Co. (from 1843) who made "The commoner class of printed, sponged and pearl-white granite wares suitable for North America, United States, West Indian and African trade." The Gold Street Works, near Stafford Street, Longton, operated by Barker Brothers, made "Ordinary medium-quality earthenware for home and foreign markets including Cape of Good Hope, West Africa, Australia, South American markets. It consists of cream-coloured, white, fancy sponged, painted and printed dinner, toilet, breakfast and tea sets." Barker, Sutton, and Till were also working the Sytch Works from 1832 to 1850 and the Barker & Till mark which is found on spatterware was used in about 1845.

Charles and W. K. Harvey worked at Longton from 1841 to 1862 and made "common and useful earthenware for North America." Spatterware with the tulip pattern marked "Harvey" is in the collection of Mrs. Douglas Sutherland of Chicago, Illinois, whose collection also includes pieces with pea fowl and blue spatter marked "Mellor & Venables" who worked the Hole House Works at Burslem after 1843, and by Samuel Alcock & Co. of Burslem, 1830–1859. A cup and saucer with a peacock design on a carmine spatter ground was in the Lorimer Collec-

TOP, LEFT TO RIGHT: Mason's ironstone plate with Chinese vase and flowers; Mason's ironstone platter with Chinese design; plate with sailboat design, Geo. Ashworth Bros. MIDDLE: Covered dish, white ironstone. Anthony Shaw, Tunstall. BOTTOM: Platter, dark-brown Chinese pavilion with floral border, Davenport. (*Courtesy Lord and Taylor*)

SPODE STONE CHINA. UPPER LEFT: Peacock pattern, polychrome. Impressed mark. LOWER RIGHT: Bang-up pattern, polychrome. Both *from the Collection of William Sherman.* UPPER RIGHT: Landscape pattern, printed in blue, colors filled in by hand. Chinese Fretwork mark. LOWER LEFT: Ship and Star pattern, printed in brown, colors filled in by hand. Both *from the Collection of Copeland & Thompson.*

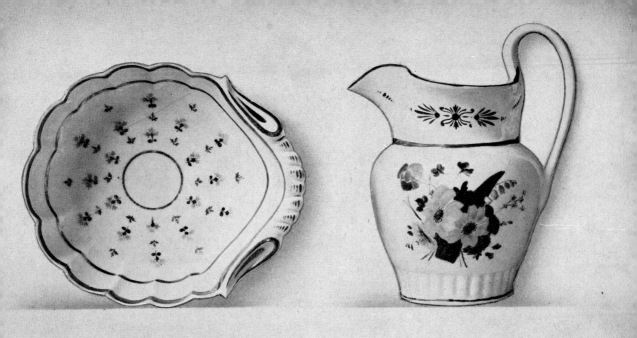

LEFT TO RIGHT, TOP: dish, sprig design, William E. Tucker; pitcher, vase shape, spider motif on the neck, Tucker and Hemphill. BOTTOM: pitcher, vase shape, with bird and flower, Tucker and Hemphill; decorative vase with painted scene of the pottery works, Tucker and Hemphill. *Courtesy The Philadelphia Museum of Art*

LEFT TO RIGHT, TOP ROW: Dutch Delft tile, blue and white. Christ's entry into Jericho; Liverpool Delft tile, pastoral scene. BOTTOM ROW: Liverpool Delft tiles with scenes from Aesop's Fables. *Courtesy The Metropolitan Museum of Art*

tion and was marked, with impress, "P.W. & Co. Stoneware." Podmore, Walker operated the Swan Bank and Unicorn Pottery & Pinnox Works at Tunstall. The Swan Bank Works (1842–1862) made pottery "both in sponged, printed, painted, enameled gilt and lustred."

In 1859 the Lane Delph Pottery (J. Pratt & Co.) made "ordinary earthenware for the foreign market." Spatterware with Lane Delph marks has been found.

Evidence of a much later date is found in spatterware marked by Powell & Bishop $\frac{\text{Best}}{\text{P\&B}}$ and "Best Goods." This dates from 1865, for until that date the firm name was Livesley, Powell & Co., and was changed to Powell & Bishop in 1865, when Mr. Livesley left the firm. They operated three factories in Hanley, the Church Street Works making common goods exclusively for the American market. Earl Robacker owns a plate with a rooster design with an impressed, "Best Goods," and Mrs. Douglas Sutherland owns a pea fowl plate marked "Powell & Bishop Pearl Ware."

The shapes of spatterware also point to a mid-nineteenth-century date. The earliest shapes are simple with rounding and graceful contours. Cups have simple bases, while late cups have ridges and are set on pedestals. The heavy-ridged hexagonal- and octagonal-sided pitchers and dishes are the same shapes as late brown transfer stoneware and Britannia metal. Heavy arms and handles are also of later date. Mr. Turner illustrates three specimens of Adams Spatterware from a private collection which are similar to those in the Tunstall Museum and illustrated by F. A. Rhead in *Staffordshire Pots and Potters*. The pieces are a baking dish, cup and saucer and plate. All three are decorated with a hand-painted peacock with green body, red tail and bright-blue neck. The back sweep of the bird is made with one long graceful stroke of the brush. The head is turned and topped with a crest while characteristic wavy lines rise from the back of the bird, and similar lines form a rest for the bird's feet. The pieces are marked with an impressed "Adams."

23

All pieces of spatterware which have been found marked "Adams" have a similar design, while peacocks on other spatterware vary in design. G. Adams & Sons also made pea fowl designs. One type of pea fowl is similar to the well-known Adams', but has two crossed, curved lines which rise from the back of the bird instead of the wavy lines; another type of bird has a separate head and an enlarged crest topping the head. The Adams bird is also found sitting upon a branch of green leaves. While the peacock is invariably painted in three colors within a black outline, the combination of colors varies, and sometimes the body is green, the neck purple, and the tail and crest red, or the bird may be blue, orange and yellow, or blue, yellow and green. A rare variation is a bird with zig-zag black lines in the body rather than plain color. The spatter background or border also varies in color and may be blue, red, green, brown, pink, purple, black or yellow, or combinations of these colors. Peacocks are found on all of the pieces of a dinner set, including cups and saucers, plates, platters, soup plates, bowls, vegetable dishes, pitchers, sugar bowls, tea and coffee pots. Vegetable dishes, gravy boats and pickle dishes are rare. A peacock on a bar and a bird on a fence are rare designs. Peacock designs have also been found marked by Barker & Till, Cotton & Barlow, Powell and Bishop, Harvey, Podmore, Walker, and F.W. & Co. (unidentified). While peacocks are rare, yellow, blue and red cocks, doves in blue, yellow and white, and green and red parrots and deer are rarer; in fact, they are seldom found.

The Schoolhouse is one of the best-known and most sought-after patterns. The house is red or blue with a yellow roof, a door, two or three white windows, and a chimney. There is usually a dark ground line and a semi-circular grass plot in front of the house, and a spatter tree near by. The Schoolhouse is found with various colored backgrounds. A Schoolhouse design has been found marked "B.T. Troutbeck Tunst," and an impressed anchor. The Schoolhouse is one of the crudest spatterware designs. Both this and the Fort and the New England design which shows a similar building, but with trees and birds, have less artistic merit than other spatterware designs which have more hand painting. Undoubtedly this design was made by unskilled workmen. The work could even have been done by a child. Although all spatterware was made for everyday use, this pattern must have been for kitchen use and even for baking purposes. Its popularity and the present prices it brings only prove the thesis .that the average collector today needs more knowledge of art .values.

Another popular pattern is the Star. The star is painted in blue, red and yellow and has a white star-shaped space around it and borders of various colors. The Tulip is also a popular pattern. The open tulip is a decorative six-petaled flower in red, blue and white or green found on backgrounds of blue; red, yellow, or purple or combinations of these colors. It is one of the most colorful and artistic spatter designs. Profile tulips are more naturalistic in design. Such a tulip is found on a plate impressed with the mark, "Opaque China, Barker & Till." A profile Thistle is also a decorative pattern, but not as popular as the Tulip patterns, nor does it bring as high prices except in the rare yellow spatter. The Acorn pattern was neglected until recently; however, with its yellow and brown acorns and light-green leaves, it is one of the most desirable patterns from the standpoint of design. It is found with blue, red, or purple spatter borders. Other patterns not so well known are the Windmill, the Cannon, the Deer, the Sailboat, the Beehive, the Bluebell, Winter Berries, and plain spatter daubs and plaids. These patterns, while rare, are not especially decorative, with the exception of the Deer pattern. They are less in demand and thus not as expensive as the better-known patterns.

Transfer patterns of an eagle grasping arrows in its feet and backed by a shield with thirteen stars and one with a flying eagle are found with blue and carmine spatter borders. Adams is known to have made transfer patterns combined with sponged work, but neither of these eagle patterns is marked "Adams."

Besides the makers already mentioned, spatterware is also found

A Handbook of Popular Antiques

with the following makers' marks: Mayer, J. or T. Walker, G. Adams & Sons, H. & G. Heath, Pearl Ware J.I. (Lane End), F.W. & Co., Ironstone, A. W. P. & Co., Cotton & Barlow, Davenport, Elmore & Fisher (Tun-

stall), E. Challinor, and Carver. Several of these makers are not listed, probably because they are too late nineteenth century to interest the historians and also because they made only crude wares. Other marks impressed are numbers and the letter "R," "Z," a cross, anchor, diamond, crown, asterisk and #.

"American Pottery Co., Jersey City, New Jersey," impressed in a circle is found on a crude chocolate pot. This pottery is known to have made spatter in the late 1840's.

The amateur collector would do well to begin with cups and saucers and plates, and later add coffee pots, tea pots, sugar bowls and such rarities as covered vegetable dishes, miniatures, cup plates and salt and pepper shakers. Old spatter has the triangular kiln spots where the points of the triangle rested during the firing, and these marks are an aid in distinguishing between the old ware and reproductions. The rarest color in spatterware is yellow, and green is next rarest. Purple and brown are not as popular as the other colors.

Gaudy Dutch——Spatterware

BIBLIOGRAPHY

The Red Hills, Cornelius Weygandt, University of Pennsylvania Press, 1929.

Pennsylvania Dutch Stuff, Earl F. Robacker, University of Pennsylvania Press, 1944.

The American Antiques Collector, Vol. I, 1939–40.

Marks and Monograms on Pottery and Porcelain, Chaffers, Reeves and Turner, 1912.

Ceramic Art in Great Britain, Llewellynn Jewitt, Virtue & Co., Ltd., 1878.

William Adams, Old English Potter, William Turner, The Keramic Studio Pub. Co.

The Magazine Antiques, April, 1930.

Catalogue of the Mary Yeager Collection, March, 1943.

Catalogue of the Alice Jones Willock Collection, May, 1943.

Catalogue of the George Horace Lorimer Collection, March and October, 1944.

I am indebted to Mrs. Douglas Sutherland for a check of the marks on her collection of spatterware.

Chapter 3

TUCKER CHINA, 1825–1838

ALTHOUGH the first American porcelain was made at Jersey City about 1825–26, the factory was discontinued after several years and thus the honor of being the first really to supply the home market with American porcelain goes to William Ellis Tucker of Philadelphia.

Tucker china was a hard-paste porcelain, translucent, dense, and tough enough to withstand extreme changes in temperature. It is similar to Sèvres porcelain and, in fact, much Tucker has been sold as Sèvres since both the shapes and the decoration of the later Tucker porcelain closely resemble it. However, Tucker china has a blue-greenish appearance when held against the light, and Sèvres is usually yellow in tint. Handles and bases of Tucker are generally a little "off," the bases being uneven and the handles often leaning toward the body. The earnest collector should have no difficulty, for almost all of the shapes and designs of this later period are recorded in the factory pattern book which is now owned by the Pennsylvania Museum of Art and easily accessible for study. Although there is not much Tucker china on the market, almost every auction sale of importance turns up a piece or two of the fine "presentation" type, and now and then more ordinary patterns are found in antique shops.

The Tucker factory had a financial struggle from the beginning, so Tucker was forced to seek aid, and it was necessary to form partnerships. Thus the products of the factory were divided into periods indicating the change in partnerships and the change in characteristics of the ware.

Tucker China

There were three periods:

First: The Tucker Period—1825 to 1828.

Second: The Tucker & Hulme Period—1828 (one year only).

Third: The Tucker & Hemphill Period—1832–1838.

At first Tucker "burned kiln after kiln with very poor success. The glazing would crack, and the body blister." However, he finally achieved a good body and glaze even on the earlier pieces, but the workmanship and decoration of the first period were inferior. Nevertheless, Tucker took the prize at the Franklin Institute in 1827 "for the best specimen of porcelain to be made in Pennsylvania," and the following year again received a silver medal for 100 pieces of gilt, painted and plain china. The china at this time is recognized by its crude and inartistic decoration. Simple landscapes and butterflies were daubed on in sepia or brown monochrome over the glaze. The landscapes were similar—a lake, a box-type house, and mountains in the distance, but no two were exactly alike in detail, since the painting was all done free-hand with a few strokes of the brush. There might be a few gold bands, but at this period gold was used sparingly and was of inferior quality and thinly applied. Much of this earlier ware was sold undecorated. The shapes were crude but original in design, and if any influence predominates it is that of the English potters in the shapes of coffee pots, tea pots and cups and saucers. In the pattern book of Thomas Tucker, 1832–1838, the pattern of a creamer marked "Old Shape" is typical of this first period. In about 1828, Thomas Tucker, the brother of William Ellis Tucker, began to learn the business, and that same year Thomas Hulme invested some money and was admitted into partnership.

With the Hulme partnership, the second period begins and there is marked improvement in the decoration. Sprays or groups of flowers replaced the old sepia landscapes and some gold and white decoration was used. Pieces made during this year were marked: "Tucker & Hulme, China Manufacturers, Philadelphia, 1828" or "Tucker & Hulme, Phil-

29

adelphia, 1828." The name was in crude hand printing painted in red beneath the glaze. Both gold and white initialed pitchers, and vase-shaped pitchers with flowers and corrugated base, were marked this way. A sugar bowl with gold and black painted emblems of the Phoenix Hose Company and the typical "Spider" design in gold is marked: "Tucker & Hulme, Manufacturers, Philadelphia, 1828" in red. From the minute books of the Phoenix Hose Company, April, 1827, is the note that they will present a "tea set of American porcelain to the value of $50.00 to be manufactured by W. E. Tucker and ornamented with sketches of the Hose House—apparatus, badge, and other subjects associated with the Phoenix Hose Company."

Although Hulme retired after about a year, William Ellis Tucker carried on alone for several years, and the quality of the ware and the decoration, of roses, bouquets of flowers, and birds, continued, with very little gold being used. However, the very rare hunting-scene pitcher dates from this era. It has a raised decoration of horses, men and hounds on the body of the pitcher and was decorated with various borders of flowers and gold. One such pitcher has "Lathrop" and the date "1828" painted on the front below the spout and a simple gold and blue scroll border on the neck. The small Round Jug Shape (#12 in the pattern book) also dates from 1828, since similar pitchers have been found with a bunch of flowers, simple gold banding, and the date, together with name or initials of the owner, under the spout of the pitcher. Of course these shapes with more elaborate floral decorations and more gold were made in the later period. The hunting pitcher of the Hemphill period usually has a gold spout and elaborate gold borders and flowers.

After Hulme left the partnership, Tucker appealed to Andrew Jackson for Congressional aid and offered his secret formula in return. But although Jackson accepted the gift of a piece of porcelain, he wrote a letter refusing the aid.

In 1832 Judge Joseph Hemphill was taken into partnership and the company appealed to Congress for a protective tariff for their porce-

Tucker China

lain. They also purchased the property at the southwest corner of Schuyl-kill—Sixth and Chestnut Streets, and erected a factory. After the death of William Ellis Tucker in the same year, Thomas Tucker took over the management of the business and the firm name became Tucker & Hemp-hill. Although Tucker was in charge of the factory, Judge Hemphill exerted a great influence upon the china output. He had just returned from Europe and was impressed by Sèvres and other European china. Due to his influence artists and artisans were brought over from France, England and Germany, and a more pretentious style of decoration was introduced. Some of the vases and pictures were close copies of Sèvres forms and it is quite possible that molders from the Sèvres factory may have brought their molds with them.

Of this later and best period we have a record in the old leather-bound pattern books. There are not only sketches of shapes showing actual sizes and quoting prices, but fine water-color sketches of the various patterns. So well executed are these sketches that their counterpart can easily be checked on the existing pieces of old Tucker & Hemphill china today.

Pitchers were the most popular output of the factory. About a dozen different styles and sizes are shown in the pattern book, and most of these have been identified in existing pieces today. The most popular shape was the Vase Shape (#7 in the pattern book). It had a raised corrugated border at the base and raised decoration on the lip of the spout with a simple curved handle extending above the rim. It was made in several sizes and its decoration varied from simple gold bands with a wreath and a monogram on the body of the pitcher or a bouquet of flowers in a wreath, to elaborate massed bandings and festoons of roses, tulips, forget-me-nots, and daisies held in by gold bands, "spider" borders, and other gold scrolls or meandering designs. One vase-shaped pitcher has a spray of pink moss roses with a bird on the stem.

The Grecian Shape pitcher was also made in several sizes. It had a squat body and wide neck with a scalloped top and a spout and handle

with raised line decoration. It usually had a spray of moss roses, yellow and purple tulips, and forget-me-nots with a Greek anthemion-like design in gold on its neck, and simple gold bands marking the base, neck, and lip of the pitcher. Often a group of apples, cherries, grapes, pears and pineapples are substituted for the flower group.

A pitcher design shown in four different sizes with a fluted top and ridged body and an angled handle is listed Walker Shape and since we know that Walker was a molder at the factory one wonders if Fletcher's Shape might not indicate a molder as yet unidentified. Neither the Walker nor Fletcher shapes are as well known as the Vase Shape or Grecian Shape pitchers. The #6 or Star Shape, which has a raised pattern on spout and handle and star flowers printed or raised in an all-over pattern, was presumably not popular, since it does not seem to exist today. However, pitchers were given to Marcus C. Stephens in 1827 by Benjamin Tucker, father of William Ellis Tucker, and he notes in a letter, "The pitchers were one pair horse pattern, one pair star pattern, and one Jug Eagle pattern—and enameled Cream Colored Jugs."

Number 1 Pitcher Shape in the pattern book has been found with simple landscapes, leaf borders on the neck, and gold-line decoration on the raised leafy spout and handle, and also with a medallion of a black eagle holding an American flag and elaborate gilt and polychrome borders, heavy gold bands and a gold spout and base. It would seem that in the variations stated the forms often remained the same from year to year, while the decorations increased in elaborateness as time went on and more skilled decorators were employed.

The same evolution of design may be traced on the simple vase with straight sloping sides and wide mouth. This vase was made in three sizes

Tucker China

to be used singly or as a pair with one larger vase for a mantel garniture. A classical design in gold and green was not as popular on this vase as the more elaborate spray of roses, tulip, daisy and forget-me-not. This vase could also be had (according to the pattern book) with a fern border, a scattered all-over pattern of sprigs of moss roses, pansies and daisies, in pink, blue and purple, or with a vertical spray of flowers and leaves, half naturalistic and half conventional in border, or with a sepia scene, of cottage and trees, or of the Tucker china works, or of a bird-hunting scene. The large vase of a mantel garniture has a view of Mt. Vernon with wide gold bands. But the *chef-d'oeuvre* was the vase with the heavy bands or festoons of roses, tulips, morning glory and other mixed flowers, with wide gold bands.

There are seventeen different sizes of cups and saucers shown in the pattern book. They vary from simple cups without a handle to bulbous French shapes with a standing lip and a handle that curves above the lip. Some have convex curves and some concave, others are straight and fluted. Handles are both curved and angular. Some cups have simple gilt bands or borders of gilt leaves and conven-tional flowers; others are bordered with the Spider design in gold. Cups and saucers with a moss rose and leaf border have gold bands and the interiors of the cups are lined in gold. Here again sepia scenes were still available and also a series of cups with gold lines and the transfer portraits of Andrew Jackson, John Quincy Adams, Madison and Monroe, on a violet-gray ground. The mark "R-VI" in gold is on one cup with these portraits, and may indicate a decorator not yet identified. While these are the only cups  with portraits which have been found and the pattern book does not in-

33

dicate portrait medallion cups, pitchers were made with portraits of Washington, a vase with "Mad" Anthony Wayne, and Tucker's ad in the *Boston Commercial Gazette* of March 8, 1827, advertised "Busts of Washington, Lafayette, Napoleon, etc."

Simple cups with gold and yellow bands and other pieces of a tea set with the same decoration have been found, but to date the fancy-shape cup and saucer in pink and gold sections has not turned up. Another design has overlapping flower petals with a circular center. This probably was made in gold.

Tea-set designs included sprays of roses and wreaths of honeysuckle, and a set with an all-over design of small blue and gold sprigs of leaves and cornflowers. The same pattern was often grouped in a border, but the most elaborate tea set had a design of flower garlands arranged to form a six-point star. It was banded in heavy gold.

The most ambitious productions of the porcelain factory were the large French-style urn vases and the decorated night lamps. The lamps came with curved and straight sides and usually had sepia or polychrome landscape decoration and simple gold bands and leaf borders.

The best-known urn vases are those at the Pennsylvania Museum. One has a scene of the old water works which was supposed to be the first Tucker factory. It has gold bands and gold handles. Of more graceful proportions is the vase with flower borders, gold- and salmon-colored lines, and leaf borders and gilt-bronze handles in the form of eagles' heads with wings meeting above. An amphora-shaped vase has scenes of shipwrecks in sepia and gold bands and still another urn-shaped vase with stand has a medallion showing Napoleon at the burning of Moscow. All of these portrait pieces belong to the Hemphill period, as do scenes which include such places as Mt. Vernon. Occasionally historic places were represented in the old sepia as is the scene of Wm. Penn's cottage and probably the view of St. David's Church, Radnor, Pennsylvania. However, the view of the bridge over the Schuylkill River, Philadelphia, is of the Hemphill period and has elaborate floral garlands in the other panels of the pitcher. A bridge view is also painted on a heart-shaped scent bottle.

A business card of the factory printed soon after Hemphill took, over gives us an idea of the stock: "Where is constantly kept on hand a superior assortment of china, comprising Dinner sets, Tea sets, vases, mantel ornaments, Pitchers, Fruit baskets, etc., etc., either plain or ornamented." While they may not have been regular stock, several types of perfume and cologne bottles were made, including a small ear shape and heart and shell shapes, powder boxes, miniature bowls and pitchers, ink stands and flower pots. Among the presentation pieces was a christening bowl "presented to First Presbyterian Church, Westchester, Chester County, February 22nd, 1834, by Joseph Hemphill of Philadelphia." That there was a great business in presentation pieces is demonstrated by the many monogrammed pieces found today. Open-work fruit baskets of several styles and designs were also made, but these usually had only gold decoration and were not marked.

Aside from the typical landscapes, which are usually recognized by their crudeness of execution and quaintness of conception, there are other patterns such as the Spider, the honeysuckle border, the fern pattern, and the laurel-leaf border that are typical and characteristic of Tucker china.

The most characteristic decoration is the compact band or garland of flowers, or the spray or bouquet of naturalistic flowers. Among the flowers used in these borders are the pink moss rose, the yellow and purple parrot-tulip, the blue morning glory, the yellow and purple clover, the blue and purple cornflower, the narcissus, lavender and white daisies and blue forget-me-nots. Bowknots of blue ribbon are used to tie wreaths, and often tassels of gold are used between garlands of flowers. These heavy and ornate naturalistic garlands were bordered in small classic gold borders such as the laurel leaf, also used on Sèvres, and delicate gold ferns and rosebuds.

Although Tucker china is not often marked, enough pieces with markings of each period have been found to enable us to identify the remaining pieces. In 1828 the mark used was: "Tucker & Hulme, Philadelphia, 1828." It was painted in uneven printing in red beneath the glaze. The same year this mark was also used: "Tucker & Hulme, China Manufacturers, Philadelphia, 1828." In 1833 and 1834 the following mark was painted in red under the glaze: "Manufactured by Jos. Hemphill, Philad-." There were also numerous workmen's marks which have been found scratched in the paste beneath the glaze; however, few have been identified. Those which are known are:

Charles J. Boulter—"B" or "C.B."
Charles Frederick—"F"
Wm. Hand— (Englishman) —"H"
Joseph Morgan—"M"
Vivian (Frenchman) —"V"
Andrew Craig Walker—"W"

BIBLIOGRAPHY

Original Pattern Book of Thomas Tucker, Pennsylvania Museum Library.

Early American Pottery and China, Edwin Atlee Barber

Bulletin of the Pennsylvania Museum, #14, April, 1906, "The Tucker and Hemphill Hard Porcelain Manufactory, Philadelphia," Edwin Atlee Barber.

The Magazine Antiques—June, 1928, pp. 480–484, W. H. Horner, Jr.; October, 1933, pp. 134–5, Samuel W. Woodhouse, Jr.; October, 1936, pp. 164–167, "Footnote to Tucker History," by Alice Winchester.

Chapter 4

DUTCH AND ENGLISH DELFT TILES

W HEN larger and more expensive articles of Delft are not available, the neglected tile offers an interesting field for collectors. Delft tiles have all the charm of color and design, if not the form, of a Delft vase or figure. Tiles may also be used to good advantage in house decoration as they were in the old Dutch houses, over mantels, around the fireplace, or as wall panels with plaster or wood paneling. Dutch tiles were used in America in the seventeenth century and from the beginning of the eighteenth century they came into popular usage.

In 1716 an advertisement of "Fine Holland Tiles" appeared in the *Boston News Letter;* in 1719 "Dutch Tiles for Chimneys"; in 1725, "Square Dutch Tiles to be set in chimneys"; in 1725, "Very good figured Dutch Tyle for Chimneys sold by the Dozen." In the *Boston Gazette,* 1738: "All Sorts of Dutch Tyles—Scripture (round and square) Landskips of divers sorts, Sea Monsters, Horsemen, Soldiers, Diamonds, etc." The popularity of Dutch tiles continued in America until the end of the eighteenth century, although Liverpool tiles were also used. Thus the Delft tile has been associated with American life for several centuries and indeed many old houses still retain their Delft tile fireplaces, and the demolition of such houses is one means of bringing these tiles into the market.

The Dutch tiles from the Beekman house, built in 1763, are now in the New York Historical Society collection. These are Biblical subjects in blue and white circles. They include such subjects as the Cruci-

37

fixion, Christ in the Garden, Adam and Eve, Rebecca at the Well, Jacob's Ladder, Moses and the Serpent and Jonah and the Whale. The backgrounds are variations of clouds and trees, and the foregrounds have the same stylistic treatment.

The earliest Dutch tiles, dating from the sixteenth century, took their inspiration from Italian tiles both in their blue, orange and red coloring and in their geometric designs of stars, crosses, medallions or lozenges. In the seventeenth century designs of plant motifs, such as oranges, pomegranates, tulips or bunches of grapes or acorns, a flower vase or a fruit dish, appeared; also medallion portraits of animals or portrait busts. The corner motif between the tiles was important, but later the designers concentrated on the picture and the corner motif became smaller. They dwindle from a large *fleur-de-lis* to volutes, rosettes, naturalistic carnations and finally the corner motif disappears altogether.

From the middle of the seventeenth century the influence dominant on Dutch tiles is Chinese blue and white porcelain, together with the native Dutch school of painting. Chinese influences are seen in the shape of medallions and the broken meander or fretwork in the corners, as well as the blue and manganese-purple coloring.

Pure tin enameled blue-and-white pottery is classed as Delft and it was at this time that this Delft proper, with a tin enamel on both back and front, began to be made. Delft was the center of this industry, but Delftware was also made in Rotterdam, Utrecht, Antwerp and other Dutch cities.

The subject matter of Delft tiles is supplied by paintings and engravings of the era, such as the work of Frans Hals. Landscapes and Dutch views were taken from engravings by J. Veerhuysen, but the sea monsters and Biblical subjects seem to be naive conceptions of the tile painters. Designs were usually pounced with charcoal through a stencil and the tile painter followed this outline, often changing it to suit his whim. For this reason no two tiles are alike. Colors and glaze blended together in one firing.

STAFFORDSHIRE—19TH CENTURY. LEFT TO RIGHT, TOP: pair of comforters; lovers in a bower. BOTTOM: John Brown; Lincoln, *circa* 1840. Upper Right: *Courtesy The Metropolitan Museum of Art*. Bottom, Left and Right: *Courtesy The Philadelphia Museum of Art*

LEFT TO RIGHT, TOP ROW: pink lustre pitcher, Sunderland; silver resist lustre pitcher, Staffordshire. BOTTOM ROW: silver lustre sugar bowl; copper lustre pitcher with painted rose, Staffordshire. *Courtesy The Metropolitan Museum of Art*

GAUDY DUTCH CHINA. UPPER RIGHT: cup and saucer, Single Rose pattern, Staffordshire, 19th c. MIDDLE: cup and saucer, Dove pattern, Staffordshire, 19th c. LOWER LEFT: plate, War Bonnet pattern, Staffordshire, 19th c. LOWER RIGHT: plate, Oyster pattern, Staffordshire, 19th c.

STAFFORDSHIRE—19TH CENTURY. LEFT TO RIGHT, TOP ROW: Gaudy Welsh plate, tulips and leaves; Gaudy Welsh plate painted over raised border: "E. Walley, Niagara Shape." SECOND ROW: Roseware cup and saucer, King's Rose pattern. THIRD ROW: Spatterware relish dish, Peacock design: "Adams." FOURTH ROW: Spatterware cup and saucer, Peacock design: "Stoneware B & T." Top Row *courtesy Lord & Taylor*. All others *courtesy The New York Historical Society*

Dutch and English Delft Tiles

While the old tile designs were continued, the popular designs in the eighteenth century were landscapes, shipping scenes, soldiers on foot or mounted, Biblical subjects, children playing games, animals, coats of arms and flowers. Purple and white was now used extensively and these designs usually were made in both colors. Some tiles had sponged or spatter backgrounds of purple around a blue scene.

Blue and white tiles in the collection at the Victoria and Albert

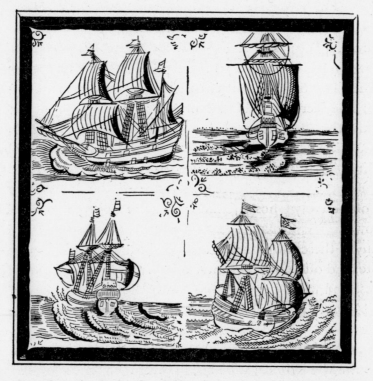

Museum, London, include the following: sixteen tiles, in each a castle beside water, within a circular frame; views of Amsterdam; the Herring-packers' Tower; the Jan Roden Gate Tower; the Moorderkerk; the Montalbaens Tower.

Tiles, each with a landscape in vignette, landscapes within circular frames and landscapes filling the whole surface of tiles were common types, as were also pastoral figures in landscapes, and sailing boats, mermen, mermaids, marine deities, whales, or dolphins, both in blue and white and in blue and manganese.

Tiles were made with heraldic arms and inscribed with names: "Amsterdam," "Hinloopen," "Huckelum," "Hartogen Bos." Biblical subjects from both the Old and New Testaments include Abraham's Sacrifice; Moses and the Brazen Serpent; The Annunciation; The Flight into Egypt; The Baptism; The Supper at Emmaus; Christ and Nicodemus; The Walk to Emmaus; The Circumcision; Christ in Triumph with Three Angels; The Kiss of Judas; Pilate Warned by His Wife; Pilate Washing His Hands; Christ Appearing as a Gardener to Mary Magdalene; The Spies Hiding in the House of Rahab; The Creation; The Fall; The Sacrifice and Death of Abel; Esau and the Mess of Pottage; Balaam and the Ass; Elisha Mocked by Children; Tobias and the Fish; The Annunciation to Zacharias; Herod and the Wise Men; Blind Leaders of the Blind; The Prodigal Son's Departure; The Prodigal Son Feasting with Harlots; The Third Reappearance of the Risen Christ; The Descent of the Holy Ghost; Jonah Under the Gourd Tree; The Parable of the Sower.

Many of these subjects are found in blue and white and manganese and white, and often in manganese and blue. One set of Biblical tiles in manganese and white has inscriptions which give references to the book of the Bible and the verse illustrated. Such a series of tiles with carnation and other motifs in the corners is in a fireplace in the American Wing of the Metropolitan Museum, New York City. Another fireplace has tiles of blue and white Biblical subjects, in ovals with flower and leaf corners. Still another fireplace in the Metropolitan Museum has tiles of figures after the manner of Franz Hals with *fleur-de-lis* borders, and painted in blue on white. These include cavaliers, ladies, monks and soldiers. Landscapes, sailing vessels, interior scenes, fishermen and birds and animals are also included on tiles in the Metropolitan Museum Collection.

Cupids, boys on stilts and boys flying a kite express a lighter mood,

Dutch and English Delft Tiles

while some of the finest early tiles have dogs, deer, rabbits or cows in circles or diamonds, with large *fleur-de-lis* corners.

Marks seldom occur on tiles. Often a letter or numeral is painted in crude strokes on the back of a tile; but these letters have never been explained and the numerals refer to a serial or class number. Patterns do not aid in dating tiles because the same patterns occur in succeeding centuries. Colors will aid in placing the general date of a tile, since even the quality of blue in the late tiles changed and the workmanship was not as good, the best painters now employing themselves with plates and other more important pieces. Old tiles are thicker than later tiles.

In the seventeenth and eighteenth centuries tiles were manufactured at the important factories in London, Bristol and Liverpool. At first their productions were influenced by Dutch pottery. Tiles were made at the same factories that made the Delftware pottery and were used for house signs and as wall pictures. Signed tiles by the Taylors of Redcliff have been found. These first tiles were polychrome and hand painted. Subjects on painted tiles include vases of flowers, birds, including the peacock, and landscapes with water, ships and buildings. The painted tiles usually had corner designs after the manner of the Dutch and fitted together to form an all-over pattern. Often the scene was enclosed in a circle or hexagonal space. However, it was not until the transfer process was discovered and perfected by John Sadler of Liverpool, in 1756, that tiles were made in any quantity in England. On the 27th of July, 1756, Sadler made an affidavit stating that he printed in six hours upwards of twelve hundred earthenware tiles of different patterns at Liverpool. These were "earthenware tyles for chimneys." These tiles are usually about 5¼ inches square and ¼ inch thick. They are glazed on the surface, which is slightly bluish-white. The body of the tile is porous, but seems harder than Dutch tiles. The designs are printed in various colors. Tones of black, from purple-black to pure black, are the most common, but tiles are also printed in shades of yellow, blue, greenish-blue, and bistre and purple-brown, and later, due to Wedgwood influence, in green. Tiles for printing were supplied by the potters Alderman Shaw and Zachariah Barnes.

Few of these tiles are signed, although they have been found with "Sadler," "Green" and "Liverpool." Sometimes the name of the town is written on the back of the tile, and sometimes the signature of the designer is put in the lower right-hand corner. Generally speaking, however, the only way to place the different kinds of English Delft is by means of the glazes, Liverpool being of a bluish cast, and Bristol greenish in color. The artists who made the engravings are not identified. However, designs were borrowed from the Chinese by way of the engravings of Jean Pillement, and the portraits in the actor series came from engravings in Bell's *British Theater,* published in 1776–7, or Bell's *Shakespeare,* and other subjects were taken from *The Ladies' Amusement,* published by Robert Sayer before 1760. The subject matter ranges from theatrical to Biblical subjects.

Some of the finest tiles from the standpoint of design and workmanship are the series of Æsop's fables. These were first made in 1760, and are usually printed in a purple-black on a creamy bluish ground. A fireplace in the American Wing of the Metropolitan Museum includes the following tiles from this series: The Ape and the Fox; Crow and the Pitcher; Young Man and Swallow; The Hunted Beaver; Mercury and the Woodman; Trees and the Woodman; Fox in the Well; Old Hound; Travellers and the Bear; One-Eyed Doe; Dog in the Manger; Owl and Grasshopper; and Fox and the Crow. Other tiles show The Boar and the Ass; Boar and the Hound; Angler and Little Fish; Cat and the Fox; Cock and the Fox Caught in Trap; Deer and the Lion; The Mischievous Dog; Dog and the Shadow; Dog and Fox; Fox, Dog, Sheep and Two Eagles in Tree; Fox and Lion; Fox and Stork; Fowler and the Ringdove; Geese and Cranes; Hare and Tortoise; Hawk and Farmer; Jackdaw and Sheep; Lamb Brought Up by a Goat; Lark and Her Young Ones; The Wounded Lion; Hunter and Fox; Lion and Frog; Lioness and Fox; Old Man and His Sons; The Sheepbider; Sow and the Wolf; Stag Looking into the Water; Wolf and the Lamb; and The Wood and the Clown.

Dutch and English Delft Tiles

Borders on this series are rococo scrolls.

Transfer tiles do not have a corner decoration and each tile is complete in itself with its border and subject. There are a few exceptions to this, such as the green vase tiles which have scroll corners and were influenced by Wedgwood.

The most valued tiles, on account of their scarcity and their interest, are the theatrical series. This series has a symbolical border and printed titles identifying the actors and the play upon a ribbon at the top and bottom of each tile. Among these theatrical subjects are such English favorites as Mrs. Barry, Mrs. Abington, Mr. Bensley, Mrs. Bulkley, Mrs. Cibber, Mr. Foote, the famous Mr. Garrick, Mrs. Hartley, Miss Hopkins and Mr. Lee Lewes as Harlequin, and various actors in Shakespearean plays. These tiles are rare and not likely to be found.

Lovers or courting scenes are in a characteristic rustic background and include figures of men and women in eighteenth-century costume. The Old Couple, after Watteau, is best known. Domestic, genre, and rural scenes are also taken from Watteau paintings and prints of the day such as The Pretty Mantua Maker by M. Darby, 1772. The Village School; Woman Churning; A Child Learning to Walk in a Go-Cart; A Man at the Village Inn; The Baby's Toilet; The Barber Shop; The Three Gossips; Girl Blowing Bubbles; Blind Man's Buff; Game of See-Saw; and Battledore and Shuttlecock are other subjects. Also included are dancing scenes, musicians, drinking scenes; Columbine, Harlequin and Pierrot; The Tithe Pig; The Fortune Teller and classical and allegorical scenes, such as Mercury Teaching Cupid. A few armorial tiles are found and scenes of classical ruins, sporting subjects, ships at sea, sailors, soldiers, shepherds and shepherdesses from Watteau are popular subjects. Biblical scenes are not as popular in English Delft as on Dutch tiles, but the Prodigal Son, David and Goliath; Abraham About to Offer up Isaac; and Christ and the Woman of Samaria at the Well are found on Liverpool tiles. Examples of most of these subjects are found in the collection of the Metropolitan Museum.

Liverpool tiles were used extensively in America, and as early as

1761, the Boston newspapers advertised: "English Chimney Tiles—A few Hogsheads of hand Delph (English spelling) Ware—English Chimney Tiles." In 1762 they advertised: "Red and white, and blue and white English Chimney Tiles." In the *Boston Gazette*, 1763: "English Delph Ware—Chimney Tiles." As late as 1784, John Rawlins advertised in the *Maryland Journal* & *Baltimore Advertiser:* "The subscriber hath just received a very neat collection of the very best Liverpool Tile or Chimney Pieces." Needless to say, many of these tiles in America were destroyed, but many still exist in old houses and museums, and enough stray ones cross the market to make interesting sport for the collector. Later tiles with blue or manganese painted on white, designs in crude workmanship and without borders, suggest the type of work on spatter-ware and were made for a less demanding public.

Delft, because of its composition, chips easily and few pieces are found in perfect condition. Cracks or chips do not mean that the piece is not collectible, because Delft is too scarce to be discarded for minor defects. However, when the design is marred or the color destroyed, a tile is certainly not desirable.

In regard to subject matter, portraits are the rarest, Liverpool theatricals, Æsop's fables, Dutch cities are next rarest, while landscapes, animals, Biblical scenes and sea monsters are more plentiful. Liverpool and other English Delft is rarer than Dutch Delft, but there has been a growing interest and a rising market in all Delft in the last few years.

BIBLIOGRAPHY

Old Dutch Pottery and Tiles, Elizabeth Neurdenburg and Bernard Rockham, Himebaugh & Browne, Inc., N. Y., 1923.

A Guide to the Collection of Tiles, Arthur Lane, Victoria and Albert Museum, London, 1939.

Burlington Magazine, Vol. VI, 1905, "Transfer Printing on Pottery: a Catalogue of Liverpool Tiles," J. Hodskin.

Connoisseur, Vols. 61, 63 and 65, History of Dutch Wall Tile as Exemplified in the Vis Collection, Conmer de Geus.

Chapter 5

STAFFORDSHIRE COTTAGE FIGURES

EARLY English pottery figures made by Whieldon and Ralph and Enoch Wood and others were usually signed pieces. They are, for the most part, in museums or well-known collections and their scarcity and price make them beyond the reach and interest of the average collector. But nineteenth-century Staffordshire figures have a more popular appeal and are available. In subject matter they are often the same as the earlier figures, although much of their interest and value lies in the fact that their subject matter is contemporary with the times.

Cottage figures were made at all the English and Scotch potteries from about 1840. Cottage figures were listed as "image toys and chimney ornaments" and were sold at country fairs and peddled from house to house. They were to be seen on the cottager's highboy or mantel shelf, and a typical mantel might have a pair of woolly-haired dogs and, in the center, a medieval castellated building with a clock enclosed. These pieces vary in quality of modeling and color and were seldom marked, although the names of some makers of late Staffordshire figures are known. John Walton, for example, was noted for his "bocage"—spreading-branch backgrounds with leaves and flowers similar to those of more refined Chelsea and Derby figures. These are marked "Walton" on a raised ribbon.

However, there was seldom any attempt to rival porcelain and thus these cottage figures in their simplicity and sincerity took on the folk spirit. They have a humor that more sophisticated figures lack. The subjects are mainly pastoral and domestic. Both figure groups and animals were made in pairs.

The figures depict the costumes of the day, the literature, and the happenings of everyday life and thus have a historical interest aside from their rustic charm and quaintness. Typical historical figures include Victoria and Albert. Victoria wears a crown and a dress with roses on the flounce. About 1845, a white earthenware figure of Prince Albert with

Death of Nelson

details in black and gold was a popular figure at both the English and Scotch potteries. Other well-known historical figures include Lord Nelson, the Duke of Wellington, and John Wesley, as well as King Charles, Cromwell, Napoleon, Benjamin Franklin and, in about 1861–1865, a figure of Lincoln on a prancing white horse with silver on the bridle and tail and a red saddle. Lincoln wears a red cloak with a fur collar. "A. Lincoln" in raised block letters marks the figure base. These mid-Victorian figures seldom resemble persons and may only be recognized when labeled. Mounted figures were made in white and gold pottery with color on the head, hands, cloak and boots. Horses are prancing, with full tails and manes, and are dappled in gold, with gold on their manes, reins and trappings. The Duke of Cambridge, Tom King and Dick Turpin are examples of familiar mounted figures. Another familar pair is a lady and gentleman in Victorian riding costumes, plumed hats, and the lady in voluminous skirts. Horses are usually white, but some figures are mounted on black horses. Other figures include: Will Watch

the Pirate, Paul Pry, William Tell, Robin Hood, Friar Tuck, A Sailor and His Lass, and Uncle Tom and Eva. This latter group shows Uncle Tom sitting on a rock while Eva hangs a wreath about Tom's head. The inscription reads: "Eva gaily laughing was hanging a wreath of roses around Tom's neck."

Other popular figures included: The Leaping Stag; The Shepherd with a Lamb; The Gamekeeper; Rebecca at the Well; African Sal. The Fortune Teller group was first made in 1840. It was of white earthenware with enamel colors and has two figures of women seated in a grape arbor. One woman holds a baby in her arms and the other, the fortune teller, has a plaid headdress. A figure of a cottage boy and girl also shows the girl with a plaid skirt. Indeed, the human interest of these figures is closely related to the cottager and his everyday life. Some figures portray the humble fishwife, the sweep, the peddler, or old-clothes man and the market woman with her basket. Minstrels, African Sal or The Hurdy Gurdy, or the figure of a boy and girl with a musical instrument illustrate the cottager's taste in music. Subjects of sentimental interest include: Mother and Child; Widow with Child; Lovers Walking; Youth with Rabbits; and the figure of a girl with flowers or a lamb. Figures of Mr. Pickwick or Ralph Nickleby and mythological subjects such as Diana and Venus as well as many Biblical subjects such as Elijah were also popular. The oriental on an Elephant dates from 1840, and figures of a cat and dog smoking, dancing dogs, and a bear with collar and chain called Bear Baiting were also first made about this time. A quaint and interesting group of theatrical figures was made in Victorian Stafford-shire. Although these figures are now rare, they are well worth the search, whether you find a quaint Tragedy Queen or a Jenny Lind, in a blue and pale-green gown standing stiff and erect upon the base which has her name in gold script. Other theatrical figures include John Kemble, William Macready, Jullien, the conductor, Charles Kean, Miss Ellsler, the dancer, and Shakespeare leaning against a pedestal with a sheet of paper in his hand.

Almost every cottager's home had a pottery cat or dog or a pair of sheep, lions, leaping stags, or spotted cows. These animal figures are some of the most charming of Victorian pottery figures. The typical Victorian pottery dog is the red-and-white-spotted comforter. He is in a sitting position and has a gold chain and padlock. These dogs are often called spaniels, but, by whatever name, their open-eyed meek expression has won the heart of the collector. They usually come in pairs and face each other. They were made in five standard sizes from 6″ to 18″, the 9″ size being the most popular. The body of the dog is white, but the dogs vary in spotting and color from red, black, brown, green and gray to copper luster. There are also poodles with baskets in their mouths, and Pomeranians, and greyhounds. A greyhound on its haunches with a bird or hare in its mouth is rare, as is the greyhound on the blue cushion inkpot. Hounds are made sitting, standing, or lying prone. Sheep, cows, zebras, lions, roosters, parrots and rare cats were also made at all potteries.

Historical buildings in Staffordshire Victorian pottery include Westminster Abbey and several buldings of local interest to the cottagers of the era, including the Red Barn at Polestead which figured in a famous murder, and Potash Farm and Stanfield Hall, which were also in the news of the day. These are rare and interesting pieces since they include both figures and buildings.

It is difficult to ascertain exactly where a certain figure was made since so-called Staffordshire pottery figures were made and imitated in all parts of England and Scotland as well. Indeed Watson's Pottery in the Prestonpans district of Scotland specialized in figures and imported English potters. They portrayed such local characters as fishwives in addition to the usual well-known subjects. A few of these figures have the name "Watson" impressed in the clay and while figures were also made at other Scottish potteries, those made at Watson's are the best in modeling and color. Rathbone's Pottery made figures set on a square base with a cable or rope used as a molding and a key-design border in deep blue. A figure of a girl and boy in plaids is set on such a base, as are many other chimney pieces of figures, birds and animals.

J. Dale of Burslem advertised: "Image Toys and Chimney Ornaments," but while both Walton and Ralph Salt often marked their names on a raised scroll, Dale has no mark. However, many spotted dogs and woolly sheep may be attributed to these men. J. Neale and Obediah Sherratt were also well-known names and the figure of Bull Baiting is known to have been made by Sherratt.

Aside from a rare marked figure, the value of a cottage figure lies in its modeling and coloring. Surfaces are given a broad treatment and the backs are often unfinished. The coloring should be restrained, but lively. Soft yellow, green, blue, brown, purple, and an orange-red are typical colorings, while animals and horsemen are often in black and white with a bit of gold or color in some article of clothing.

These cottage figures were also made in America of stoneware. The inspiration and subject matter usually showed Staffordshire influence, however. In both England and America these figures were made in the early part of the twentieth century, so that one must be critical in order to find a really old figure. However, if you are sensitive to the color, the new figures are garish in comparison to the older figures and the modeling is not so good.

The type of lettering used in the inscription of a Staffordshire figure is helpful in dating the piece. Bold script in gold is used on figures from about 1820 to 1860, while the Egyptian style of block lettering with gold decoration was used from 1860 to 1880, and later crude variations of block lettering were used or brush letters instead of modeled or relief letters.

Staffordshire was made of soft paste which is lighter, more porous and duller in color or tone than hard paste. The glaze is also soft and is warmer and more clinging to the touch. To this soft paste is due much of the charm and rustic quality of Staffordshire figures. On the base of old Staffordshire can be detected the lines made by the stilts which held the piece in the firing kiln. There were so many old figures made that there are still some to be found, but it is often difficult to get a matching pair. However, with patience, the mate may often be located months or even years later.

Staffordshire houses are another interesting subject for collectors. There are pink and lavender English cottages with vines and flowers growing about their doorways. There are also churches of English architecture and Gothic buildings and castles. As fascinating as these houses are, they are not for as wide a public as the other figures, since they are rather expensive when located. However, several might be included in a collection of dogs or other figures.

Staffordshire Cottage Figures ·

BIBLIOGRAPHY

Portraits in Pottery, Albert Lee, The Stratford Co., Boston, Mass., 1931.

Scottish Pottery, J. Arnold Fleming, O. B. E., Maclehose, Jackson & Co., Glasgow, 1923.

Chats on English Earthenware, Arthur Hayden, T. Fisher Unwin, London, 1909.

The Earthenware Collector, G. Wooliscroft Rhead.

Staffordshire Pottery Figures, Herbert Read, Duckworth, London, 1929.

Catalogue of Willett Collection Illustrating Popular British History, Public Museum, Brighton, England.

Chapter 6

ENGLISH LUSTRE OF THE
NINETEENTH CENTURY

LUSTRE ware was first made by John Hancock in the late eighteenth century and was soon produced in the Staffordshire potteries, at Brislington near Bristol, and at Leeds, Sunderland and Swansea. Lustre originally was made for cottage use, and the shapes, designs, and decorations are generally simple and unsophisticated. A great quantity of lustre was made over a long period of time so that there is still considerable lustre on the market. Really fine lustre is not cheap, but if you have been led into the field by grandmother's copper lustre cream jug with the bright-blue band there is still a supply of these quaint pitchers in the shops, and the prices are comparatively low.

A collection of small lustre pitchers may be modest. Larger jugs are harder to find and higher in price. Goblets and mugs also exist in sufficient quantities to lure the more discriminating collector, and tea pots, cups and saucers and even complete tea sets are available as well as bowls, occasional vases, candlesticks, salt dishes and figures. The Sunderland lustre plaque or picture is another field of interest.

Lustre is produced by the application of a thin coat or glaze of metal, reduced by chemicals, to a pottery surface. From the chemist's viewpoint there are three kinds of English lustres: gold, silver and copper. Gold lustre is produced from a solution of gold and copper on brown clay. There are many shades and effects due to the difference in the pottery ground and the amount of metal used as well as the time and heat of firing. When gold is used upon a white or cream ground, it produces a lilac or metallic pink. Wedgwood produced a ruby glaze upon a thin Queen's ware body, and the result is mottled or splashed.

Silver lustre is made by platinum in chemical solution. A thin coat produces a steel appearance and thus an inferior product. Copper lustres vary in shade and some resemble gold while others are dark copper-brown. Ordinary copper lustres were made in the Staffordshire district until about 1875 and reproductions are still being made, so beware when you buy copper lustre or any lustre, since there are fakes and reproductions. Since there is considerable discussion concerning the chemical makeup of gold and copper lustre and since they do vary and seem to overlap, gold often looking like copper and copper looking like gold, I prefer to consider lustre by its methods of decoration or surface design.

Considerable lustre was made in both silver and gold, which was intended to produce the effect of plated wares. Candlesticks, goblets, chalices and other communion dishes as well as tea and coffee pots and complete tea sets were made in both silver and gold lustres. These pieces not only resembled the plated wares, but were actually made in the old silver or Sheffield molds. Thus many fine old Queen Anne and Georgian shapes are covered with silver or gold lustre, and the tea pots are especially interesting. The sets were also made in a pineapple pattern, and a molded design similar to the hobnail pattern, also a diamond molded pattern. And we find such decorations as fluting—both horizontal and vertical—beading, and gadroon borders in relief. Some goblets are plain and some have a single band of beading. The insides are sometimes gold or silvered or they may have a plum or ruby lining.

Pitchers and tea pots with classic reliefs and fluting similar to jasper or basalts of Wedgwood were covered with lustre. Also the Wedgwood mask in relief has been found on both gold and silver lustre jug spouts. Plain gold and silver without pattern or design is often of distinctive shape—especially is this true of goblets, pitchers and even tea and coffee pots. It is difficult to find pieces of this plain lustre in "mint" condition since it may be rubbed with age or may have originally been a second. Next to condition, the shape and contour of these pieces is especially important in making a choice.

Gold and silver resist or stencil patterns are another interesting class of lustre. The resist design was painted on in an adhesive fluid of brown shellac and spirits of wine. Then the piece was dipped into the platinum or gold bath and all the surface except the resist would be covered with lustre. When the piece was washed a background design remained. Resist patterns of a tropical bird with flowers and foliage and vine borders may completely cover a jug, or tea pot, or cup. However there is often a panel which encloses a bird or several birds and foliage. Birds are painted red, blue and green, and red and green are also often put in by hand on silver resist patterns. Designs include naturalistic birds and flower patterns, grape and leaf patterns and borders of scrolls, interlaced ovals, Greek fret, leaves and delicate scrolls and brushwork in silver. There are also designs of Chinese influence and the Morland sportsman designs. These subjects are hunting, farm and field scenes, and deer. These designs were printed in a blue underglaze and often tinted by hand. Designs were usually in one color —black, sepia, violet, brick-red or purple—and often other colors were put in by hand. Views of country residences in Queen Anne style and Masonic emblems are also found in panels surrounded by resist lustre decoration. Sometimes blue or red are added to the resist pattern. Silver resist is most often found on a white or cream ground and this ground presents the clearest pattern outlines. Silver resist is also found on a buff ground, a rare canary ground, with or without a bit of red in the decorations, and a turquoise and a rare blue ground. A pink or an apricot ground is very rare in resist lustre. Presentation pitchers have names and dates of the owners in a space beneath the spout and these dates tell us that silver resist was made as early as 1791.

Copper resist is usually of a lilac shade. The patterns are floral and the grounds are white and sometimes pale blue. Many late nineteenth-

English Lustre

century copper lustre goblets have resist bands of lilac. Sprays of gold on a white body produce a golden-pink resist.

The stencil is the reverse of the resist. The stencil pattern appears in lustre on a white or colored ground. A gold stencil is usually on a blue ground. Stencil is found more often on borders or small surfaces rather than a large all-over stencil decoration.

For many years pink lustre was not included in most collections because of its childish patterns and general peasant character. However, now that we are especially interested in folk art, pink lustre has come into its own; in fact, it is considered the height of sophistication to collect it. While not all pink lustre is Sunderland, the group of potteries that grew up along the Tees, the Wear and the Tyne, including Sunderland and Newcastle, did produce lustre with individual designs and a character different from the Staffordshire lustres. These wares have a salty tang. They were made for a sailor clientele and their designs are definitely geared for such appeal. Especially is this so of the Sunderland and Newcastle jugs and mugs with transfers of ships and verses. Jugs were made in twelve sizes and were sold as gift china for weddings, anniversaries, birthdays, etc. The most popular subject was the iron extension bridge over the Wear. Pitchers and mugs are found with a transfer print of the bridge, a mariner's compass and a verse relating to marine life or drinking. The pink lustre is in wide bands at the neck and splashed around the panels. Other jugs have a seaman in kilts and the verses, The Hardy Sailor and When Round the Bowl. Still other jugs have Masonic emblems or scenes from the Crimean War with splashed pink borders. Sporting jugs have a raised scene of dogs, birds and horses or horsemen in pink lustre, with green shrubs and a pink lustre vine decoration around the neck. Other sporting pitchers have a raised hunting scene in white, and the only lustre is a band of pink around the neck of the jug. The handles of these sporting jugs are often in the form of a hound. Some of the pitchers have initials and a date beneath the spout. Still other pitchers have a spray of flowers or small sprigs of flowers with lustre bands.

55

Drinking mugs of several sizes were made with designs of ships and verses, the Wear bridge, and the cottage design. Many of these mugs have a molded frog on the interior and are known as Frog Mugs. Some of the lustre decorations are plain and others are mottled pink, made by oiling the piece before firing. The Sunderland plaque framed and decorated in pink lustre is another distinctive piece of this section of the country. It was a pottery plaque with a religious inscription such as Praise Ye the Lord, Thou God Seest Me, or Prepare to Meet Thy God. This text usually had a garland or wreath of flowers printed around it. These plaques are rectangular, square, or round, and have a hole in the frame for a cord. They were hung in fishermen's cottages. Some plaques also have transfer scenes of landscapes, express trains, ships and probably the Wear Bridge may be found on such a plaque, as well as portraits of well-known preachers of the era.

Designs on Sunderland tea sets include variations of the cottage pattern, the grapevine pattern, a transfer of Queen Victoria and Prince Albert, an all-over sprig design, the aster design and the strawberry design. All of these designs are in the characteristic pink and green, that is, pink lustre with green-painted leaves, vines, trees, or other accents. Sometimes a blob of foreground in a landscape is painted green. Another design in pink lustre is the blackberry flower and leaf which is especially striking with its white flowers and green leaves upon a pink-lustre band with fine gold veinings; however, such a delicate pink-lustre design was probably made in the Staffordshire district rather than at Sunderland. All these designs are further banded in pink lustre and also may have decorative borders of sprays and leaves in lustre. The scenes vary from a primitive cottage to a country estate, a castle, and a bridge over a mountain stream; all of these variations may appear in one tea set. The shapes of cups vary. Some have handles, but the earliest are without handles. Saucers are round, without the usual ridge in the bottom to hold the cup. The basins or bowls are of two shapes, rounded, or with a line or ridge which breaks the curve. Some of these basins have verses and some have armorial designs and coats of arms. Others have simple aster and leaf designs, or blackberries and leaves, while some have Victorian transfers of such subjects as The Mother's Grave, To Lucy in Heaven, and The Monument to Washington, all with pink-lustre borders. The latter type of design was also made at Staffordshire potteries. Rare transfer patterns are on yellow with gold-lustre bands.

White pottery with pink lustre bands and leaf borders which have a printed pastoral subject or a semiclassic design is called New Hall type, although it was also made by both Leeds and Sunderland. These subjects were often taken from blocks used by wood engravers of the period, including Adam Buck, who did a series of maternal amusements that include such well-known prints as the battledore and shuttlecock game, mother and child, children playing with each other, and reclining maiden, and a series of scenes of women in classic costume, in a setting with Regency furniture, reading or playing with children, birds or dogs. Scenes of a woman with a child, and a woman at the piano appear in a black transfer on yellow with gold bands. Scenes from *The Peacock at Home,* a popular children's book, were also used.

Copper lustres are found decorated with sprig patterns in an overglaze decoration in various colors. Sometimes floral borders of blue or lavender and green and other colors are in raised enamel decoration. A transparent blue floral-painted border is also associated with copper lustres. The grapevine border and the strawberry border are found on bands with both blue and white grounds. Goblets are also found with an openwork basket with raised flowers of several colors on a blue ground.

Copper lustre relief designs on reserve grounds of blue, tan and turquoise include the figures of the four seasons and such classic subjects as *putti* and other figures at a sacrificial fire. These classic subjects which always include trees, vases, an altar, or similar subjects, were undoubtedly taken from Wedgwood plaques which in turn had their inspiration in the *"Recueil d'antiquities Egyptienes, Etrusques, Greques, Romaines et Gauloises"* by Comte de Caylus. A farm and field subject in relief under copper lustre was also popular. Ordinary copper lustre with relief patterns in colors show wreaths of leaves and small classical and flower designs. Swansea relief patterns show fruit in rare green, orange and red-vermilion colorings.

Much copper lustre with relief, brightly colored, was made in later years in Sweden, Denmark and Germany. Still other relief patterns are in white upon copper grounds. Gold or copper lustre with raised white ornaments in relief are typical of Wilson in the Staffordshire district. The designs show *putti* dancing with flowers and trees as part of the design, or *putti* rollicking with a bear or goat in ribbon harness or with lion or goat either in white or in various colors. Sprays of flowers and raised borders of vines and strap design also appear in relief. Sometimes the relief is in pale blue on copper, but usually the grounds are blue, cream or tan. A boy with sheep appears in blue relief on copper. Also pink roses with copper leaves are in relief on a blue band on copper pitchers and flower pots. Very often a lion head in relief forms a handle and a spout may have a leaf design or a mask in relief in copper. The scenes from The Peacock at Home appear in colors on a blue ground on small copper pitchers. An unusual pitcher in the Buck collection at Home Sweet Home, East Hampton, Long Island, has a lavender lustre relief of a basket of grapes, a dog and men in a tavern scene on a white ground. The pitcher also has raised borders of lavender lustre.

Painted borders on copper lustre include: copper flowers and leaves on a blue border, an orange spatter on a light-blue border, lavender and green flowers on copper, an aster and leaf design and blue and green flower borders. Early gold lustre had reserved belts of blue, yellow, dark green and pink lustre.

Often copper lustre has bands of blue, cream, tan or other colors of various widths and these are the only decoration. Horizontal bands of color also alternate with borders of horizontal ribbing.

While it is difficult to identify the lustre of different factories unless a rare piece is found with a mark, enough marked pieces have been found to allow us to attribute certain types to definite factories or districts.

Swansea gold lustre has a brilliancy of glaze and was made over a mottled ground of blue or purple. Red and green designs of fruit on a pale-blue ground incised with gold are typical of Swansea lustre, and the strawberry and cottage design was made at Swansea as well as Sunderland and other factories. Old Leeds farm and hunting scenes in relief often have a small ring impress on the bottom. A pitcher with a farm scene of pink lustre cows and green trees which is in the Buck collection is marked, "Clews Warranted Staffordshire," with impressed crown above the name. A rare jug with a transfer of Cornwallis and of Lafayette is marked "B" and refers to Longton lustre made by Thomas Barlow.

Relief designs painted in lustre and color are typical late-nineteenth century from St. Anthony's Pottery, Newcastle-on-Tyne. Cauliflower or sanded borders are late and are not as desirable as borders with a painted design. Purple-mottled lustre of Wedgwood in shell form is rare and so are silver resist crocus or bulb dishes. These bulb dishes are half-circle shape and have covers with holes and a classical relief design which divides the vase into panels which are filled with silver resist designs of flowers in a vase and birds and fruit. They are so fine in workmanship and sophisticated in design that they suggest Wedgwood or Swansea or Leeds origin.

Although we know many makers of lustre, marked pieces are very rare. Thus we must train ourselves to recognize old lustre and to spot the fakes. Such well-known copper lustre jugs as the Polka jug with dancing figures in copper relief on copper with blue decorations, and a diamond-fauceted jug with a raised floral decoration in turquoise have been faked. Gold and copper goblets have also been faked. Fine old lustre is smooth and clear and should be without bubbles, which begin to appear about 1850 or after. Shapes of lustre will help to date a piece. Fakes are often made on modern molds as well as shapes that did not exist when old lustre was made. The structure of handles and the weight of the piece will aid in ascertaining the place where it was made. For example, Wedgwood lustre was light and thin, while Wilson copies were heavy. The subjects of transfers on old pieces will aid in dating, since many scenes were taken from children's books or relate to certain historical events such as the Crimean War or Cornwallis and Lafayette. Canary color usually indicates fine workmanship, while apricot is more

common, and dark green and tortoise shell are associated with coarse colors and designs and later dates. Finely painted floral sprays are usually more desirable than flowers in relief. A pink ground is rare but purple and lilac are Victorian and thus date around 1850 or after.

Remember that the most important feature of lustre is the decoration. If the decoration is in good color and good design, then the piece is worth owning.

No lustre was made in America, but pieces were marked for the American market with an eagle imprint.

A great deal of present-day lustre is being made, but anyone acquainted with really fine old lustre will never be fooled by it, although even some of the ten-cent store variety is not bad in itself.

Few pieces of lustre are marked, but those that are have an impressed name or letter. The following marks have been found on lustre:

English Lustre

"A"—either Aynsley or Allerton—Staffordshire

"Allertons" — Staffordshire — c. 1831

"Aynsley"—Staffordshire—c. 1800

"B" — Barlow — Staffordshire — c. 1800

"B" scratched in clay (cursive) — Silver Staffordshire—c. 1820

"Bailey & Batkin" — Longton — Staffordshire

"Bailey & Harvey"—Staffordshire

"Bott & Co."—Staffordshire

"George Bratt"

"Cambrian"—1769–1790

"Copeland and Garrett"—1833–1847

"D"—Davenport—c. 1800

"Dawson"—Sunderland—c. 1810

"Dillwyn"—Swansea—1802–1870

"Dixon & Co."—Sunderland—from 1780

"Dixon, Austin & Co."—Sunderland—c. 1820

"Fell"—Newcastle—c. 1813

"G" (Masonic pattern) —unidentified maker

"Harley"—Staffordshire—c. 1800

"Hartley Green & Co."—Leeds

"Lakin & Poole"—Staffordshire—1770–1795

"Leeds Pottery" or "L.P."— (silver) —c. 1790

"J. Lockett & Sons"—Staffordshire—c. 1829

"Mayer & Newbold"—Staffordshire—c. 1800

"E. Mayer"—Staffordshire—c. 1790

"Meigh"—Staffordshire—c. 1790

"Minton"—c. 1790

"P. & U." (Poole & Unwin) —Longton—c. 1870

"Scott & Sons—Southwick"

"S. & Sons, Southwick"

"Scott"—Sunderland—c. 1789

"Spode"—c. 1770

"Warburton"—Cobridge—c. 1802

"Wedgwood"

"Wileman"—c. 1860

"J. Phillips—Hylton Pottery"

"Wilson" — Staffordshire — 1786–1802

"W"

"E. Wood"—Burslem—c. 1783

"Wood & Caldwell"—1790–1818

"Enoch Wood & Sons"—c. 1818

"Moore & Co."— (Southwick— Sunderland) —c. 1820

"Pountney & Goldney" and impressed cross—Bristol—c. 1831

"London" (Middleboro Pottery) —c. 1831

However, almost all the well-known English potteries made lustre, as did Prestonpans and others in Scotland.

BIBLIOGRAPHY

Collecting Old Lustre Ware, W. Bosanko, W. Heinemann, London, 1916.

Bulletin of Art Institute of Chicago, November, 1941.

Connoisseur, December, 1907, pp. 218–224; May, 1904, p. 3.

Pink Lustre, Atwood Thorne, B. T. Batsford, Ltd., London, 1926.

Collecting Old English Lustre, Jeanette R. Hodgdon, The Southworth-Anthoensen Press, Portland, Maine, 1937.

Chapter 7

PINK AND OTHER LIGHT-TONED STAFFORD-SHIRE WITH AMERICAN HISTORICAL VIEWS

To THE collector interested in china and in the American scene, pink and other light-toned Staffordshire is a good hunting ground. To be sure, it is not as plentiful nor as easy to find as blue Staffordshire, but also it is not nearly so expensive, and, to date, few collectors are specializing in it.

Pink Staffordshire does not have the same quaint charm as old blue. There is no depth of color or rough pottery texture, for pink Staffordshire is a later product. The lighter colors were introduced into the potteries about 1829. From this date on through the 1850's American historical scenes were printed in pink, light blue, green, mulberry, purple, gray, brown and black. These colors replaced old blue, but many of the interesting scenes of the earlier period were used, with some variations, in the paler tints. Of this later pottery, Simeon Shaw wrote in 1829: "This pottery has a rich and delicate appearance and owing to the blue printed having become so common, the other is now obtaining a decided preference in most genteel circles."

It is strange that light-colored Staffordshire was neglected for so many years, for from the artistic standpoint it is not far below old blue. The drawings are by the leading artists of the period; artists of equal ability with those who did the old blue. In fact, in many cases the artists and the designs are the same. The borders on light-colored Staffordshire are more delicate and naturalistic, the best, perhaps, being the series on Adams views on Celtic china in which the contrast between the light and dark pink and the use of the conventional shell, as well as the inner border framing the scenes, seems to give greater unity than the Jackson scenes and borders. The Adams American views usually bring higher prices than any other light prints, while the Columbus series is more in demand than either the William Penn or the Richard Jordan.

Although most of the scenes listed as pink also come in various other light colors, the pink is considered the more desirable and more collectible. For this reason the emphasis in this chapter is on pink. Those who think that old blue is the only decorative Staffordshire should set a collection of old pink against a green wall or a wall of deep contrasting pink like the darker pink of the plates. Such backgrounds bring out the delicacy of the color. However, pink Staffordshire is not only more delicate in color, but in design as well. The borders are more sophisticated and the shapes more refined. Where the edges of platters and plates in old blue are simple curves, the edges of the lighter-colored plates and platters are often rounded into scalloped or bracketed curves. Finally, there are scenes on pink Staffordshire which do not appear on old blue at all. Consequently most collectors of old blue include several pieces of old pink to complete their collection of the American Scene, and most museums also have a few pieces of pink Staffordshire.

While it is desirable to have only pieces in perfect condition, there are exceptions. When a rare plate such as Bunker Hill Monument by Jackson is discovered, the rarity is so great that a slight crack does not reduce the intrinsic value. When pieces are not marked, the border is a means of identification as each maker usually had his own border for a special series and seldom used any other.

Many well-known potteries and artists made pink Staffordshire. Especially well-known are the series of American views by Enoch Wood & Sons. This series was made in black, medium blue, light blue, pink and mulberry. However, as is the case with all of these views, the complete dinner set was not made in all colors, but plates might be one color, platters another, and hollow ware another. Then, too, some views have so far been found only in one color when it is almost certain that they were made in various colors.

Light-Toned Staffordshire

The Enoch Wood series of American views has a border of fruit and flowers. It is often stamped with a printed eagle facing right, with a scroll attached to a shield in its mouth, and, above, a scarf with "E Pluribus Unum." Of this series the pink vegetable dish with the scene Buffalo on Lake Erie is one of best known and most-desired pieces of pink Staffordshire. The view is a scene of the waterfront at Buffalo showing the Niagara River as it flows out of the lake toward the falls at the right, with buildings in the middle distance, and masts of sailing vessels in the background. The scene is based on a sketch by Captain Basil Hall and included in Hall's *Forty Etchings from Sketches Made with the Cameria Lucida in North America in 1827–1828.*

Pink plates with a design from the same source were made by Ralph Stevenson; here, however, only half of the scene is used. The plates have a lacy border, and are marked with an oval wreath enclosing the name of the view and the words "Lace Border" and "R.S." A small plate with a harbor scene of New Orleans has the same border and is also marked "R.S." This scene is only on the light-colored Staffordshire.

Another view in Wood's Celtic china series which has been found in pink is the Pass in the Catskill Mountains. The scene shows the Hudson River in a diagonal through the picture. In the foreground is the river bank and a white road outlined by trees. A man with a staff on his shoulder appears in the center. Sailboats and a steamboat are on the river and the Catskill Mountains form the background. There are also several other interesting designs in pink by Wood. One is the Eagle on the Rock. The scene is of a large eagle perched on a flower-covered rock, with water and ships in the distance. A wide border of light and dark checks overlaid with vines and flowers surrounds the scene and covers the body of the piece. The pink design is found on small creamers while the same design in mulberry has been found on a tea pot, sugar bowl and cups and saucers. The pink creamer is unmarked, but pieces have been found marked "Wood."

Several of the most interesting and sought-after pink Staffordshire views are found in Clews series of Picturesque Views. The designs for this series were taken from Wall's Hudson River Portfolio. The series was made in black, brown, light blue, purple, pink and lavender, and has a border of birds, roses and scrolls. Pieces are marked with a printed view of a lake, sailboat and trees, with Picturesque Views and the name of the view in script on a white band across the center. Baker's Falls (on a plate in the Morse Collection in the Antiquarian Society at Worcester, Mass.) shows the falls and rapids, pine trees and grist mills, with a man and woman on a flat rock in the foreground. Fort Edward, Hudson River, is found on small pink plates. The scene shows the banks of the Hudson with two cows grazing and the village of Fort Edward and mountains in the background. Pink soup plates have been found with Fort Miller, Hudson River, and give a view of the Hudson north of Albany and a few houses in the background indicating the village of Fort Miller. A small pink pitcher has a scene of the Hudson with men hauling seines, and sailboats and rowboats and the village of Hudson, New York, on the hills in the background. It is a quaint and attractive scene and is fenced by a delicate lacy frame. Another pink pitcher has a view, Near Hudson, showing an expanse of countryside, a horseman and the river in the middle distance. Still another small pink pitcher by Clews has a view of Newburgh on the Hudson. It shows a farm wagon with oxen on a country road, a hillside and sheep, and, in the background across the river, the town of Newburgh with hills and mountains behind.

One of the most decorative series on pink Staffordshire is the Tunstall Views, by W. Adams and Sons. These designs were mostly in pink, but were also made in black and brown. They have a lovely border of baskets of roses and fan-shaped medallions. Of the fourteen drawings for the series, seven are by Thomas Cole. The mark on the Tunstall Views is an impressed "Adams" and a printed eagle surmounting a bar with two cornucopias filled with fruit and flowers. Monte Video, the residence of D. Wadsworth, Esq., Hartford, Connecticut, shows a large two-story house against a background of Talcot Mountain and the observatory tower. In the foreground, by the edge of the lake, two figures sit surrounded by trees and ferns. The scene is by Cole and is found on plates of several sizes. The View Near Conway, New Hampshire, shows a log cabin set in mountain scenery and, in the foreground, two figures and a tree stump which are typical of Cole's drawings. A small lacy frame encircles the view on the plates. White Mountains, New Hampshire, from one of Cole's best paintings shows two men and a dog, with Mt. Washington towering in the distance. It has been found on a pink platter and vegetable dish. Pink plates with a view of Catskill Mountain House were also from a drawing by Cole and the view is similar to that on a pink plate by J. & J. Jackson. One of the loveliest views of Niagara is on the pink platter entitled Falls of Niagara, U.S. The engraving is from a painting by Cole. Another pink platter shows a view of West Point framed in a foreground of trees and shrubbery. The drawing is by J. Milbert and is more naturalistic than Bennett's painting of the same scene on the old blue platter by Wood. Still another pink platter has a scene of Harper's Ferry, W. Va., from a drawing by W. Goodacre. It shows the Potomac River with two figures on a tree stump by the banks, and the slopes of the Blue Ridge Mountains. Headwaters of the Juniata, U.S., showing a rustic bridge across a stream, is by T. Cole and is one of the scenes that is not found on dark-blue Staffordshire. Shannondale Springs, Va. shows a view of the hotel and cottages of the Springs. The drawing is by Charles Burton and was also used on pink plates by J. & J. Jackson. But one of the quaintest of all scenes on pink Staffordshire is that entitled New York and found both on plates and on cups and saucers. It shows a sailor boy and girl, with ships and the buildings of New York in the background. The border has medallions of a sailor boy and a ship and conventional sunflower decorations.

The largest series of views in light-colored Staffordshire was made by J. & J. Jackson, who did not make dark blue. Their views number about forty and include scenes from New York, Pennsylvania, Connecticut, Massachusetts, Virginia and even Ohio. The border on this series of views shows a spray of fine flowers, a beaded band and a white margin with sprays of roses on the inner edge. On the back, the name of the view is printed in script, and on a scroll are the words, "Jackson's Warranted." This series was made in light blue, black, brown, green, pink and maroon. One of the most interesting views and one that does not appear elsewhere on Staffordshire is the view of the Battle Monument, Baltimore. The view of Hancock House, Boston, is also found only in light-colored Staffordshire, although on brown and maroon as well as on pink plates and soup plates. The drawing was by the architect, A. J. Davis, who also did the drawing of Harvard Hall, which was used by so many potteries.

Bunker Hill Monument by Jackson, from the drawing by A. J. Davis, is perhaps the rarest of all pink plates. It shows the granite monument surrounded by a fence with huge posts, and trees and houses in the background, with a group of people in the foreground. This plate is listed as blue and is rarely seen in pink. Jackson's views also include a plate of Monte Video and a scene of Hartford, Connecticut with two cows in the foreground and the city on the distant river bank. A view near Conway, N.H., which is often unmarked, has been found on pink plates and is attributed to Jackson. It is a variation of the T. Cole drawing which appears on an Adams plate of the same title. New York scenes which have been found on Jackson's pink Staffordshire include: New York, Castle Garden; Cattskill Mountain House; New York, City Hall; Little Falls, Mohawk River; View of the Canal and Skenectady, Mohawk River.

However, the scenes most often available and therefore most popular in Jackson's pink Staffordshire are the Philadelphia scenes. Among these is a plate with the Philadelphia Deaf and Dumb Asylum. It is a building of Greek architecture with six Doric columns in façade and a two-story wing at each side. Hitching posts and a group of people are in the foreground. The drawing is by C. Burton and a variation is seen on a plate by Enoch Wood. Another Burton drawing shows Girard's Bank, Philadelphia, another easily identified building with Greek columns. The Race Bridge, Philadelphia, which arches over the Schuylkill River, is a popular subject as is the old Water Works, Philadelphia. The Jackson view has a house and buggy in the foreground. Another ever-popular view is Virginia, Shannondale Springs, which is similar to the view on Adams plates of the same subject. Jackson also did a rare view of Richmond, Virginia, showing the Episcopal Church after a drawing by W. Goodacre, and a quaint view of the President's House, Washington, as well as a view of Fort Conanicut, R.I. A beautiful unmarked pitcher with a border of flowers and peacock feathers and a view of Schenectady, Mohawk River, has been found and is attributed to Jackson.

Thomas Godwin also made a series of American Views in pink, blue, brown and maroon. They are from drawings by W. H. Bartlett. The border of the series is a morning glory and a nasturtium upon a delicate flower background. The title is printed in color on the back in script along with a printed lion and unicorn with a crown between, and below the British coat of arms and a garter bearing the words, "American Views" and "T. Godwin, Wharf" on a scroll. However, although the series includes ten views, only two—Brooklyn Ferry and Fort Hamilton, The Narrows—have been found in pink.

An interesting scene of Franklin's Experiments with Electricity has been found on pink pitchers. There is a border of flowers and deep pink and the mark "Davenport" is often printed or impressed on the bottom.

Mellor, Venables & Co. also put out a series of American views in about 1843, and while most of the views have only been found in light blue, purple or lavender, one item, New York, Fort Hamilton, has been found in pink, and this certainly brings up the question whether the whole series was not originally made in pink. The scene on the pink plate shows the Fort with a flag with figures and a mounted horseman in the foreground, and the Hudson River in the background. The border which is similar to the border on the whole series of plates shows the arms of Maryland, Pennsylvania, New York, Virginia, Massachusetts, Delaware, New Jersey and North Carolina in wreathed medallions alternating with a spray of four flowers resembling dogwood.

One of the plates which should certainly be included in a collection of pink Staffordshire is the view of The Residence of Richard Jordan. A simple farmhouse is shown with a man in Quaker costume in the foreground. The design was made in a complete dinner service in blue, black, brown, lavender, purple, maroon and pink. It has a border of scrolls and large roses and tatting edge, and the mark is an umbrella with the name of the print and the maker, "J.H. & Co." (Joseph Heath & Co.) partly in print and partly in script, below.

Two series of imaginative landscapes also offer interesting items for the collector of pink Staffordshire. They are the William Penn series by Thomas Green, and the Columbus series by Adams. The William Penn series consists of seven variations of William Penn's Treaty with the Indians. The series was made in black, blue, brown, green and pink, of which colors the pink and the green are the rarest. The scenes show Penn and Indians set in a landscape of tropical trees and Chinese pagodas. The border is a stenciled diamond pattern and the print is framed in a lacy circle. The Columbus series by W. Adams & Sons is perhaps the earliest American historical china printed in light colors. The series was made in blue, black, brown, green, pink and purple. The border is made up of alternating medallions with deer and bison and large roses. While all of the scenes have not yet been found in pink, there are several sizes of plates of the boat scene, two fleet scenes and Indian scenes, and platters of the landing scene, pavilion scene, and the dramatic cavalry scene in pink. A pink bowl of the greyhound scene is also on record.

When William Henry Harrison became a candidate for President in 1836 and 1840, various souvenirs were made for the election, including glass, pottery, buttons and textiles. A series of plates, tea pot, and bowl, creamer, cups and cup plates was made by John Ridgeway. The scene is a log cabin with a man plowing and the border is of large stars set upon a field of small stars. The design was made in black, brown, light blue and red or pink. There are three variations to the view. The platter shows the end view while the side view is on the cup plates, cup and tea pot. The printed mark is a star-covered belt with "Columbian Star, Oct. 28th, 1840, Jno. Ridgeway" on the buckle and the impressed mark, "Jno. Ridgeway."

A log cabin scene was also made by W. Adams & Sons. It shows a log cabin with a barrel, two figures and a dog in the foreground, and a river scene in the background. The border has medallions of Harrison, and vines and flowers on a latticed background. It was made in pink and brown. The mark on a printed scroll is "Log Cabin" printed and "Adams" impressed. Plates, bowls, cups and pitchers have been found.

The Texian Campaign, made in pink and marked "J.B. Texian Campaign," on a scroll was made in black, green, pink, purple and blue. The border has war trophies alternating with medallions of Ceres. In the center of the plate is a battle scene with Zachary Taylor mounted on a horse. The source of the view is not known.

I have made no attempt to name every pattern of pink Staffordshire, for only those connected with American history are considered here. Perhaps, however, the Statue of Washington by Canova should be included. The design shows Washington in Roman attire holding a scroll and pen and sitting on a platform. The background is Venetian. The mark is an urn inscribed "Washington" and "E.W. & S." It was made in the 1830's in both pink and green with a border of clusters of flowers and Venetian scenery. Many collectors also include the Ruins of the New York Merchants' Exchange, a pink plate with a border of fire engines and phoenix, and Thorps & Sprague, Albany, which has a border of large flowers and vases with plants. Both subjects are by unknown makers.

BIBLIOGRAPHY

American Historical Views on Staffordshire, Ellouise Baker Larsen, Doubleday, Doran & Co., Inc., New York, 1939.

The Standard Catalogue of Anglo-American China, Sam Laidacker, Scranton, Pennsylvania.

Old China, Keramic Studio Publishing Company, Syracuse, N. Y., 1901–4.

Anglo-American Pottery, Edwin Atlee Barber, Patterson White Company, Philadelphia, 1901.

The Magazine Antiques—various articles.

Chapter 8

PARIAN WARE

IN COLLECTING Parian, it is well to remember that it is a Mid-Victorian product, and like all articles of the era, is likely to be over-decorated and much of it is bad design and in questionable taste. Yet enough Parian is beautiful so that, if you are a judge of art values (that is, if you know good line, form and design when you see it), you can let your instinct be your guide.

Parian or Statuary Ware was first made by Copeland in England in 1842. Parian is a hard porcelain that was invented so that marble figures could be reproduced for a larger market—thus its second name of Statuary Ware.

Parian is translucent and vitreous, and Parian proper is unglazed and is easily recognized by its granular surface. Parian ware is molded. The liquid slip is poured into the mold or sometimes pressed in by hand. The pitted background surface is made by points in the mold. Handles and ornaments are added before firing. Parian proper has no outside glaze, but the insides of pitchers and many vases were glazed for utility purposes. At least one well-known authority would not apply the term Parian to any pieces with color; but for the purpose of the average collector, and for the added interest color gives to a collection, it seems simpler to call these colored pieces Parian. When the color was included in the slip, as it was at Bennington, there was no difference in the ingredients, except that the color was added. However, one may still be technical if one calls these colored pieces Parian upon a colored ground.

As to the pieces that were gilded and hand-colored, there were many

Parian Ware

that were painted and decorated by the owners after they left the factories, and they were made for just this purpose.

Parian ware was made in England and America and to a lesser extent in other continental countries. In England, principal makers were Copeland, Charles Meigh, Minton, Wedgwood, Boote, Rose, T. Booth at Hanley, William Adams and Samuel Alcock. There were also many lesser-known factories. English Parian was made mostly in statuary form, but pitchers and vases, as well as other articles, were made in all the factories.

Copeland was so proud of this Parian that he put out a special catalogue of "Copeland's Statuary Porcelain." In this catalogue were listed such figures as Apollo; Paul and Virginia; Little Red Riding Hood; Psyche; The Four Seasons; and Cupids Supporting a Basket. Also listed were candlesticks; The Convolus Jug; The Vine and Grape Jug and The Vintage Jug, Artists employed, or whose designs were copied, included Gibson, Wyatt, Foley, Jones, Durham, Cumberworth, Marshall, Cellini, Flamingo and Marochetti. Derby models used for Copeland Parian, 1846, include: Infancy of Jupiter, Lady Godiva, Nora Creina; Flute Player, Reading Girl, A Mother, Love, Night and Morning—all by Monti; Young England, Young England's Sister—both by Halse; Shepherd Boy by L. A. Malampre; On the Seashore by Masterton; Spring, Summer, Chastity, Innocence; Santa Filomena, Jenny Lind—all by Joseph Durham, R. A.; Ino and Bacchus by J. H. Foley, R. A.; Greek Slave, Narcissus and Venus after John Gibson, R. A., 1851.

In 1846 William Adams made Parian and marked it with an impressed "Adams." Subjects included figures of a Spanish Brigand; Jacob and Joseph; Shepherd; Musician with Flute; Venus; Pointer and Setter; Stags; Harvesters; Boy with a Dog; Girl with a Lamb; Italian Fruit Girl and Spanish Flower Girl. Florence Nightingale figures were made by Copeland and Garrett in 1854–6, and G. M. P. Bell of Glasgow turned out figures of Diana (marked with a Bell impress) between 1850 and 1860. A figure called Rock of Ages, which is similar to the sentimental picture of the same name, and a portrait bust of Queen Victoria, were made by Robinson and Leadbeater, one of the largest makers of Parian in England after the middle of the century. Among other subjects by this firm are busts of Gladstone, Disraeli, Dickens, Tennyson and Cobden. Groups include Innocence Protected, in color, Penelope, Cupid Betrayed, Cupid Captive, Virgin and Child. They use no mark.

Statuettes by H. Minton & Co. include Una and the Lion, Triton and Nautilus, Babes in the Wood, Shakespeare, busts of Michelangelo and Raphael, all by John Bell.

Charles Meigh and Sons made Parian statues of Templar and Companion, Falconer and Companion, Flora, Cupid and Venus, and Prometheus, as well as heads of Dr. Adam Clarke, Sir Robert Peel, Shakespeare and Napoleon.

Parian subjects by T. & R. Boote in 1851 include vases with raised vine and flowers, rustic and allegorical figure groups and statuettes, twenty inches high, of Shakespeare, Milton, Venus, etc. A Parian bust of Sir Robert Peel was taken from the picture by Sir Thomas Lawrence.

Parian statues by John Rose & Co. include Wrestling Figures, The Pleiades Adorning Night, Puck and Companions, Basket Supported by Female Figures and a Flower Vase supported by Dolphins.

Wedgwood employed such artists as Wyon and Beattie to model Parian figures from the antique, such as Venus, Mercury and Cupid.

American Parian ware included pitchers, vases, boxes, as well as animal and human figures. Motifs of design were usually taken from nature, but they were combined with classic borders, such as fluting, and the acanthus leaf, and with geometric flutework designs. From marsh and pond life there are designs of water lilies, cattails, frogs, and kingfishers. Fruits of the harvest included grapes, acorns and hops, and garden and field flowers include morning glory, lily, poppies, rose, ivy and tobacco leaves, daisy, and the palm tree. Pitchers with the Water Lily, Love and War, and Palm Tree, are well known, and were made at both English and American factories. They are made in white Parian

Parian Ware

and also in Parian with a colored pitted background of blue, brown, sage green, or pink with the design raised in white. These pitchers have a glazed interior. Also the same designs are found on glazed or semi-glazed pitchers which are not Parian proper, but should be classed as hard porcelain, which is the same family that Parian belongs to.

Fine pitchers are often expensive and hard to find. The same design may be found in as many as three or four sizes and also on syrup pitchers with a pewter top. The Water Lily pitcher design was probably first made by Fenton at Bennington, but Samuel Alcock in England also made the same design. It is one of the loveliest designs on Parian ware, since the lines of the design seem to conform to the contour of the pitcher. The Water Lily is sculptured in white on a pitted blue or gray ground. The blue on Parian ware varies, as it does on Wedgwood, and while there may be a difference of opinion, I think the darkest blue is the finest, and it is certainly the rarest. The Bennington Lily Pitcher is usually marked with the raised ribbon mark with the letters "U.S.P." or "U.S. Pottery," and the serial number, together with the number indicating the size. The Love and War pitcher shows a scene of the Knight and His Lady on one side, and the Knight at War on the other side of the pitcher. This pitcher is rare. Those made at Bennington have the medallion mark: "U.S. Pottery, Bennington, Vt." Cupid and Psyche pitchers were made in blue and white, pink and white and smear-glazed white.

The Ivy Leaf pitcher and the popular Niagara or Waterfall pitcher also have the medallion mark: "U.S. Pottery, Bennington, Vt." The rare Rose pitcher, which has a tree trunk as a spout and a tree branch handle, and the Daisy pitcher, both have the early medallion mark: "Fenton's Works, Bennington, Vt." Because of their glaze these pitchers are not generally classified as Parian, but as hard porcelain.

The Sunflower pitcher has the ribbon mark, and a pitcher with Acorn and Leaf design has a blue pitted ground and a tree trunk spout and handle, and is also marked with the Bennington ribbon mark. The

75

Paul and Virginia and Palm Tree pitchers also have the well-known ribbon mark. Of course there were many pitchers from Bennington that were not marked and there were also similar pitchers made at other factories which were not marked.

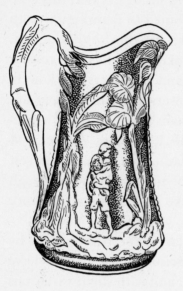

Parian boxes were made in white and also combinations of blue and white, brown and white, green and white (which is rare), and pink and white (which is the rarest). The size, shape, and decoration is so varied that boxes alone would form an interesting collection. The most ordinary boxes have grapes or flowers on the top and the remainder of the box may be covered with a shell pattern, Gothic tracery, geometric fretwork, or classic fluting, or acanthus-leaf borders. One box has a bird's nest on the cover with two birds and eggs, and a companion box has only one bird and no eggs in the nest. There are also box tops with dogs, doves, the lion of Lucerne, hens, foxes and lambs. A rare book box has a lamb with a hobble. Perhaps the most inter-

esting boxes are those with the sleeping child and drapery. This design was originally English, and was probably brought over by John Harrison, who was brought from Copeland's factory in England by Fenton in 1843.

The first piece of Parian known to have been made at Bennington was a presentation piece for Mrs. Norton, sister of Fenton, who had a child in 1843. Harrison made the piece as a gift to Mrs. Norton. It is a

Parian Ware

basket with a moss-covered top holding a sleeping child, surrounded by fruit and flowers. The same piece without the child was also made by Harrison. The later boxes follow this type. And for this reason this type box, when of good workmanship, may be attributed to Bennington or to Copeland, England. Those of inferior workmanship, but similar design, were probably made at other factories. Some boxes have the child resting its head upon a basket of fruit and flowers, and on others the flowers are at the side of the sleeping child. The flowers and the drapery are varied and the child's features vary in workmanship. The child is usu-ally sleeping on its side, but the position of its feet varies. A later box shows a similar child and flowers on a Victorian couch with a head rest and a sloping back. The couch is too small for the child, and although the workmanship is good, the proportions make the general appearance of the piece ugly.

The baskets on these box tops are similar to the baskets held by the Parian poodles which are attributed to Harrison. These poodles have cauliflower manes with a top knot on the head, and with slight variations served as models for the Rockingham dogs made at Bennington. The poodles are rare and expensive. The pair that I know of was only located after years of search. They are definitely museum pieces. They are not marked, nor are any of the American Parian figures of animals or people. Figures of animals, besides the rare poodle, include sheep, ram, eagle, dog, swan, a small bird's nest with a bird on the side and three eggs in the nest, owls, a greyhound reclining on a cushion with tassels (rare). Other Parian figures made at Bennington include a fine Red Riding Hood, The Tight Shoe (on a rare pillow base), Child Kneeling at Prayer (on a pillow base), an Indian Princess, and Eagle and Child. Dickens busts may have been made at Bennington or more probably they were imported from England and sold in the Bennington district. The same is true of busts of George Washington and his Mother. However, Daniel Greatbach is thought to have made the bust of Fenton and the Mother Handing the Bible to a Child on the Bennington Monument, which was exhibited at the New York Fair in 1853. Although Greatbach had no great originality, he had a certain quaintness and whimsicality and a feeling for the popular taste. He later worked at Kaolin, South Carolina, and at the Peoria Pottery Company in Illinois, when Fenton was interested in these factories. However, Greatbach is more remembered for his work in Rockingham (brown ware) than for what he did in Parian, yet the fact that he worked at Kaolin and Peoria might account for the similarity of some pieces to those at Bennington. Some pieces at Kaolin, South Carolina, were marked with an impressed shield with the words "Southern Pottery Company, Kaolin, S.C.," or simply the initials "S.P.C." Farrar, who was interested in the Kaolin factory, later started a factory in Syracuse, New York, and in 1871 made Parian souvenirs for the dinner of the stockholders of the company.

Outside of Bennington, Charles Cartlidge and Company of Greenpoint, New York, made the finest American Parian. Josiah Jones, who modeled there (1848–56), made excellent busts of Daniel Webster, Zachary Taylor, John Marshall and Henry Clay. The work of this factory was not marked. D. F. Haynes at Baltimore is given credit for the figures representing the seasons and the Ear of Corn vase. Parian was also made by Ott and Brewer at the Etruria Pottery in Trenton, New Jersey. In about 1876, Isaac Broome, an able artist at Trenton, made a bust of Cleopatra and several excellent baseball figures, also busts of Franklin and George Washington. Also, Karl Müller modeled for William Boch and Brother at Greenpoint, Long Island. Hood's Song of the Shirt, and Forrest as William Tell are his best-known figures. George Priestman also made Parian plaques, which are of some artistic value, for the Chesapeake Pottery Company. The well-known sculptor, Daniel Chester French, modeled for the American Porcelain Works, Gloucester and East Liverpool, New Jersey, from 1854–62. He is known especially for his figures of owls and dogs. Parian figures by D. C. French also include Farewell, Dolly Varden and Joe Willet, Imposing on Good Nature and Retribution (both figures of a cat and dog). These two subjects were made in

Parian Ware

England. "Owls" dates from 1870 and French also made figures of Dick Swiveler and the Marchioness, and Sara Gimp. These figures were signed, "D.C. French."

Parian vases might well be collected, since there is enough difference in shape, color and decoration, as well as size, to give a collection interest and variety. Vases are of three general shapes. Some vases have large shoulders and small necks, sometimes with a pair of handles rising from the grape decoration on the shoulders but often without handles. The shape of the top or mouth of the vases varies in its scallop and is sometimes crimped, as are many other types of Victorian vases. Another type of Parian vase is the tall classic pitcher and still a third and rarer shape is the cottage vase. Not many cottage vases were made in Parian. The only ones I have ever seen are decorated with grapes and grape leaves, and have a center group of morning glories.

The decoration on these vases of various shapes is again in a mingling of naturalistic leaves and geometric borders. Tobacco leaves with puffs, magnolia leaves and shells, were often used, fruit and flowers with bandings, fluting and borders of classic or geometric origin dividing the vases into panels or leaving a center medallion for decoration. These medallions often hold a group of flowers, such as roses, poppies or morning glories, or a medallion head. One vase has a relief profile of Victoria and Albert. This vase evidently did not sell as well as expected, for some have been found with a bunch of grapes, partly covering the portraits, and other vases plainly show where the medallion has been scraped off. These vases were made in blue and white. An eagle in relief is often seen in the medallion of a vase. After the Mexican War a design of a rather sad-looking eagle with an oak leaf in its bill was made and, after the fire at the Bennington factory, a vase with a phoenix in relief was appropriately made. The Kingfisher design is also well known.

Vases were made in cornucopia shape and a figure of a swan often holds a vase as does the ever-popular Victorian hand. These hand vases were first made in England in Parian and were said to have been modeled from the hand of Queen Victoria. A hand holding a pineapple is often found marked: "T. Booth, Hanley." Vases of all types were made in many different sizes and even in miniature. Indeed, there are enough miniature vases to form a collection. There are miniature cottage vases as well as pitchers, and a tiny perfume bottle with a wicker pattern, and miniature tobies. Also, there are baskets of fruit and flowers which are exquisite in workmanship, and again may be related to Harrison's baskets held by the Parian dogs, and to the porcelain jewelry with grapes and various flowers.

Some collectors of Parian are only interested in the pieces from Bennington. To be sure, that is the earliest and by far the finest Parian made in America. However, since so few pieces of Parian were ever marked, one must be warned of the exchange of molds and workmen. The instance of Greatbach has been mentioned in this chapter. Also, much Parian is not Parian proper, and each collector must weigh the facts and make his own definition for his particular collection.

The quality of workmanship is the only real basis for identification, for many factories bought molds from near-by factories. Workmen also migrated from one factory to another, taking molds with them. However, the color is one means of identification, since Bennington was the only factory where the color was mixed and blended in the slip and put into the mold and fired. William Bloor at Trenton made Parian with painted blue backgrounds, and the paint often runs over the lines since it was not baked in the mold.

The white or pure Parian is the most desirable, but certain pieces of dark blue and white are of fine quality. Of the colors, pink and white is the rarest, then green and white, tan and white, and blue and white.

Designs which conform to the shape of the vase or pitcher are the best. However, pitchers, because they are marked and can be traced to the much-sought-after Bennington factory, are valued on the present-day market according to their marking and scarcity, rather than for their design.

Parian Ware

If you like to collect figures, remember that enough good artists were connected with the Parian industry to make this a good field even though it be of Victorian and sentimental interest.

BIBLIOGRAPHY

The Potters and Potteries of Bennington, John Spargo, Houghton-Mifflin Co., Boston, 1926.

Early American Folk Pottery, A. H. Pitkin, Hartford, Connecticut.

Early American Pottery and China, John Spargo, The Century Company, New York, 1926.

Pottery and Porcelain in U. S., Edwin Atlee Barber, G. P. Putnam's Sons, New York, 1901.

Official Descriptive and Illustrative Catalogue of the London Exposition of 1851, Vols. II and IV.

Collection of Dr. Charles Green.

Chapter 9

AMERICAN VICTORIAN SHAVING MUGS

OLLECTING shaving mugs requires little knowledge on the part of the collector and no strain on his purse strings. Antique shops and some barber shops still have good examples.

A collector of old shaving mugs will be interested in a picture of the old barber shops. The usual equipment of a Victorian barber shop was a single green-upholstered tonsorial throne, a row of chairs along the wall, perhaps an old leather couch, and cuspidors a-plenty for waiting patrons.

Barber-shop air was redolent of bay rum. On a shelf near the barber's hand stood slender bottles, perhaps adorned with roseate pictures of popular actresses: red bottles for bay rum, blue for witch hazel, and white for water. But the most enlivening feature of the place was a black-walnut cabinet divided into small cubicles which held the customers' decorated mugs, each emblazoned in gold letters with the name of its owner. These mugs were tantamount to a business directory of the locality, for many of them, in addition to carrying the owner's name, bore some gaily painted and obvious symbol of his occupation.

It is the mugs revealing such symbols that the collector seeks, for though these bits of porcelain can boast no great antiquity, they picture modes of doing business almost foreign to our day. Thus the milkman's wagon is filled with milk cans (dating his mug before the time of milk bottles), and the vegetable peddler's cart is piled with vegetables innocent of protection. All of the delivery wagons, carts and other vehicles are moved by horsepower, often supplied by quite fiery steeds. Horses were a popular motif and appear on the mugs of undertakers, firemen,

street-car drivers and conductors, as well as gentlemen of sporting pro-
clivities. The last-named personages are usually shown in stylish attire
driving a spanking pair attached to a light carriage.

Among the indoor trades most frequently symbolized are those of
the butcher, the paperhanger, the shoemaker and the bartender. An-

other group of mugs is dedicated to members of the sporting fraternity.
A recent example was painted for Bob Wernick, a boxer. It is dated 1924.
Another interesting mug once belonged to Harry Townsend, one of the
first six-day bicycle riders. From the design on another mug, we know
that its owner, T. P. McKinney, was a jockey. Other sports mugs were
made for baseball men, billiard players and bowlers. If you can get a
mug of any well-known sportsman, it is valuable. Immigrant citizens
occasionally insisted on proclaiming their nationality with mugs exhibit-
ing the flag of the fatherland, sometimes composed with the American
emblem. Certain collectors confine their attention exclusively to these
flag mugs. Again, we find mugs which show boats of various types: sailboats, tugboats and ferryboats. Those showing old historical types of
boats are rare.

Every kind of musical instrument appears on mugs. Usually the
instrument portrayed was appropriate to the owner's specialty, but the
Barber's Journal (Vol. I, p. 52) tells of a lawyer's mug in a Philadelphia
shop tastefully decorated with a lyre. Some of the symbols employed
were curious. We hear of a dentist's mug exploiting a gaudy set of false
teeth; and an editor's mug on which was painted a pot of paste and a

pair of shears. Many such cups show the tools or symbols of a trade: a butcher's tools, a hand and hammer, a horse's head framed within a horseshoe, a skull and crossbones, or a loan broker's three balls. The large number of barroom scenes suggests that many a man-about-town liked to be known as an amiable and peripatetic tippler. Still others preferred to identify themselves by the insignia of the lodges of which they were members. Lodge cups were expensive, for an example beautified with the order of the Masons or the Elks cost as much as five dollars. But today lodge cups are less highly prized than those representing the trades.

Occasionally a single mug was used jointly by the members of some one society or club. Thus, a mug illustrated with a hook-and-ladder decoration, served the volunteer firemen of Union Hill, New Jersey, from 1860 to 1901. It is particularly interesting and would be a valuable addition to any collection, since it shows the old-type fire apparatus.

Many of these barbers' mugs were decorated by unskilled artists, yet their lettering is always meticulously executed, and if the item chances to carry a floral design, the latter is usually well done. From this fact we may safely conclude that the majority of mug decorators, who came here from Germany or Austria, were trained china painters who specialized in floral decorations and fine lettering and striping. It is even possible that, in many instances, the master did the lettering, and finished the pictorial additions, after an apprentice had applied the stenciled outline. These stencils, or pounces, were small bits of tracing paper on which the designs were outlined in pinholes. Decorating shaving mugs was a humble and homely trade. If tracing paper was lacking, a woodcut print would be pierced, or a piece of tinfoil would be made to serve as the pounce. The transfer of the design was effected by holding the stencil against the mug and patting charcoal through the pinholes. The outline thus obtained was then painted in by hand and individual touches were added according to requirement. Bands of gold surrounded the rim and the bottom of the mug, and floral or scroll decorations flanked the design, while the remainder of the cup would be in solid color, usually blue, red, green, or black. Sometimes scrolls and flowers would be painted free-hand on the porcelain.

The pictorial scenes and symbols on these mugs reveal no evidence of creative gifts. Most of them were taken from newspaper or magazine advertisements. Again, a buyer would send his letterhead to the artist and direct that a device or a monogram be copied from it. Recently I had the opportunity to look through a file of old pounces, covering a period from the 1860's to the present. In this accumulation could be read the evolution of the shoe and the hat, not to mention the automobile, the fire engine, and the street car. Although customers often ordered from stock designs in the decorator's catalogue, they would quite as frequently supply their own patterns and even designate the colors to be used.

The mugs to be decorated were imported in blank from Bavaria or Limoges and, after 1890, from various parts of Germany. They were heavy white porcelain, in shape and size resembling the sturdy coffee cups used in cheap restaurants. The average mug was about six inches high, with a four-inch diameter; but a slightly larger size was sometimes favored.

Concerning some decorators of shaving mugs I have gathered the following information. In 1889, William Haehnel arrived in this country from Germany. He found occupation painting shaving mugs for a man named Riedel. Riedel owned a basement shop in lower Manhattan. He conducted a flourishing business and is listed in Wilson's New York Directory of 1884. When Riedel died, William Haehnel took over the business, then located at 186 Center Street. In the *Barber's Journal* of 1899 appears the following notice:

"Wm. Haehnel, 186 Center St., has devoted almost a lifetime to the art of decorating shaving mugs and an examination of his work clearly shows that it bears the imprint of artistic merit. He devotes his time ex-

clusively to the decoration of shaving mugs and is prepared to execute work at short notice in a satisfactory manner and can be depended upon to charge the right price."

Some years later, when Haehnel moved to Lafayette Street, he issued a broadside sheet of numbered designs. These he sent out to the various barber shops as a means of soliciting trade. At the bottom of the sheet he proclaimed: "These are some of our trade designs. We have hundreds of others and can reproduce upon a shaving mug any trade design or society emblem wanted." A later sheet showed new ideas in flower decorations, and names only. Later still, Haehnel was offering silver and nickel-plate borders with initials.

In the *Barber's Journal* of the late 1890's we find the announcement of J. Holzsager, photographer and decorator on china and glass, located at 34 East 7th Street, New York, and of George Bassett and Co., of 49 Barclay Street, as well as that of Charles Wedell of 361 Fourth Street, Rochester, New York. The *Barber's Journal* was a national trade periodical and published news notes and advertisements from all parts of the country. But the artists whom I have named are the only men of their profession mentioned during some fifteen years of the *Journal's* existence. It seems safe to say, therefore, that the business of glorifying shaving mugs was largely centered in and about New York City, although St. Louis was also a center. At its height the trade was so extensive and decorated cups were in such demand that each shop must have had several men in its employ. R. F. Habel, who came over from Austria in 1900, started in the capacity of helper to a decorating establishment. He worked for William Haehnel and took over the business when his master retired.

Though the decorators whom I have named were active hardly more than fifty years ago, it is safe to say that painted mugs were in popular demand as early as the 1860's. Several of the examples illustrated show volunteer-fire-company engines and hose carts of that decade, and the style of the milk wagon and its cans on one mug tallies with that in a

TOP: Pink Staffordshire platter, West Point, after a painting by Jacques Gerard Milbert. W. Adams & Sons. BOTTOM: Pink Staffordshire plate, Bunker Hill Monument, after a drawing by A. J. Davis. J. & J. Jackson. *From the collection of Dr. Arthur H. Merritt*

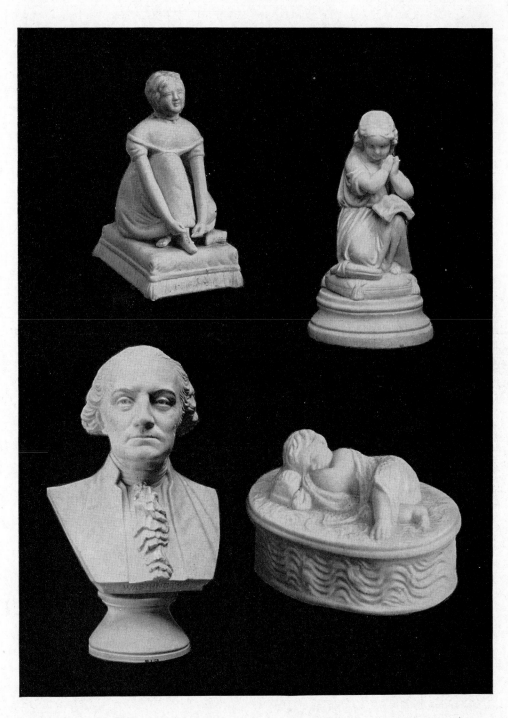

PARIAN FIGURES. LEFT TO RIGHT, TOP: The Tight Shoe; Girl Praying, Bennington. BOTTOM: Bust of George Washington, Isaac Broome, sculptor; oval box with sleeping child on cover. Left, top and bottom *Courtesy The Metropolitan Museum of Art*. Right, top and bottom *Collection of Dr. Charles W. Green*

LEFT TO RIGHT, TOP: blue and white Parian boxes. BOTTOM: Lily pattern vase, white Parian on blue ground; pond lily pitcher, white Parian on blue ground, Bennington. *Collection of Dr. Charles W. Green*

TOP ROW: occupational shaving mugs. MIDDLE ROW: unfinished occupationals. BOTTOM ROW, LEFT TO RIGHT: coat of arms; eagle; Lincoln; bride and groom. *Collection of W. Porter Ware*

street scene in *Valentine's Manual* for 1862. A Currier & Ives print of the same period portrays P. T. Barnum and a shaving mug. If this mug exists, it is naturally valuable.

The most valuable mugs are those with names of famous people. Next come the occupational mugs, and of these, the ones with old-type railways, steamboats or fire engines are the most sought after. The sports mugs, especially those with horses, are desirable. About 1870, mugs with glass labels were in vogue and these are interesting to include in a collection. Shaving mugs are not marked and although the same design may have been used many times, no two mugs are alike in color. Names and initials also make mugs individual and one of a kind.

BIBLIOGRAPHY

The Magazine Antiques, May, 1938, article by the author, Katharine Morrison (Kahle) McClinton.

Chapter 10

OLD GLASS PAPERWEIGHTS

PAPERWEIGHTS, because of their color, beauty of design and meticulous workmanship, are a fascinating field for the collector. Although paperweights were made over a comparatively short period of time, from about 1820 at St. Louis, France, through the first few years of the twentieth century, their subject matter is varied. No two old weights are ever exactly alike. Designs include both conventional and naturalistic flowers, animals, reptiles, butterflies and cameo portraits and scenes, and thus give a wide range of interests for the collector.

Collecting paperweights had not really been taken seriously until recent years and there is very little text on the subject. Perhaps the story of American paperweights has been told, but the field of European paperweights is open for further research and discovery. The finest paperweights were made at Baccarat, France. Others were made at St. Louis and Clichy, France, and at Bristol, Nailsea and Stourbridge, England; in Venice, Bohemia, Belgium, Germany and America.

Paperweights are of several types. The *mille-fiori* or thousand-flower type is made up of conventional flower forms or canes set up in a pattern. The designs of paperweights were made first. In the case of *mille-fiori* the glass rods or canes were made and cut into short lengths and then arranged in a mold of clay or iron. No matter how many canes were identical their selection and placement varied the design. When the design was set in place, the background of *latticino*, or filigree, or lacy beads was put in. Then pattern and background were encased in a dome of solid clear glass. This was then smoothed and polished. Candy-cane paperweights are scrambled *mille-fiori* designs made from odds and ends.

Paperweights

Cameo or sulphide weights have a ceramic cameo portrait which has been incrusted in a mixture of silver and glass so that it glistens as silver when looked upon through its glass dome. Familiar cameo subjects are Victoria and Albert, Napoleon, Lafayette, Count de Chambord, Louis Philippe and George Washington. Cameo portraits were often made by well-known artists. They were first carved in a wooden mold then cast in iron; then the white ceramic was poured in and baked. The glass incrustation was done by reheating; the cameo requiring a higher degree of heat for fusion remains intact. Sulphides were first made in Bohemia and at the various French factories. The process was perfected by Apsley Pellatt in England. A Victoria and Albert cameo on amber by Apsley Pellatt is rare. Also a Joan of Arc with a double laurel wreath on a royal-blue ground. Cameos were also made at the various American glass factories. Naturalistic flowers, glass fruit, flowers, animals, butterflies and reptiles are also familiar types. These usually have *latticino* or white lacy backgrounds.

The finest paperweights from the standpoint of workmanship, color and design were made at Baccarat. They have more variety of pattern and subject matter than those of any other locality.

The finest Baccarat paperweights are in overlay or case glass and are beautifully cut. Baccarat was the only factory that made incrusted overlay. Single overlay usually was red, dark blue or green glass upon white, while the colors of double overlay were usually light and dark blue on white or rose and emerald green on white. The design within the dome was usually *mille-fiori* type.

Snakes and salamanders in various positions are found on Baccarat paperweights. A red and green snake with a raised head, coiled upon a lacy white background is considered a superior weight. Another rare Baccarat weight has three ducks in a clear pond with a border of green glass. Only a few of these were made.

Other subjects included fruit and vegetables in a lacy basket, a cluster of cherries and green leaves upon a lacy ground, and a butterfly, with cane insets in its wings, perched upon a flower. A dahlia—white, pink or yellow—upon a *latticino* background, was a typical Baccarat paperweight. A cross of green leaves with a flower in the center and a *latticino* ground and faceted crowns is also from Baccarat. The Baccarat pansy has two purple and three dark-blue petals with white veining and a white rim. It has a honeycomb cane center and often a border of *mille-fiori* canes. The Baccarat butterfly also has honeycomb canes in its wings.

Next to lizards and snakes, the *mille-fiori* paperweights are the rarest, and Baccarat made the finest of these. Baccarat *mille-fiori* weights have canes set in conventional circles or sometimes scattered in rhythmical order over a lacy background. Typical Baccarat canes had star-shaped set-ups in the cane center. A Maltese cross and canes with small animals such as monkeys, birds, elephants, and butterflies are also used, as well as the typical Baccarat honeycomb cane. Sometimes the whole surface of the weight is completely covered with small canes, and again considerable lacy background is seen between the canes, or large canes may accent the pattern. The color and the workmanship decide the value. Of course if you find a signed weight, and many Baccarat weights were signed, it is valuable.

Mille-fiori Baccarat weights were signed with a "B" or "B," plus the date. Most of those found date between 1845 and 1850. In canes upon a lacy background you may find a "B" in red or blue in the center of one cane. Other marks within the cane are: Red "B 1846" (numbers 1 and 4 are blue—8 and 6 red). Blue "B 1847" (1 green—8 and 7 blue—4 red). Blue "B 1848" (1 and 4 green—8's red); "1849" (no letter) (1 and 4 green—8 and 9 red).

Several paperweights are typical of the St. Louis factory. One is a naturalistic aster in purple, pink or yellow. The aster is often full blown and covers the whole weight. Again it is small and has a bud and light-green foliage and a cane border. Spiral crown weights are typical, although they were also made at other factories. One beautiful cameo from St. Louis has a portrait of Josephine within a *mille-fiori* cane border.

Paperweights

St. Louis *mille-fiori* weights are in wheel formation and a dancing figure in the center of a cane is a means of identification. Salamander weights are usually rare and may have an overlay or frosted dome. St. Louis weights are signed in white or red on a black cane—S.L. 1845—or in black and red on a white cane.

The third French factory that made fine paperweights was located at Clichy, near Paris. Clichy weights are recognized by the presence of a white or sometimes a pink rose incorporated in the pattern. It is a rose which in design resembles those made of rows of narrow ribbon sewn closely together. It is often seen among the canes of a *mille-fiori* pattern. Clichy canes are usually opaque flower-shaped backgrounds of rose, green, purple or white. A typical Clichy blown-fruit weight has orange pears on green leaves set upon a background of white lacy canes lying in straight lines.

The Clichy double overlay weights have opaque light-blue or deep-rose overlay. These as other double overlay weights are rare and valuable. Clichy snakes are usually set up on a lacy ground. Swirl weights in all combinations of color and with cane centers were made at Clichy, but these are not as rare as the overlay, reptile or *mille-fiori* weights. Several fine sulphides were made at Clichy. One of Napoleon and Eugenie has a Clichy rose border. A full-length portrait of Napoleon is set on a blue background and has a border design of red and green canes.

Clichy weights are often marked with a black, green or red "C" in the center of a cane. While there was seldom a date, even inferior candy-cane weights often are marked with a "C." "Clichy" in small letters is a rare marking. A word should be said about the popular storm weights. The old ones are rare and now contain no liquid. They were mounted on china or marble bases. They are French and date from about 1850. They usually show a castle with tree and a figure in a red costume. One from Baccarat has a red figure with umbrella standing before the castle door. Modern snow weights have wooden bases and were made in Switzerland.

English paperweights were made at Bristol, Nailsea and Stourbridge. They were not as fine as the French weights and there is also less accurate information concerning them. The dome or case glass of English weights was dull and this tended to gray the colors of the encased design. Bristol colors were the well-known Bristol sapphire blue, yellow and opaque white. A butterfly made of canes and set upon a blue ground within a border of canes is typical. Another weight has a butterfly and fruit. The Bristol pansy is purple and yellow with a stem and green leaves and a star center. A snake upon a *latticino* background is rare. Less interesting weights from Bristol are colored spirals and a sage-green high dome weight with a flower growing in a pot. A *mille-fiori* weight with a date in the center cane was a fake of a much later date, but is now old enough to be collectible.

Stourbridge weights resembled those from St. Louis, but have softer colors. Canes had animals and a filigree background. Stourbridge weights are considered good.

Nailsea weights had high crowns and the typical high-crown green-glass weight with bubbles or a flower pot with pearled flowers and leaves is probably from Nailsea. The greens are softer than those of Bristol.

American paperweights followed the European pattern generally since many workmen came to American glass factories from Baccarat and other European factories. However, there are also types of American paperweights which are unlike any made elsewhere. In some of these weights the workmanship is crude and the color and design unsophisticated, but they have historical interest and a certain folk value.

The blown-glass pear and apple, said to have been made by François Pierre, a Baccarat workman employed by the New England Glass Company, are entirely original and distinctive. They are blown from tubes of red and yellow glass and set upon a crystal vase, not encased. Often they have a leaf blossom, or stem, or, like the Gravenstein apple, they may be set directly upright upon the base. A blown yellow quince is rare. The New England Glass Company also made candy-cane

Paperweights

weights and a cameo of Victoria and Albert, and cameos of Washington and Lincoln, which are rare. During the Civil War they made green-glass turtle weights.

The weights of the Massachusetts glass companies are naturally similar since one man, Deeming Jarves, was interested in the factories of the New England Glass Company, Sandwich, and later the Mt. Washington and Cape Cod Glass Works. It is probable that both workmen and designs of these factories were interchangeable. The weights of Sandwich are known for their brilliance of color and for the introduction of flecks of gold.

Mille-fiori and candy-cane weights from Sandwich are a common type, but the flower and fruit are more distinctive. A pink poinsettia and a purple or blue dahlia or pansy or fuchsia on a *latticino* background are well known. One of the loveliest Sandwich weights has five strawberries with leaves and blossoms and dew bubbles in red, green, orange and yellow colorings on a fine lacy ground.

Timothy Collins and Nicholas Lutz were known workmen at Sandwich. Sandwich weights were not marked or dated.

A weight much sought after has a frilled salmon-pink rose held by a hand with a gold ring on one finger. There are also leaves, fruit and two butterflies in the composition. The weight was made at Mt. Washington.

The Pairpoint Company of New Bedford, Mass., made weights with pinwheel, stars and fan designs. Also a cobalt-blue and ruby-red spiral weight. But the rare weight from this factory is a cameo portrait of Robert E. Lee within a spiral wreath of red, white and blue.

From about 1860 to 1912 paperweights were made at Millville, New Jersey. While several workmen were employed, the best known was Ralph Barber, and Barber rose weights are the most sought after. The roses are a naturalistic pink, red or rare yellow or white. The roses have opalescent tips, free petals and are with or without leaves. They usually have a footed base of plain or rare baluster type. These were made from 1905 to 1912.

93

Other rare weights from Millville are the hunting scenes by Michael Kane. One weight has a hunter with a gun and a dog. On a log are two quail, and a fence completes the scene. The colors are delicate and the casing is cut and faceted.

The other scene has a white dog with orange-brown spots, pointing quail, and three green trees in the background. Weights with eagles, horses and boats were also made at Millville.

John L. Gilliland of Brooklyn made faceted *mille-fiori* type weights. These often had pink, green and white in the center and dark blue on the rim.

The popular Three Little Pigs weight came from Somerville, Massachusetts.

Louis C. Tiffany in 1880 made a weight of sea urchins and waves. This was intended to be a doorstop.

Late in the nineteenth century sentimental weights were made at almost all factories. These include weights with names and inscriptions such as "Remember Me," and "Home Sweet Home" or "Friendship" set within a white wreath on a clear ground. "From a Friend" has a hand, dove and letter within a wreath. It is blue and white and the lettering is black. "Maud S" has a white design with amber backing set in a clear casing. "Hope" has an anchor set in two wreaths in white on a clear ground.

Clasped hands, patriotic and Masonic emblems were also popular, but inferior weights. However, these commercial weights including flags, insignia of wars, etc., were typically American even though they are of historical rather than artistic value. Animals in American paperweights include the horse, lobster, rabbit, butterfly, eagle and snake.

Paperweights with enclosed scenes were made of Pinchbeck metal in England and France in 1850. The scenes of Pinchbeck were enclosed in a glass dome with a screwed-on base or pewter on a marble base. The scenes include village-tavern scenes and landscapes with figures and a portrait of Queen Victoria. The designs were usually taken from paintings; some

Paperweights

were all gold and some gold together with other colors. Paperweights were also made of pressed glass; the Victoria and Albert (1851) of Cambridge glass is the finest of this type. A bulldog and a miniature Plymouth Rock were also made as souvenirs for ads. Later, coins were put under glass and porcelain plaque inserts with photographic or painted designs closely related to that Victorian horror, potichomania work, were common late in the nineteenth century.

Here are several points for consideration in collecting paperweights:

Workmanship

Color and design

Condition—fine old weights do not show scratches

Weight should be heavy

Tint of glass should not be too yellow and glass should not have too many bubbles or swirls which might interfere with the clearness of the design

Pontil marks were usually smoothed, but a frosted base is modern. Many fine weights have cut stars on their base.

BIBLIOGRAPHY

Old Glass Paperweights, E. R. Bergstrom, The Lakeside Press, Chicago.

Cambridge Glass, Lura Woodside Watkins, Marshall Jones Co., Boston, Massachusetts.

American Glass Paperweights, Francis Edgar Smith, The Antique Press, Wolaston, Massachusetts.

Curiosities of Glass Making, Apsley Pellatt, David Boyne, London.

Chapter 11

PICTURES ON GLASS

Both for their subject matter which is mainly historical, and for their decorative value, pictures on glass are of unusual interest to the collector.

There are two types of these pictures. The first type is painted directly upon the reverse side of the glass. The second type is transferred from a mezzotint. Direct painting on glass is done with oil paint ground in shellac, varnish or linseed oil. Often the colored pigments are backed by a ground of white which reflects light back through the pigments and gives the work its characteristic warm and brilliant color. The smoothness of the glass increases the richness and vibrancy. In the William and Mary period frames of mirrors were made of recessed moldings of glass painted with roses, tulips and leafage touched with gold upon a greenish-cream ground. These were similar to the old courting mirrors brought from China by East India traders. This type of glass painting was known as early as the fourteenth century and was revived and became popular in Austria, Germany, Poland, Switzerland and other European countries in the eighteenth and nineteenth centuries.

It is this later glass painting that is available and of interest to collectors today. It was usually of peasant workmanship and the subject matter, following the old patterns, was mostly religious, but also included allegorical subjects, heroes of the day, and some landscape. These paintings are primitive in conception, but often brilliant and vibrant in color. Vermilion red, blue and yellow are combined with gold and silver. Religious votive paintings were often found in peasant homes and included such subjects as The Virgin and Child, The Crucifixion, The Resurrec-

96

tion, the Saints, The Last Supper and other scenes of Biblical interest. Background spaces are embellished with typical peasant floral decorations and scrolls. At first a great deal of gold was used, but later opaque paint was used with accents of gold or silver. These paintings were also made on mirrored backgrounds, as in China and Persia. "Soot" paintings were made by blackening the glass with candle smoke, fixing the soot, scratching the picture in and filling the spaces with gold leaf. These paintings were framed in crude home-made wooden frames. In the late eighteenth century and early nineteenth century secular subjects became more popular and portraits of women symbolical of spring, summer, autumn and winter were popular, as well as portraits of kings, queens and other well-known personages.

The influence of this type of glass painting spread to America and was particularly popular among the Pennsylvania Dutch, who carried on the religious tradition and also painted crude portraits of men and women and national heroes such as Washington, Andrew Jackson and Van Buren. At least four different portraits of Washington, especially those after Gilbert Stuart, were popular for glass painting in nineteenth-century America.

Various portraits of Washington on glass are owned by the New York Historical Society and by the Gallery of Art, Reading, Pennsylvania. Other subjects include Andrew Jackson on horseback, Napoleon and portraits of women in early-nineteenth-century costume. Several portraits of Washington after Stuart were also painted in china for the American trade.

Reverse glass paintings in the Reading Museum collection include the following subjects: General George Washington on horseback, Lafayette, Napoleon, Jesus Christ, General Andrew Jackson, Joseph, Martin Van Buren, Isabella, Dr. Martin Luther and Daniel Webster.

Although some of these may have been imported from Germany for sale in the Pennsylvania Dutch country, the crude workmanship and misspelled words such as "Englenderin" or "Englandrin" indicate the work of an itinerant amateur who sold his wares from house to house, including an occasional portrait of a customer done from life, together with his usual stock of religious, patriotic and symbolic subjects.

In New England, still life was more popular than portraits, and flower paintings or pictures cut and pasted combined with tinsel work were made. Other subjects included naval engagements, such as the Battle of Lake Erie and the Monitor and the Merrimac. These pictures are not signed and thus have no marks of identification. They were done by amateurs or itinerant painters and have very little value except as folk art and a certain decorative quality, yet they bring high prices. They are not plentiful, but have been faked so that the collector should beware and buy only from a reputable dealer. Paintings on the back of glass were also made for mirror and clock decoration. For this purpose the subject matter was usually flowers or fruit still life or a simple flag or eagle design. Later transfer designs of local scenes, such as the Boston State House, Mt. Vernon, Independence Hall, Christ Church, the Merchants Exchange and other well-known landmarks were painted on mirror tops and clock glasses. Much of the value of these paintings on glass depends upon the condition. Peeling and cracked glass destroys the value of the painting.

Transfer painting on glass is distinctly English in origin and is linked with the story of mezzotint engraving beginning at the end of the seventeenth century with the work of John Smith and continuing into its decadence in Victorian days. The first transfer-glass pictures known were made from mezzotints by John Smith after paintings by Sir Godfrey Kneller. These were portraits of Mary II, Queen Anne, George, Prince of Denmark, and William, Duke of Gloucester. However, although the earliest of these mezzotints dates from 1690, the process had become popular and well known several years before, for, in 1688, John Stalker printed his *Treatise of Japanning and Varnishing* which included full "directions in painting mezzo-tinto prints" on glass. He says: "This most ingenious way of painting justly claims applause and admiration, if skill and dexterity are called to the performance. . . . We think a piece of limning lies before us, but more strict enquiries will evince that 'tis Mezzo-tinto at the bottom. . . . This manner of Painting is lookt upon to be the Womens more peculiar province and the Ladies are almost the only pretenders." Then he proceeds to advise as to the selection of prints, frames and glass, paints and other materials for the work, then the actual process. "First, let your prints be steeped in water four or five hours; second, with a pliable knife spread Venice turpentine thin and even over the glass. Next take the print out of water, press the water out, and lay the print face downward on the glass, then wet the back of the print and rub off paper with a sponge. Then let dry, varnish and let dry over night and color in."

Although Stalker states that this work is ladies' amusement, it was also done commercially, and several dealers of the early eighteenth century advertised mezzotints painted on glass. Also the number of duplicates and the excellence of much of the painting further reveal the fact that the production of these paintings was on a commercial as well as an amateur basis. In 1764, the catalogue of John Bowles includes "The greatest variety of glass paintings," and in 1786 R. Sayer and J. Bennett in the *Artists' Assistant* printed directions for painting mezzotints on glass and included the following notice: "All sorts of metzotinto and other prints proper for painting on glass may be had at the place where this book is published."

Thus the subject of transfer-glass painting divides itself into two parts: that done by professional painters and that done by amateurs. Also broadly speaking, there are two kinds of transfers on glass: the older type, which includes mezzotints from well-known painters and the later transfers which are unsigned and crude in workmanship but interesting from the historical viewpoint. The old signed mezzotints bring high prices and are rare as well, and a good collection deserves space in any art museum.

The range of subject matter on transfer-glass pictures is extensive and varied. It includes portraits of royalty, noblemen, naval heroes, and eighteenth-century English beauties. It also includes allegorical pictures and decorative pictures, hunting scenes, pictures relating to the theatre and religious subjects, and a few landscapes and sea pictures. Fox-hunting and hare-hunting prints were issued in series of four. The finest fox-hunting glass pictures are after J. Seymour, engraved by Thomas Buford. They were published in 1766. Hunting prints of not as fine workmanship but with a certain naive appeal were published in 1800 by P. Stampa & Son at 71 Leather Lane, London, while rare prints of Eclipse and Marquis after Sartorius were engraved by R. Houston. Decorative glass pictures with women in fancy costume depicting the time of day, the months, or the seasons were popular from about 1730. The earliest of these were taken from the pictures of the artist Rosalba and engraved by J. Simon and published by C. Bowles. Other series were put out by R. Sayer and John Bowles as well as C. Bowles. The Metropolitan Museum of Art, New York City, owns one of the Element series—The Element of Air by Amigoni and engraved by J. Simon. Emblematic pictures include An Emblem of Africa and An Emblem of America, published in 1800, several years after Washington's death, which are decorative although produced later when glass painting had reached a low ebb.

Scenes from mythology, such as Cupid and Psyche, The Judgment of Paris, Venus and Bacchus, and religious subjects, such as the set of the Prodigal Son, Judith and Holofernes' Head, were not as important and are easier found today because they were of later make.

Fine old mezzotint glass pictures have inscriptions of their subject matter, their painter and engraver and usually of the publisher and date of publication. Such data are especially satisfactory from the collector's standpoint, whether he collects for subject interest, from an interest in mezzotint or even from the standpoint of listing publishers of the eighteenth and nineteenth centuries.

Painters from whose works mezzotints were made include: Rembrandt, Romney, Sir Joshua Reynolds, Sir G. Kneller, Van Dyke, Rubens, Teniers, Boucher, Lancret, Watteau, Chardin, Molenaer,

Pictures on Glass

C. Rosalba, Mercier, T. Hudson, H. Morland, J. Seymour, H. G. Hamilton, Amiconi, J. Zoffany, G. Wilson, and many others who are listed in *The Story of Old English Glass Pictures* by H. G. Clarke. The list of engravers includes the important names in mezzotint history from John Smith, and includes such well-known engravers as T. Buford, J. Faber, E. Fisher, R. Houston, Valentine Green, J. McArdell, R. Purcell, C. or P. Corbutt, J. Simon, John Raphael Smith, C. Spooner and James Watson. Several of these engravers were publishers and print sellers as well. The best known of these publishers were J. Faber, Robert Sayer, J. Bowles, T. Buford, H. Overton and J. Boydell & Son.

That glass pictures were as popular in eighteenth-century America as in England is evident from newspaper ads of the time. As early as June, 1728, William Prince advertised in the *Boston Newsletter*: "Prints and maps and fine Metzotinto for painting on glass in frames or without." In 1738 Peter Pelham, the well-known English engraver, advertised in the *Boston Gazette* that he would give lessons in painting on glass. Similar notices of other teachers are found in New York and Philadelphia papers. Prints listed for sale in Boston newspapers of this date include: "Battles, Riding, Hunting, Fowling, Fishing, History and Scripture"—*Boston Gazette*, December 23, 1728. Peter Pelham also issued the first of his series of New England ministers, Reverend Cotton Mather, and since he taught glass painting and issued "mezzotinto in the most convenient size for glass pictures," it was probably used "for the ladies to paint."

In 1757 "Metzitento Pictures painted on glass from London" were offered for sale in Boston. These included the following subjects: The Royal Family, Judges of England, The Months, The Seasons, The Four Parts of the Day, The Five Senses, The Elements, Sea Pieces, Rakes' and Harlots' Progress, after Hogarth. In 1759, the same dealer, Nathaniel Warner, lists "a neat assortment of Metzotinto Pictures such as: The Hon. William P.H., Esq., The King of Prussia, Prince Ferdinand, Marshal Keith, Admiral Boscawen (from Reynolds by J. MacArdell), Mr.

Garrick, Actor, Mr. Beard, Singer, The Sciences, The City of Quebec and the Draught of the River, The Idle and Industrious Apprentice, Beautiful Prospects, coloured and without—as also a neat Assortment of Pictures painted on glass."

Mezzotints issued in America at the time when mezzotint painting on glass was at its height were by Peter Pelham, the same man who taught dancing and painting on glass. Before coming to America, Pelham was well known as an English engraver and at least one of his mezzotints has been found painted on glass—The Children of Charles II.

Stauffer lists sixteen mezzotints of American subjects by Pelham. All are portraits except the map of Louisburg. A series begun in 1735 includes the well-known clergymen of New England. The last of the series—Reverend William Welsteed, 1753—is by Copley, the stepson of Peter Pelham. Just how many of Pelham's mezzotints were used for painting is not known.

A rare English mezzotint glass painting of Sir Hans Sloane after T. Murray and engraved by F. Faber in 1728 was found in a house in New Jersey and is now in the collection of the New Jersey Historical Society.

Subjects relating to American history and which must have been popular in America were portraits of George and Martha Washington; Major-General James Wolfe by Richard Houston, published in 1760; Rt. Hon. Major-General Robert Monckton, Governor of New York, by James MacArdell after T. Hudson. Also popular were a group of pictures of naval engagements between English and American ships such as the *Argus* and the British sloop, *Pelican*. These are later pictures and the execution suggests amateur rather than professional coloring, as also do such late prints as Britannia or the Continents or the memorials to the death of Queen Charlotte, which were done by unknown and unskilled engravers and date from the nineteenth century.

Much of the value and beauty of the old mezzotint pictures is due to the framing. John Stalker gives his ideas about the proper frames. "Your frames for glass-painting are usually made of stained Pear-tree,

LEFT: The Hon. Robert Monckton, Governor of New York, mezzotint on glass, English 18th c. RIGHT: Washington, reverse painting on glass, Pennsylvania German, 19th c. *Courtesy The New York Historical Society*

LEFT TO RIGHT, TOP ROW: Clichy double overlay, Millville rose on footed base, faceted bouquet with filigree border. CENTER ROW: Clichy rose floral spray, Clichy millefiori, Baccarat millefiori, Sandwich dahlia on latticino background. BOTTOM ROW: St. Louis millefiori, Baccarat floral spray of dahlia, buds and flowers, Baccarat snake on pebbled background. *Collection of S. Welden O'Brien*

LEFT TO RIGHT, TOP ROW: Baccarat fruit on latticino background; St. Louis red and green crown; Baccarat Joan of Arc, white against dark-blue ground. BOTTOM ROW: Clichy millefiori; Baccarat amethyst pansies; Baccarat pink dahlia with border of dahlias. *Courtesy C. W. Lyon, Inc.*

LEFT TO RIGHT, TOP: Bohemian overlay glass vases, painted decoration and cut spearhead prisms. BOTTOM: opaque green vase, dumbbell prisms; opaque pink crimped-top vase, arrow prisms. *Courtesy B. Altman & Co.*

with narrow mouldings for little pieces, which increase in breadth as the size of your picture does in largeness; they are made with Rabets and are afforded for 6, 8, and 12 pence or more according to their several dimensions. If you approve of black frames, command the frame-maker to work them half round with Pear-tree; would you stain or Japan them, gild or raise their carved work; this Book will sufficiently inform and direct you." From New England newspapers we find mention of gilt frames, pear-tree and pine frames as well as double frames neatly carved and gilt, and ebony or bird's eye maple frames were used in the nineteenth century.

The value of mezzotint glass pictures is determined by the subject and the excellence of the engraving, and by the quality of the painting; that is, whether it was painted by a good professional or a poor amateur. Also the picture must be in good condition.

Genuine old-glass pictures are on thin glass known as crown glass. This glass has an uneven surface that reflects the light in such a way that it enhances the colors. New glass is heavy and even in surface. Old prints have a soft velvet quality and depth to the color. New or faked prints lack depth and have no brilliancy and do not seem a part of the glass, but merely a print pasted on and colored, and are thus dull and flat. In a fake the back often smells of paint. Also the condition of the paint will show how old the picture is. Fine old glass pictures are usually still in their old frames since they are so delicate that destruction of the frame would mean that of the picture too. However rare they are, some of these old glass pictures can be found and their value will not diminish for it is based upon true art values of color, design and good workmanship.

BIBLIOGRAPHY

The Story of Old English Glass Pictures, H. G. Clarke, Currier Press, London, 1928.

The Antique Collector, June, July, 1931, "Old English Pictures on Glass," L. Loewenthal.

A Handbook of Popular Antiques

Artists' Assistant, R. Sayer and J. Bennett, London, 1786.

Treatise of Japanning and Varnishing, John Stalker, London, 1688.

Arts and Crafts in New England, George Francis Dow, The Wayside Press, 1927.

Arts and Crafts in Philadelphia, Maryland and South Carolina, A. O. Prime, The Walpole Society, Topsfield, Massachusetts.

Arts and Crafts in New York: 1726–1776, New York Historical Society, 1938.

Reverse Glass Painting, Earl L. Poole, Reading Public Museum and Art Gallery, Bulletin 18.

Chapter 12

AMERICAN FANCY GLASS, ART GLASS AND LUSTRES

IN THE late nineteenth century American glass factories produced a wide variety of glassware. They made glass that looked like old Chinese peach bloom, or that had a sheen like mother-of-pearl or with the iridescence of a butterfly's wings, and other such novelties. Much of the fancy glass was blown and the effects gained are those of the blower's art and the results of varying heat and blowing. Acid finish also gave unique effects and the use of metals such as gold and copper together with various colors and types of glass gave effects not seen except in antique glass from China, Persia and other ancient countries. Sets of pitchers and tumblers and berry dishes and bowls and other tableware were the staple products of the factories but rose bowls and pairs of fancy mantel vases and lustres were also made in great quantities. There is much of this glassware on the market today and the prices are comparatively reasonable.

Fancy vases in pairs, designed for a place on the mantel shelf, were made in plain, frosted, or opaque glass in various shapes and colors— both with and without painted decoration, and often with cut-crystal drops. These latter are now called "lustres."

Lustres were made from the early 1800's and until the end of the century in Bohemia, France, England and America. However, many of the lustres in use in America were from Europe and the crystal drops were almost all of European manufacture. Lustres were made with opaque white, blue, green, pink and black bases. Also with frosted vases in various colors. They were also made of Bristol blue and other colors, and Bohemian glass, as well as other overlay glass, and fine old Waterford and Irish cut glass.

Bohemian glass lustre vases were made in the mountains of Germany. The glass was blown, cut, and polished on wheels, and finished by hand painting with scrolls of gold and wreaths of flowers, cupids and vines. The most popular colors were ruby-red, emerald, topaz, turquoise and chrysoprase. This glass had heavy deep cutting and often a white incrustation, with grapevine, and hunting scenes or bold flowers. Other vases had hand-painted flowers and gold decoration.

Overlay glass vases were also made in England, France and America. These vases were made of several layers of colored glass over clear glass and the design, usually of bold circles, diamonds or other geometric lines, was cut through to the clear glass. White cut to pink, emerald-green, and turquoise, and amber and red were often cut to crystal. Some overlay vases had a glossy finish and some a dull acid finish. Gold lines and enameled decoration were often added to the remainder of the vase surface as in the Bohemian glass.

The cut-glass drops or pendants of lustres were made in England and France. As early as 1835 glass drops for use on Irish cut-glass lustres were ordered from Follet Osler of Birmingham, England, and at the London Exposition in 1851 A. & C. Osler exhibited a candelabra with glass pendants or drops which was purchased by Queen Victoria.

Apsley Pellatt also exhibited chandeliers with white–, ruby– and blue–crystal drops. Other English firms that made crystal drops were Messrs. Perry & Co. and James Powell and Sons at Whitefriars, and drops were undoubtedly made at Bristol, Stourbridge, Whittington and Waterford, the other centers of cut-glass manufacture. Although most writers on old cut glass ignore the forms and cuts of drops or pendants, we do know that the oldest forms were the flat leaf or pear shape pendants and cut crystal beads with a star, daisy or rosette. The combination of a hexagonal bead and a pointed, fine cut elongated diamond drop is early—about 1775. Then come flatter notched drops and tear drops. Icicle drops date to the

American Fancy Glass and Lustres

Regency. Fine prisms have small star cuttings, while later prisms are long fingers that may be notched, or end with an arrow or a heavy round ball. Prisms earlier had four, six, or eight sides; later in the century they are triangular spears, well known in late-Victorian times.

Fine lustre bases of blue and white Jasper ware were made by Adam and Wedgwood made bases with metal mounts and pendant lustres. In the late nineteenth century, lustres were made with brass, bronze and gilded metal standards and had marble bases. These were made in mantel sets of three pieces. The metal standards usually had figure designs with allegorical, patriotic or sentimental significance. Subjects included Paul and Virginia, an Indian chieftain, a Viking, a cavalier, a pioneer, Pocahontas, Robinson Crusoe, the one-legged soldier, Washington, a hound, lovers, a vase or basket of flowers, a group of cupids. The crystal drops were heavy and long and usually attached to a metal *bobêche*. The beauty of these late Victorian lustres is in the crystal drops rather than in the base design, which was machine made. These were made in France and England and in America in the last half of the century. American designs include Jenny Lind and a weeping willow tree.

Satin or mother-of-pearl glass is one of the best-known and most sought-after late Victorian glasswares. This glass was invented and made at the Phoenix Glass Co., Pittsburgh, by Joseph Webb who came over from Stourbridge, England. Satin glass is acid frosted and was made in plain or shaded colors with a white lining. It was blown in a pattern mold; then transparent color was blown over it and finally the acid vapor. Satin glass was made in shades of blue, green, rose, yellow, light brown, amber and old gold, as well as such combinations as yellow and white, and stripes of blue and pink and blue and white. But the most sought-after satin glass is that with a diamond quilted, herringbone or polka-dot pattern. Satin glass was often painted or enameled and some vases have a frosted leaf applied in blue and yellow. It was made in many shapes, including round rose bowls with pinched-in tops, card trays, fruit bowls,

107

pitchers, tumblers, sugars and creamers, berry sets and fancy vases with fluted tops and perfume bottles. Robin's-egg blue is a rare color, as is a deep bittersweet tone. Satin glass was also made by Thomas Webb & Sons, England.

Another type of fancy Victorian vase was the mercury or silvered vase. These vases were made by blowing nitrate of silver into the pontil hole of a clear glass vase. These silvered vases were made in pairs and were both plain and decorated with floral and bird designs in white and colors. They were made by the Boston and Sandwich Glass Co. and also at various other factories.

A small amount of tortoise-shell glass—pale brown–amber in color with splotches of darker tone—was made by the Sandwich Glass Co. A shell plate of this glass is rare.

Hobnail glass, which was originally called Dewdrop, was made by Hobbs, Brocunier & Co., at Wheeling, West Virginia, after 1886. It was first pressed, then the color blown in and it was finished by hand. It was made in a variety of forms, including pitchers and tumbler sets, berry sets, cream and sugar sets, card trays, barber bottles and salt and peppers. The opaque white is rare.

American Fancy Glass and Lustres

Spot and resist spot glass, which had an opalescent design on a transparent ground, was blown in a mold and expanded in a larger mold which spread and flattened the spots. It was made as early as 1875 by King, Son & Co., Pittsburgh, and Hobbs, Brocunier & Co., who made both crystal opaque and colored spot pattern mostly in ornamental novelties. The New England Glass Co. used the same design on Amberina and Pomona glass. It resembled an overlay or cut pattern but was molded.

From 1880 on, glass vases of all types and colors of opaque, frosted, and clear, were decorated with painted flowers, fruit, butterflies and berries. There were painted Bristol type and frosted vases in all colors, also black vases painted with striking red berries and designs painted on amethyst, sapphire blue, light brown and emerald-green vases.

Vases of various colored glass, especially green, turquoise blue, blue, amber and clear glass had a white painted decoration of a boy or girl. These are called Mary Gregory vases after a decorator of the name who worked at the Boston and Sandwich Glass Co. Sometimes the child represented is a girl. She may be in a swing or skipping rope. Again the child holds a parasol or a wreath of flowers. Again the figure may be a boy, holding a hoop or shooting a bow and arrow. Or two children may be shown seated at a tea party, or chasing a bird or butterfly; or the boy may be handing the girl a flower. The background is of flowers and trees and the design is in white, regardless of the color of the glass. These similar designs are on pitcher and glass sets, barber bottles, vases, powder boxes, jewel cases and many other shapes. It is in such quantity that it must have been made and decorated at many factories and Mary Gregory herself could only have been the originator of the sentimental series. If you collect this glass, you will probably have an open field, as I know of no collectors at present.

Certain types of Victorian glass were known as art glass. Foremost among these is Peachblow glass which resembles Chinese porcelain of a similar name. Peachblow originated at the New England Glass Co. but was also made at Mt. Washington where it shaded from pink to yellow or blue-violet and was called Rose Amber. The New England Glass Co. Peachblow is marked: "N.E.G.W. Wild Rose patented March 2, 1886." It shades from rose to white at the base and is the same inside as out. It usually had an acid or velvet surface. The pontils were ground off on all New England Peachblow, although it was made here both with and without the acid bath. Hobbs, Brocunier & Co. made Peachblow with a white lining. It shades on the outside from yellow at the base to red with a glossy finish. The copies of the famous Morgan vases were made at Wheeling. Baskets, rosebowls, fingerbowls, tumblers, sherbet cups, decanters, salts, peppers, pitchers and many Chinese-shaped vases were included among the twenty styles of vases made at Wheeling.

Agata glass was a variation of Peachblow, which was made in small quantities at New England Glass Works in Cambridge, Massachusetts. Vases, bowls, pitchers and tumblers were made in this opaque rose glass with an iridescent mottled and glossy surface.

Burmese glass shades from lemon yellow at the base to rose at the top and is often mistaken for Peachblow. It was made with both glossy and dull finish, and the bowls have a crimped top. It originated at Mt. Washington Glass Co. in 1885, and was made up to 1891. It was made in many decorative shapes and tablewares as well as gaslight shades. Candlesticks are rare.

Amberina glass, a yellow amber glass containing gold, was also popular. A portion of the article was reheated to give it a ruby tint and the remainder was amber. It was made by Joseph Locke at the New England Glass Co. and was also made at Mt. Washington. Amberina glass was blown into a mold. It has swirled ribbing, a diamond or star and diamond or a thumbprint design and a variation has incised tracery made by masking part of the surface during heating. Amberina was made in many shapes and patterns. Tumblers and pitchers have a swirl effect which was made by manipulation during the blowing process. The Venetian diamond pattern is mottled with air pockets which produce the

American Fancy Glass and Lustres

pattern. Amberina glass was made in vase forms, pitcher and tumbler sets, berry sets, toothpick, spoon and celery holders, fingerbowls, trays and fancy dishes. Amberina glass has a metallic ring.

Other art glass of the late nineteenth century includes Pomona glass, which is a clear-etched or stained glass with or without pattern and often with a band of gold around the top of the vase and a garland of blue flowers and straw-colored leaves. It was blown in a mold and expanded and had a ruffled top. Tumblers and pitcher sets are often found, but bowls are rare.

Spangled glassware was made by Hobbs, Brocunier & Co. It was made of a mica and glass mixture and was ornamented with spangles or flakes of any desired color or shade. Vasa Murrhina, made at the Art Glass Co., Hartford, Connecticut, also had mica, and metals such as gold, silver, nickel and copper mixed with the glass.

One glassware which deserves special mention for its beauty of color, decoration and form is Tiffany's Favrile glass. It was originated by the artist, Louis C. Tiffany, of the Tiffany Glass and Decoration Company, Corona, Long Island, in 1893, in an effort to produce a glass suitable for his stained-glass window designs. Various colored glass rods were blended by heat and then exposed to the fumes of vaporized metals. The designs were made in the process of blowing. Thus the designs are imaginative and fanciful, such as spirally twisted lines and veins which suggest leaves or waves or a peacock feather. These were made by spinning and twisting the glass as it was being blown. Thus no two pieces are alike. The colors are bluish green and gold which suggests metal, a light mother-of-pearl, and a red which suggests pottery rather than glass. Favrile glass has a silky texture and is iridescent and brilliant. The shapes are unusual and beautiful in form. Besides vases, simpler glass, yellow, rose and green in color, was made into goblets, toilet boxes, trays, vanity and snuff and cigarette boxes, tea sets, bon-bon dishes and lampshades.

One type of Tiffany glass has flowers and leaves in the bottom of

A Handbook of Popular Antiques

a clear glass vase, and it is known that Tiffany experimented with paperweights.

Golden bronze and blue are the most common colors, but such unusual colors as mazarine, aquamarine and turquoise blue and Samian red are seen on finer pieces. The colors were combined with oxides of copper, iron and gold. Pure cobalt produced the blue; manganese, the violet shade; gold, the red; while iron and gold made green; and manganese and iron produced yellow. Besides the famous peacock design, the pond lily and iris are well known.

Tiffany glass is thin and has a ringing note. It has been imitated in Bohemian and other glassware, but the really fine pieces of Favrile were signed. Marks were scratched in the bottom of the glass and are as follows, plus a serial number: "L. C. T.," "Louis C. Tiffany," "L. C. Tiffany-Favrile," "Louis C. Tiffany Inc.," "Favrile."

At the Chicago World's Columbian Exposition in 1893, The Tiffany Glass & Decoration Co. had an exhibit which was described thus: "A new process in which glass of various colors is blown into a framework of silver and silver gilt, producing the effect of jewels, crystal and precious stones." Tiffany glass also won acclaim at the Paris Exposition and at art expositions in England.

BIBLIOGRAPHY

The Magazine Antiques, August, 1934; March and December, 1936.

Victorian Glass, Ruth Webb Lee.

American Glass, George and Edith McKearin, Doubleday, Page & Co., Garden City, N. Y.

The Art Work of Louis C. Tiffany, Louis C. Tiffany.

Chapter 13

GLASS SLIPPERS, BOOTS AND SHOES; HATS AND OLD SALTS

THE size or humbleness of the object does not limit the scope or variety of a collection. Small objects such as slippers and boots, hats and old salts have been made in all countries and in various materials as far back as the eighteenth century. Thus a collection of these articles could be international in scope.

Originally these small articles were made for utilitarian purposes. In Germany, in the seventeenth century, tall glass boots were made to hold beer, and often had engraved or painted inscriptions suggesting their use. English hunt clubs had drinking glasses or loving cups in boot form. These were usually of clear glass, engraved, often with a vintage pattern of grapes and leaves, or of swirled glass. Glass boots or shoes for drinking often rest on a circular stand. French lacy glass shoes or slippers held perfume and Dutch Delft slippers with a floral decoration painted in blue or blue and red on a white ground were used as toilet-water containers. In America slippers were made in both china and glass and used as perfume bottles, ink bottles, pincushions and even thimble holders.

The glass slipper or shoe of nineteenth-century American manufacture offers the most fertile field for the average collector. The price range is low and examples are available in the average shop. Of course reproductions have also been made, so one has to be wary. All types of glass were made into shoe and slipper forms, including blown glass, case glass, engraved glass, spatter glass, red cranberry glass, opaque white milk glass, black opaque glass, pressed glass, and cut, threaded and engraved glass.

The oldest types of glass footware are the blown bottles in the shape of boots which were used as rummers. These were made in a swirled pattern in crystal and sapphire blue. They were six to ten inches in height. Boots of Nailsea type blown glass with delicate swirls of blue, red, white and yellow were also made in America. These boots are in bottle form with a neck and stopper. Frosted boots in the shape of a bottle, and plain clear glass large "rubber" boots in crystal and red cranberry color may also be found. There are no markings on these shoes except for the pontil mark on the bottom. Any number of factories made these trinkets and it is even hard to distinguish between the old blown boot and the occasional blown boot of today.

The largest selection of glass shoes and slippers is found in pressed glass which was made in many patterns from around 1840 to the end of the century. The most common pattern of pressed-glass shoes and slippers is the Daisy and Button. The usual type of slipper in this pattern has a smooth sole and plain toe and heel. This slipper is 4 5/8 inches long and 1 1/4 inches high and comes in clear glass and in colors. Variations of this type are found in different sizes and different colors. The most common colors are yellow, amber, blue, amethyst, aquamarine and crystal. Various combinations of color are also found, such as crystal with red button dots, and red toes, heels and borders. Other designs found in pressed-glass shoes and slippers are the Sunburst and Fine Cut or Diamond Block and Cane patterns. A rare slipper with a plain glass ribbon bow has sides decorated with Sunburst pattern. A shoe with Cane pattern has hobnail buttons and has been found in amber, crystal and blue. Some pressed-glass shoes are mounted on trays, while others have skates or sleighs as bases. These are rarer than unmounted shoes or slippers.

Slippers and shoes were also made in various shapes and sizes of opaque glass. White milk-glass slippers often had floral decorations

Glass Shoes, Hats and Salts

painted on the toes and some had molded designs of flowers and leaves or scrolls. Black opaque glass shoes are rare as are shoes of marble glass. Opaque blue or lavender glass shoes or slippers are also rare.

Elaborate case glass shoes with applied decorations of crystal were made in spatter glass in the 1880's. Slippers of swirled case glass with applied leaf decoration are rare. Frosted glass shoes and shoes with a satin-glass finish are also found.

Shoes and slippers as glass novelties were made at practically all of the American glass factories; thus patterns and types of glass are hard to place. The only marks are initials that do not often have meaning, and "patent applied for" dates. The old factory catalogues are a means of identification; that is, they will confirm the fact that such a style was made at a certain factory, but that will not authenticate your particular piece unless it is marked.

Certain pieces are rare. Among pressed-glass footware the rarest—Daisy and Button—is a high blue-glass boot with a spur. The high shoe

in Cane pattern in amber is also rare. Among opaque items, black glass is more scarce than white or marble glass. Boots with horizontal ribbing are rare, the rarest being a man's boot in blue with horizontal ribbing on the heel. Lacy and threaded-glass slippers are rare and are of Continental make, while the rarest and oldest of all are the blown-glass boots.

An amethyst slipper in Daisy and Button design has been reproduced, and as late as 1901, small glass slipper thimble holders were made for the Pan-American Exposition at Buffalo, New York. The amber one has white enamel dots on the toe. It is rare only because few are now found.

Glass hats offer more variety of shape and are made in more types of glass than shoes and slippers. In shape, they run from the witches' hat to the brown derby and they are made in fine English glass and Baccarat as well as the later American pressed glass. Again there are seldom any marks or factory names, so we can only classify them according to types and judge their value from their quality of workmanship. Thus a collector with good taste and discrimination may gather a sizeable collection without spending large sums, for while the rarest and finest items may take some patience to find, the more common hats are found in the average shop. For this reason and to keep his enthusiasm fired, the collector should start with more available hats, such as those of nineteenth-century pressed glass.

The patterns available in pressed-glass hats include the Thousand Eye, Cube, Raindrop, Daisy and Button, Diamond and Fine Cut. Daisy and Button hats are the easiest to find, but the collector should be warned against reproductions of this pattern. Daisy and Button hats in toothpick size may be found in clear blue, amber, canary, amethyst, smoke, light red and opalescent blue. There are also variations with bands of other colors such as clear with blue or red buttons and clear with hat bands of amber and other colors. Small salt-size Daisy and Button hats are found in amber, blue, clear and canary and large-size hats are found in the same colors. Green is the rare color in Daisy and Button hats. Daisy and Button hats may also be found with the buttons decorated in colors such as red and clear, and amber and clear. Often hats are found with a variation of the Daisy and Button, with a star instead of a button. These may be found in bright blue, amber, canary, pale blue, clear, lime green and emerald green.

Diamond pattern hats with all or part of the hat in diamond pattern

Glass Shoes, Hats and Salts

are found in amber, clear, and light blue, cobalt blue, and opaque white. Raindrop hats are found in blue, amber, canary and emerald green. This pattern is rare. Cube pattern hats are found in blue, clear, amber, canary, emerald, lime and a rare frosted opaque white.

Thousand Eye hats are found in amber, clear, blue and canary. Horizontally ribbed hats were made in both milk glass and clear glass. These hats come in a variety of colors and often have plain rims or hat bands.

Various souvenir hats from places such as Asbury Park and world's fairs, as well as hats used as favors at parties, form another classification, but not a very important one. They are usually marked with the place and date.

If the collector has gotten this far, he is then ready for some of the finer, rarer, and harder to find varieties of hats. Thus he may consider early blown-glass hats. In this classification, he may find witches' hats of deep blue, or clowns' hats, or hats blown into bottle or tumbler molds. These hats are found in the deeper colors, such as cobalt blue, dark amber, bottle green or black. Some of these hats are swirled, or vertically or horizontally ribbed.

Early blown-glass hats from the old bottle factories are rare. Interesting shapes include tall crowns, monks' hats, tricornes, and other primitive shapes. The quality of the glass suggests its age. Many of these hats were made by individual workmen after factory hours and were not commercial hats, thus the scarcity. They are often marked with interesting pontil marks or such irregularities as holes in the tops where the glass snapped off in the making. It is possible to obtain these old blown hats made by workmen in the various early glass factories throughout the country, but they were not marked and thus cannot be definitely authenticated.

Sandwich glass hats blown in the same molds as the Sandwich ink-wells or tumblers were made in many of the well-known Sandwich designs, including the rare Bull's Eye Sunburst, with fluting below, the Diamond Sunburst, with rows of herringbone below, the Diamond  Quilted Sunburst, the Diamond Sunburst Banding, the Waffle Sunburst and diamond quilting with diagonal ribbing. Hats in these patterns are found in crystal and sapphire blue and occasionally in a rare darker blue. The shapes and sizes vary because they were taken from the molds and finished by hand. The miniature hats are difficult to find, thus the rarest. There is beauty of workmanship in these hats, and that should be the collector's interest. The Sandwich hats are not marked but are identified by pattern.

Among unusual hats are those which illustrate the different types of glass manufacture, such as paper-weight hats, overlay glass hats with cut decoration, blown striped glass hats, spatter glass, Amberina and Burmese art glass, threaded glass, glass hats with gold flecks, cut and engraved hats of European make and Bristol glass hats. All of these hats are rare and hard to find, but they lend interest to any collection.

The collector of old salts has a field of almost endless scope. One collector who does not claim to have covered the field has 780 old salts and another collector has over 500. For this reason, and because of availability, it seems best for the American collector to limit his field by specialization. For example, there are enough blown-glass examples to be found for a valuable collection of this type. Pressed glass might be divided into early and late. A collection of lacy Sandwich glass salts will not deplete the average pocketbook.

An amusing but not very important collection could be made of novelty salts of the late nineteenth century and this type of collection would be within the price range of the collector of modest means. Salts of this type are found in the average second-hand shop. Blown-glass salts were made at all the early glass works, including that of Stiegel. Many

Glass Shoes, Hats and Salts

were made in Ohio, in Pittsburgh and in New Jersey. Stiegel salts were set on pedestals of various heights. They were blown in the following designs: spiral-ribbed, swirled and quilted diamond. They were made in various sizes and in both clear and blue glass and expensive and rare amethyst and emerald green. Stiegel glass is not marked. Early blown-glass footed salts were also made in amber and sea green at Zanesville, Ohio. These may be found diamond-faceted, with broken swirls, globular and perpendicular swirls, and of plain blown glass. They are not marked. Some blown-glass salts are made without feet. A rare cased-glass salt has a deep-blue inside with a white outside and regularly spaced air bubbles. Some salts are blown with horizontal rings and others are blown in a mold. A clear glass salt with a row of beading and a molded pattern is marked: "R. & C.A. Wright, Philadelphia." The finest salts blown in a mold are those with Sandwich designs. These include footed salts with variations of the diamond quilted design. These are found in clear, amethyst and dark blue; all rare pieces and not marked.

Of the molded salts the earliest were the heavy salts in tulip shapes. These were made in crystal and blue in 1825 at Sandwich. "Moulded salts for cutting" were also made in the same year. Some had round bases and others had petal feet as well as rims. They were footed and came in opalescent and canary, as well as milk glass. One rare early Petal and Bull's Eye salt comes in a beautiful canary color. Models from the Sandwich Glass Factory show several of these heavy early types, but the salts are not marked and the same types were also made at other factories even in the late nineteenth century.

Lacy salts are rare and much sought after. There were about fifty patterns made. The early ones are larger and heavy and clumsy as compared to the later delicate, lacy patterns. Lacy salts were made at Sandwich and at many other factories. Some of them have historical significance such as the "Lafayet" boat. Some of these were pressed "Sandwich" on the inside base and "B & S. Glass Co." on the end, but few Sandwich pieces were ever signed. This boat salt in several variations was made in clear glass, blue opaque, opalescent and dark-blue glass, and canary yellow. Another early lacy boat is found in clear glass without any markings.

A rare early lacy salt has a portrait of Washington on one side and one of Lafayette on the other with the names inscribed. Another rare salt has a design of a locomotive in its base and the inscription, "H. Clay."

The Providence salt is also rare because of its marking, as are the early clear salts marked "N.E. Glass Co., Boston." A lacy salt with the basket of fruit on each side and a flower on each end comes in crystal and other colors and has this mark. A similar oblong salt has a bowl of flowers on each side and a thistle on one end and a beehive on the other. It comes in clear glass and is rare. Some are marked "N.E. Glass Company, Boston" on the base. Another salt with a basket of flowers on its side is marked "Jersey Glass Co. Nr. N. York." A similar salt is marked with a twelve-pointed star and is found in light green as well as clear glass. Other rare oblong lacy salts include one with an eagle and thirteen stars on each side. It is held up by columns and has a border of fluting at the bottom and one of laurel leaves at the top. The Chariot Race, a design of laurel branches on a rare stippled background, a salt with a cable edge and a heart on one side and a clover on the other with a star in the base, are other designs in clear lacy salts. Other variations of the Eagle design are the rare Eagle Sofa, and the eagle end supports with a shield. Other early oblong salts have a design of Gothic arches. There are at least three variations of this design.

Rarest of all salts are those with covers. They are found in lacy clear glass, milk glass, opal and opaque powder blue. One such salt has a fruit basket on its sides and lacy beaded double scrolls at the ends. This type has been found in opal, dark blue, crystal, opaque light blue and green. Another covered salt has a harp design on its sides and scroll ends. Many other scroll-end lacy salts must have originally been made with covers.

There are several salts with a diamond-waffle pattern in both oblong and sofa shapes. They vary in their top and base designs. The rarest is the crystal salt with the band of leaves, ribbed base, small round feet, and the eight-pointed star imprint on the base. Others are found in sapphire blue, light blue and opal.

The carriage salt and the sleigh salt in clear glass, while not desirable from the standpoint of design, are much sought after, and are hard to find.

Among the delicate lacy salts in oblong shape with scrolled ends are many with designs of baskets of flowers, lyre, and a conventional anthemion. All are distinguished by their shape, their delicate lacy beading and scrolls.

Lacy salts are also found in round and oval shapes both with and without a footed base. Among familiar patterns in these shapes are variations of the Diamond pattern, the Peacock Feather, a conventional design of leaves against a stippled base, the grape design, as well as many other conventional designs. Many of these designs are found in both clear and colored glass. The rarest of the early round salts are the variations of the Eagle-Cadmus pattern. The one with the laurel top is rarer than the scalloped edge.

From about 1840 to the end of the century, pattern glass was made in much larger quantities. Much pattern glass exists and is on the market today and thus it is not as rare as earlier glass. There are about 300 listed patterns; thus it will be impossible to list or describe them in a book of this scope. However, a few of the most popular are the early Petal and Loop, the ribbed group which includes the Bellflower, Ribbed Grape, Ribbed Palm, Ivy, and Fine Rib, and the variations of the well-known Lincoln Drape both with and without tassel. These patterns are all recognized by their background of fine vertical ribbing. The salts are round, footed, and have scalloped or beaded tops. These patterns come in clear glass with a few occasional pieces in color.

Other well-known designs in round, footed pattern salts include the Popcorn, Dewdrop and Star, Cable, Jacob's Ladder, New England Pineapple, Horn of Plenty, Barberry (with oval or round berry), Cabbage Rose, Princess Feather, Blackberry, Waffle, Honeycomb, Flattened Sawtooth (one of most common in old salts), frosted Lion, frosted Three Faces, English Hobnail and Diamond Cut with Leaf. Daisy and Button salts are three-cornered and are found in green, blue, amber and vaseline in small sizes.

Still later salts were of heavy glass, usually thick and plain with cut designs of star, rope, diamond, squares, honeycomb or raindrop on their bottoms. They are found in round and oblong in both large and individual sizes.

BIBLIOGRAPHY

Early American Pressed Glass, Sandwich Glass, Victorian Glass, all by Ruth Webb Lee.

Old Salts, A Portfolio of the Collection of Mr. and Mrs. A. E. Coddington.

Salt Dishes, Clark W. Brown.

Chapter 14

BUTTONS

BUTTON collecting can become the most fascinating of hobbies, for the field is so wide that it touches on almost all materials and methods of artistic workmanship. Those interested in history find a wealth of historical material in buttons. A knowledge of French buttons includes a study of French history, manners and costumes. Military buttons not only include history, but a study of insignia and heraldry. The button pathway runs from natural materials such as wood, metals and stones, to porcelains, china and miniature painting; from the jeweled masterpieces of the French Court down to the lowly Shaker buttons and the calicos of the nineteenth century, and from the simple etched star to the painted scenes on eighteenth-century enamel and ivory. Whatever field you choose will depend upon your own individual interests. I shall cover the field from the standpoint of countries, materials and artistic methods of decoration.

From the beginnings of "buttonry" the French have excelled in producing not only elaborate buttons, but buttons which at the same time were distinctly French. One of the most interesting of this group is the late eighteenth-century button made of metal foil, thread and paillettes. These show a variety of leaf and geometric design whose charm lies in the limitations of the gilt-thread needlework. They are backed on gold, crimson, green or bright-blue metal foil. But the most essentially French buttons were the ones with paintings, in the French manner, of portraits, pastoral landscapes, etc. These paintings were on enamel and porcelain, ivory and even paper. Of course the finest painted miniatures were those on ivory. The artist, Jean Baptiste Isabey, is known to have been employed for a year painting buttons from designs after Boucher and Van Loo—lovers, flowers and landscapes.

Another type of French buttons was painted on paper and mounted in brass or other metal under glass. There were profiles painted white on black paper, a series of the French monuments, and buttons with inscriptions in French.

A group of buttons depicted the balloon ascension in 1783. Another group, with scenes painted on paper under glass, included the symbols of the French Revolution, including the taking of the Bastille, the Phrygian Bonnet and the three orders (sword, cross and spade).

In the Musée des Arts Décoratifs in Paris is a series of buttons with colored lithographs illustrating the taking of the Bastille. There are eighteen views in all and each is marked on the back: *"Garniture de Bouton au Revolutions de Paris le 14 Juillet, 1789,"* and with the maker's name, "Chez Guyot Rue St. Jacques." The buttons of the monuments of Paris were sold exclusively by Mme. Lecomte, a clothier in the arcades of the Palais-Royale. Paintings on glass included flowers, birds, landscapes and even geometric patterns to imitate fabrics. Insects, shells, moss, etc., were also mounted in brass under glass in the nineteenth century. Little hand-painted flowers were set in borders of gold and silver tinsel under glass and mounted in brass. One of the most interesting types of these fancy French buttons is the white paper cut-out scenes against a colored background.

Another group of buttons was painted on satin, or other silk materials; in fact every conceit of the French designer seems to have been employed in the eighteenth and nineteenth centuries to make French buttons unique, fanciful, gay and intriguing. These buttons are all very rare.

Battersea enamel buttons are so rare that you may be certain you will not find one since the factory was in existence only three years. However, there are buttons of English enamel which were made after the closing of the Battersea factory in 1756 when the enamel work was car-

Buttons

ried on at Bilston, Liverpool, London, and at various Staffordshire factories. The advertisement of the Battersea factory in 1756, however, included buttons. "Coat and sleeve buttons and other curiosities mostly mounted in metal and gilt." Thus Battersea set the style for enamel buttons in England. Subjects on English enamel buttons included portraits of well-known persons, among them Franklin, after the Cochin portrait, and Washington by W. Nutter, after the Stuart painting. Landscapes and hunting scenes as well as the favorite seasons series were popular. Most of these enamel buttons were transfer printed upon a white, pink, blue or yellow ground. Some were printed in black and others were filled in with hand coloring. In 1869, Lady Charlotte Schreiber bought "two small enamel buttons painted with a vase," and later in the same year, "twelve buttons of enamel with hunting subjects in black transfer printing."

Later transfer-printed buttons are now found with a magenta lake, or blue print on a lighter ground of the same color. Sepia and white transfers are also set on black enamel. Such subjects as dogs, swans and other animals are found, but the most common subjects are usually heads from mythology. Portraits of women and children have also been found. These are often set in a mounting of brilliants or cut steel. Similar buttons were also made at Meissen and of Limoges enamel. There is a series of late enamel buttons with a landscape background and a girl in shepherdess costume, also a girl with a bird, which are decorative and colorful. These were set in cut-steel mounts. A series of a cavalier and his lady was made in different colorings, and there were deep-blue enamel buttons scattered with gold stars and conventional patterns and borders. Still later enamel buttons had naturalistic flower sprays set in a steel border and sometimes the flowers were cut out or pierced.

Nineteenth-century transfer buttons were usually on porcelain or glass bases and included portraits of women, usually from French sources such as Greuze, late Roman, rather than Grecian heads, and realistic scenes of landscapes with animals or figures.

125

A Handbook of Popular Antiques

In 1785, Thomas de la Mayne took out an English patent for "buttons of burnt earth or porcelain." These china buttons had interesting subjects, including French pastoral scenes, flower sprays, wallpaper or  chintz patterns in gold and delicate colors, and birds and flower sprays. Large white china buttons of late date with heads of George and Martha Washington in black silhouette and some with flowers and other designs in gold have been found. However, some of the loveliest china buttons are those with wreaths of flowers and quaint brushwork borders. These buttons have a hole in the center which usually held a paste brilliant. One such button has a wreath of leaves and brownish-red berries or rose hips which is reminiscent of the decoration on Victorian painted vases. Another button has a pink-china background dotted with little circles with red centers and a center medallion with a rose. Several other buttons have pink roses with crude but decorative brush-line borders in blue or brown. Another button is white with quaint gold brush-work. Both the design and the painting of these buttons make them appealing and worthy of a place in any collection. The ones with the hole and jewel center are undoubtedly the older type because of their construction.

Wedgwood cameo buttons are rare, but if you are rewarded with a "find" you have a real collector's item. Mr. Wedgwood, ever with an eye for business, put the following note at the top of his list of cameos in his catalogue of 1787: "The cameos are employed for various ornamental purposes . . . as also for buttons, which have lately been much worn by the nobility in different parts of Europe." The list of cameos which is a ready reference for anyone wishing to identify the subject of a Wedgwood cameo, includes subjects from Egyptian, Grecian and Roman mythology, ancient poets and philosophers, sovereigns of Macedonia, heroes of Greek and Roman history and illustrations of modern kings, queens, and other well-known people, including Washington, Dr. Franklin, Shakespeare and Cardinal Richelieu. A pattern of a flower is also found.

Buttons

The buttons were made in several sizes, from ¼ to 2½ inches—evidently waistcoat and coat size. Some buttons were mounted in brass, but more often they were mounted in gold, cut steel, marquisite or mother-of-pearl. A very lovely button in the Cooper Union collection has a Wedgwood flower set in the center of a mother-of-pearl button, with blue glass stones. Real Wedgwood buttons have "Wedgwood" imprinted into the back of the button, but there were Wedgwood-type buttons made in England, Belgium, France, and perhaps other countries. Wedgwood buttons are made in round, oval, and curved rectangular shapes.

As early as 1878, Lady Charlotte Schreiber was collecting buttons along with her other great collections of porcelain and pottery. In her journal she makes the following notation: "Paris, September, 1878—A little lot of near 1,000 Wedgwood buttons, which Fournier (Paris dealer) had put away in a drawer. . . ." The colors of Wedgwood buttons vary from light to deep purple-blue. They were also made in pink and lavender. Buttons of Wedgwood type show a greater variety of design. Especially lovely are the small flower and rosette designs. Sometimes the flower covers the whole button and sometimes a border of dots or leaves completes the design. Often a hole is left in the center, probably for a gold or jewel bead with a metal shank. French Wedgwood-type buttons illustrated the storming of the Bastille and other Revolutionary subjects.

Pearl buttons of France and England, cut from the pearl of shells, are among the finest buttons made, both from the standpoint of design and workmanship. The earliest ones—about 1785—were large, about an inch and a half in diameter. The decoration of the simpler type ranged from fluted and gouged lines, checkerboards, diamond criss-cross to leaf and flower forms. A familiar design is a decorative star center with a border of leaves or simple lines. Sometimes the star takes the form of a flower or a sun, and often a black transfer or an inlay of dark metal marks the design. Incised decorations of scenes and sprays of flowers and initials are also found on mother-of-pearl buttons. Sometimes part of the pattern is cut out or pierced which gives the button the effect of several

127

levels. Many pearl buttons are mounted in steel, brass and other metals and often have a center hole which is filled in with a bead of metal or a brilliant stone in white, blue, green, amber, red, amethyst or such precious stones as opals. Often the center is larger and the metal bead is etched with a design, or perhaps a Wedgwood button or a Delft pottery button with a scene in blue and white may be used in the center. Metal such as brass is often set beneath the cut work and often the button has a border of brass, steel or wood. Aside from the design and workmanship, the beauty of these mother-of-pearl buttons lies in the beauty of the pearl, and in the contrast of metals, gems and other materials.

Silver buttons were made in all countries of Europe as well as America. They were among the earliest buttons made. The first silver buttons were large, flat discs with simple engraved or etched designs. Fine English silver buttons were made in the reign of Queen Anne. English silver buttons were cast or molded. There were flat engraved sporting or hunt buttons with dogs, horsemen, and scenes of hunting. The designs on a set for a coat varied, with seldom more than two buttons alike. Other English silver buttons had engraved dragons, flowers or cupids' heads. Many old livery buttons were silver.

Among the most interesting silver buttons are the flat Dutch, engraved with quaint flowers, horsemen, birds, ships, stars and crests. Especially fine are the variations of the horsemen. These buttons are small and are both round and octagonal in form. Later Dutch silver buttons were stamped and had designs similar to the engraved buttons, but more sophisticated. There were also dome-shaped silver buttons with conventional patterns.

One of the most fascinating fields of silver-button collecting is that of silver peasant buttons. These were made in Russia, Norway, Sweden, Italy, Austria, Hungary, Spain, Portugal, Switzerland and in provincial France. The most typical peasant button is domed and has an openwork or filigree conventional design made of silver threads. Some of these buttons have jewels of paste, or glass; some are round and are called hanging

Buttons

buttons. Peasant buttons from France are flat and are of both brass and silver with flowers, grapes, animals and star designs. Among the finest silver filigree buttons are those from Spain which were imported and used in England in the eighteenth and nineteenth centuries. Especially interesting for a collector's item is the dome-shaped Spanish Bull Breeders button of silver-silt. The designs on these buttons are variations of interlacing circles and knobs. Even the Balearic Islands had flat engraved silver buttons with simple flower designs.

A neglected field of silver button collecting is the old Navajo silver button with engraved design and perhaps a turquoise.

Sheffield buttons were first made by T. Boulsover, a button maker of Sheffield, England, who invented the plating process in 1743. The copper plate was first silvered, then the buttons cut, soldered and polished. These buttons were plain with borders, and also had crests, initials, animals and birds. Some were made from old dies which were used for silver buttons in the time of Queen Anne. Other manufacturers of Sheffield buttons included Firmin & Sons, London, who even today make uniform and livery buttons; John Roche, Dublin; Joseph Hancock and Matthew Bolton and John Taylor of Birmingham. John Taylor first made gilt buttons, and Robert Hickman in 1787 took out a patent for a different method of making gilt and plated buttons. James Dixon in 1790 first made Britannia metal in an effort to find a substitute for Sheffield and from that time on buttons were made of this material. Among the most interesting plated buttons are the English livery buttons. The designs are heraldic, but include wild animals, such as the boar, porcupine, deer, elephant and lion; birds, dragons, winged horses, ships, castles and heads  as well. It is possible to collect buttons with many well-known Sheffield marks including: Firmin & Sons, London; Doughty & Co., London; Armfield, Birmingham; C. F. Bullivant, Birmingham, and C.P.H. & Co., London.

Matthew Bolton of Birmingham, England, is credited with the invention of cut-steel buttons toward the close of the eighteenth century. While the English excelled in this type of button and exported many to France and other countries, France also had her own industry. In 1772, M. Le Gay was specializing in cut-steel buttons *à l'anglaise,* and steel from the mines of Montbard was used. The fashion was so widespread that at least nine important stores specialized in steel buttons or gilded metal buttons.

The simplest steel buttons were plain circles or star shapes with a faceted design stamped on, and perhaps only one cut-steel button in the center. Some of these plain steel buttons were cut out or had borders or circles or stars of steel attached. The background disc was decorated with incised and faceted patterns in various geometric designs—wheels, stars, flutings, etc. Many buttons, however, had a hundred or more separate faceted bits of steel which were arranged in patterns and riveted onto the steel disc which served as a back for the button. The more bits, the choicer the button. Steel was often colored blue, and bronze, and the separate steels were arranged in a variety of patterns.

Large copper buttons of the eighteenth and nineteenth centuries show almost as much variety of design and workmanship as steel buttons. They are plain or engraved with designs, from fine lines to flowers, leaves and star designs. Some are even set with enamel centers which have colorful flowers on a background of white or blue or yellow enamel. Engraved white metal and metal alloy buttons also offer an interesting field for design. The designs are usually direct and simply executed, and include not only geometric patterns, conventional flowers and leaves, but a variety of animals and birds. A series of rare metal buttons in the shape of an inverted soup plate has bone carving of birds and animals. Early gilt buttons also have interesting designs including fruits, flowers, horsemen, animals and heads.

Buttons

From the seventeenth century on, buttons of wood, horn, tortoise-shell and semi-precious stones were made both in large and small sizes.

Semi-precious stones were often mounted on gold or brass or had a flat metal bead in the center. They were of various shapes: round, square, horn-shaped. Such stones as lapis lazuli, carnelian, malachite, cairngorm, bloodstone, cat's-eye, agate, alabaster and goldstone were made into buttons in the early eighteenth century, and later, in the Victorian era, these stones were made into mosaics of flowers, animals and landscapes and set in a gold mount.

Wooden buttons range from simple turned buttons, sometimes decorated with steel, brass, bronze or pearl, to those carved with heads or animals which, of course, are rare. The Irish bog-wood buttons are the most unique. These were carved from the black or dark-brown bog-wood and are crude carvings of Irish windows, doorways, gates, castles and churches. These were made in about 1883. In appearance the material is similar to gutta-percha. Some wooden buttons have a primitive effect and show the natural burl and outline of the wood, and some wooden buttons are inlaid with designs of silver flowers or arabesques.

Early American buttons were made of silver, pewter, steel, bell metal, copper and even gold; also gympe, thread and silk. The metal buttons were plain or might have a chased design of a star, a leaf, a figure or merely dots or lines in a simple geometric pattern.

The inventory of Henry Landis, a Boston shopkeeper in 1651, includes: "Breeches buttons, silk breast buttons, hair buttons and great silk buttons." Another shop advertises "gold cloak buttons." "The Statutes of the Realm," London, 1660, lists the following buttons for export: "Brasse, steel, copper or lattin, of crystall, of glass, of thred, of silke, of fine damaske, of Bugle, for Hankirchers, of Hair." While some few buttons may have been made by individual workmen in America, the following advertisements from the Boston paper will show the variety and quantity of English buttons that were used in America. 1742: "Fine mohair newest Fashion Buttons." 1747: "Bath metal and other sleeve buttons, Crystal set in silver." 1757: "A great assortment of white and yellow mettle coat and breast buttons, sleeve buttons. White stone and other kind of sleeve buttons. Best double Regimental Coat & Breast buttons and a variety of cheaper kind for the country sale. Best London-made silver sleeve buttons set with Brilliant stones and all other sorts of sleeve buttons." 1761: "A very great assortment of metal and breast buttons, black and colored horn buttons, Mathewman's & Wild's buttons, all sorts of colour'd stone sleeve buttons." 1762: "Silk lace for button lupes—plain and worked buttons, yellow & white buttons." 1763: "Scotch Peble Buttons."

From this list of imports, it would seem that colonists, at least in the Massachusetts colony, had almost as many kinds and types of buttons as people in Europe. What kind of buttons they actually wore, whether gold, silver, and silk, or pewter, copper, and horn, depended upon their circumstances and what their purse could buy. The gold and silver buttons and even the pewter buttons might be plain or chased with a simple design and even the horn and tortoise-shell buttons had variety. They might be round, oval, square, pea, concave or pyramid shape and some were as large as a watch. While there is no mention of Sheffield buttons, they undoubtedly must have been used in America.

Although there may have been button makers in America at this time—the *Boston News Letter,* 1716, lists a button maker among Irish servants arriving in America—the industry was not well developed. However, Caspar Wistar was making brass buttons and buckles in Philadelphia before 1750 and one John Fitch of Trenton made sleeve buttons from brass kettles and peddled his wares before the Revolution. Joseph Hopkins of Waterbury, Connecticut, made plated silver sleeve and vest buttons and Henry Witerman manufactured metal buttons near the Fly Market, New York, in 1850.

Benjamin Randolph, the cabinet maker at the Golden Eagle, Chestnut St., Philadelphia, in 1770 manufactured wooden buttons of "apple, holly and laurel wood hard and clear." There is no other description of these buttons, whether they were simple hand-turned buttons or whether, in view of Randolph's furniture, they might have had leaf carvings.

The button industry in America had too much competition with English manufacturers and in order to sell their buttons many of the manufacturers turned their buttons over to tin peddlers. Importation continued even after the Revolution. However, Richard Lee, of Taunton, Massachusetts, who manufactured pewter buttons as early as 1770, also supplied buttons to the Continental troops in the Revolution as did several other American manufacturers. The American-made pewter buttons of the regular soldier during the Revolution were of flat pewter or lead, and of solid construction, since they were cast in crude molds. They were of two sizes and were plain or had a beaded rim. They had simple lettering or insignia. Revolutionary officers' buttons were bone-backed and silver faced. The initials and insignia on these were usually engraved and they were of fine design and workmanship. These were probably made in France.

The collecting of military buttons involves a knowledge of the insignia and heraldry of the various troops. There are several books and articles on the subject listed at the end of the chapter, but the subject is too detailed for more than passing mention here. However, there is enough interest in the design and workmanship of some military buttons to include several in any general button collection. There are the Loyalist buttons with crowns and borders of laurel. The buttons with crossed swords, flags, drums, skull and cross bones, eagles and even a bounding stag are also among the subjects of interest. Navy buttons are usually of brass and may have eagles, anchors, wings and stars. A collection of American military buttons could be limited to the Revolution and the War of 1812, or it could include the Civil War and other succeeding wars even down to the present war. After 1800, there were numerous button manufacturers in the United States and most of them made army or navy buttons at one time or another.

Other interesting American historical buttons which do not require so much knowledge on the part of the collector are those concerning well-known men in American history. Washington inaugural buttons issued at the time of the first and second inaugurations are of four different designs. Each has the initials "G.W." and the phrase "Long Live the President," but the design and lettering varies on each type of button.

In 1824, Leavenworth, Hayden and Scovill, all of Waterbury, Connecticut, issued gold buttons with a head of Lafayette in celebration of his visit to America. These were made again from a re-die in 1876 for the Centennial at Philadelphia, and these are available today.

Campaign buttons, many of which were made by R. W. Robinson, include a head of Henry Clay and two of Zachary Taylor, one with "The Hero of Monterey" printed on the back and the other with the inscription "Rough and Ready" on the face around the portrait head. A button with the head of Franklin Pierce and flags and an eagle was also made as was one of U. S. Grant, marked "N.R. Co. Goodyear P.T." The Cleveland and Hendricks, and the McKinley and Roosevelt campaigns were also celebrated on buttons as were the Jackson campaign which is marked "American Standard" on the back. The Harrison campaign was the most popular from the standpoint of campaign buttons. There are eighteen different buttons showing the Log Cabin, both with and without the cider barrel. These were made by E. W. Robinson, E. E. Pritchard, and Scovill, all of Waterbury, Connecticut. Jacksonian vest buttons of gilt brass are early and therefore valuable, and at the present time they are obtainable. All are plain with separate rim turned over the edge and the center design includes a horse, a deer, a bird, a squirrel, an eagle, ships, anchors, wheat, a tree, a horn of plenty, a flower basket, a basket of fruit, grapes on a vine, a sheaf of wheat, a rose, and many other designs. These buttons came out at the time of Jackson's victory at New Orleans and were popular during Jackson's lifetime.

A unique center of button making in America was the Shaker colony at New Lebanon, New York, where buttons were made as early as 1789. The buttons were for use on brethren's garments, but there was

TOP, LEFT AND RIGHT: Sandwich glass hats, diamond sunburst pattern. *Courtesy The Metropolitan Museum of Art.* MIDDLE: Blue Bohemian glass slipper. *Collection of Mrs. Hazel Webster.* BOTTOM: four lacy Sandwich-glass salts. *Collection of Mr. and Mrs. A. E. Coddington.*

LEFT TO RIGHT, TOP: U. S. 19th c., wooden mold covered with silk threads; English, late 19th c., tortoise shell; U. S. 19th c., porcelain with painted decorations. MIDDLE: French, 19th c., pearl disc, brilliants and copper strips; French 19th c., pearl shell with glass; U. S. 19th c., pearl shell carved and inked. BOTTOM: French 18th c., copper and engraved nickel; U. S. 19th c., copper with nickel band; French, 18th c., cut steel. *Collection of the Cooper Union Museum*

UPPER LEFT: Papier-Mâché tray, green ground and floral decoration. LOWER RIGHT: Papier-Mâché tray, red background, Chinese-style decoration. *Courtesy J. E. Treleaven, Needham's Antiques.* UPPER RIGHT: Stobwasser Ware snuff box, Van Dyck and his mistress. LOWER LEFT: Stobwasser Ware snuff box, La Belle Polonaise. *Courtesy James K. Lewis*

TOP: Tucker family register, executed by Elmira Edson, Halifax, Vt. *circa* 1834. *Courtesy The New York Historical Society.* BOTTOM ROW, LEFT TO RIGHT: paper cutting by Martha Ann Honeywell. *From the collection of Mrs. M. L. Blumenthal. Courtesy The Magazine Antiques;* Pennsylvania German birth and baptismal certificate, printed by G. S. Peters, Harrisburg, Pa., *circa* 1840. *Courtesy The New York Historical Society*

also some outside sale. Jacket, coat and sleeve buttons of different sizes were made. Some were of polished brass or pewter, bone and ivory, and others were horn molds covered with cloth. These would be interesting in a collection of early-American buttons. They were simple in design and excellent in workmanship.

Victorian buttons include paste, mosaics, tin-types, pearl, lustre, cameo, glass, carved ivory, black glass, gutta-percha, hair- and cloth-covered buttons, also hand-painted and papier-mâché. However, the most popular Victorian buttons, both then and now, are the story buttons. These buttons were of brass or gilt and began to appear about the middle of the nineteenth century. Their  subject matter is sentimental, including scenes from operas and books, animal groups, like kittens in a basket and the cow jumping over the moon; Kate Greenaway children, lovers, musicians, Jenny Lind, hands and flowers, and such literary figures as Little Lord Fauntleroy. These buttons have been carefully listed and recorded in button books. Many were made by the Cheshire Manufacturing Co., Connecticut, between 1880–90. They are only of sentimental interest and a collection has no lasting worth except for what historical record might be connected with it. Few of the buttons have any beauty of design or workmanship and no intrinsic value. They are bringing prices today which are far beyond what they are worth.

If eighteenth-century papier-mâché buttons were made, there is no record. But we do know that papier-mâché buttons along with other papier-mâché articles were especially popular in mid- and late-Victorian times. In 1851 James Souter and James Worton of Birmingham took out a patent which mentions papier-mâché buttons. They were called paper buttons and usually were molded with several planes of surface with a metal plate at the back for strength. Many papier-mâché buttons had a hole in the center and fluid glass was poured into the hole and set like a jewel. Papier-mâché buttons are also inlaid with mother-of-pearl. The broken chips of pearl are set in a circle or border, or sometimes just scattered over the surface. Inlays also were of flowers, birds and butterflies and even landscape and buildings. These are not to be confused with the Chinese mother-of-pearl buttons with Chinese figures and scenes. Papier-mâché buttons are also painted with flowers and birds.

Tôle or painted tin buttons are also Victorian. J. Peele, in *The Art of Painting on Glass,* gives a recipe: "To Japan Brass such as is used to gild brass buttons or Bath-Metal." This recipe was intended for ladies who wished to spend leisure time in painting. All the tôle buttons to be found are of late nineteenth-century make. Some simple tôle buttons were painted by the Pennsylvania Dutch. These have geometric or flower designs.

Few collect silk- and cloth-covered buttons, yet here is an interesting field. The first cloth-covered buttons were plain, but in England, even in Elizabethan times, some buttons were covered with embroidery, and both long and oval buttons were worked in chevron pattern in red and green. The fish-bone stitch was also used and a silk-weave stitch made a ribbed effect. In the seventeenth century silver and gilt thread-decorated flat buttons had a strap pattern. Silver wire was also used in striped and plaided effects. By the eighteenth century flat buttons were embroidered in silk, bullion, metal thread and sequins. Both satin stitch and darning stitch as well as buttonhole and chain stitches were used. Some buttons were worked on a mold, but waistcoat embroideries together with matching buttons could be bought with button designs ready to cut and put on molds. The beauty of these embroidered buttons is in their color, the variation of the stitch and sometimes the exquisite needlework. However, although the color and design matched the coat or vest, usually the work was not as well executed as the embroidery on the article itself.

Simple thread buttons were made over a mold of metal or bone by the cottagers of Dorset, and similar buttons were made in Germany.

Cloth-covered buttons had a revival in mid-Victorian times. They

Buttons

were covered with hand embroidery and later machine embroidery tapestry patterns and profile portraits in black on colored silk and satin. Our grandmothers wore buttons which were covered with silk or other woven material over a padded mold and had padded designs of stars, anchors, flowers, a dove, a chevron, and other designs raised in their centers. The backs were metal. Florentine buttons with embroidered figures were popular, according to *Godey's Lady's Book*, in 1854.

To be a discriminating collector you will have to train your eye to recognize good design, color and workmanship, for it is only in this way that fine buttons can be identified. A knowledge of historic patterns will aid in identifying and dating certain buttons. Also a knowledge of how the button was made is an aid in dating. Flat one-piece buttons of pewter, silver and gold are older than buttons of two-piece construction.

BIBLIOGRAPHY

Les Accessoires du Costume et du Mobilier, Henry René d'Allemagne, Paris.

Buttons: Historical Notes and Bibliography—The Chronicle of the Museum for the Arts of Decoration of Cooper Union, Vol. I, No. 6.

New York Historical Society Quarterly Bulletins: Button Articles, William L. Carver, January, 1922–April, 1932.

The History of American Manufacture, L. Leander Bishop, Vols. I and II, Edward Young & Co., Philadelphia, 1868.

Arts and Crafts in New England, George Dow, Essex (Mass.) Historical Society.

Button Handbook, Florence Zacharie Ellis Nicholls, privately published.

A Button Collector's Journal, Lillian Smith Albert.

The Button Collector's History, Grace Horney Ford, privately published.

Button Classics, L. Erwina Couse and Marguerite Maple, Lightner Pub. Co.

Sheffield Plate, H. N. Veitch, George Bell & Sons, London, 1908.

New York State Museum Bulletin, 1932.

Chapter 15

ENGLISH PAINTED ENAMELS; BATTERSEA AND STAFFORDSHIRE

FOR collectors whose tastes call for sophisticated textures and designs, and delicate coloring, the painted English enamels of the eighteenth century have a strong appeal. Lady Charlotte Schreiber collected them and her collection is now in the Victoria and Albert Museum. Indeed it is safe to say that all larger and more important pieces of English enamel are in museums, but such small items as mirror knobs, wine labels and small boxes are still available. Other small enamel articles not so plentiful are scent bottles, bodkin cases, writing cases, *étuis, bonbonnières* and *nécessaires* with scissors and other instruments.

English enamels are not cheap. While you may be fortunate enough to pick up a piece among the stock of a second-hand dealer, the most likely place to look is in a good established antique shop. Do not expect to buy enamels in perfect condition. Most available pieces have cracks, but these should not be considered objectionable unless the enamel is cracked off to the copper base.

English eighteenth-century painted enamels are made on a copper base. The metal base is prepared with a hammer and acids. The opaque enamel is then laid over the front and back of the surface and the piece is fired. When the background or first coat of enamel is fixed, the design is painted on in transparent enamels and then the article is fired again. The majority of the eighteenth-century English enamels had the design applied by transfer and when other coloring was added it was put on by hand within the transfer outline. The transfer impressions were taken from engraved copper plates and printed on paper with special adhesive inks; then the paper imprint was pressed upon the enameled base leaving an outline design in black, red, brown, purple or mauve, as the case might be. This transfer process allowed for large production at little cost since many articles had little or no hand coloring.

Transfer printing on enamel was first discovered by John Brooks at the York House factory of Stephen Theodore Janssen and used on Battersea enamels, which are the finest transfer enamels made. The Battersea factory actually only operated for a period of three years—from 1753 to 1756. The name of the factory in 1753 was Jansen, Delamain & Brooks. John Brooks was a Dublin engraver. Other men known to have worked at Battersea are James Gwinn, John Hall, the well-known French artist, Simon François Ravenet, and John Hancock, the English engraver.

Battersea enamels are distinguished from other English enamels by their color. A thick, warm white with a brilliant surface is the best-known background. Upon this white surface the brighter colors melt with a wet translucency. The most characteristic colors are a clear bright blue, a deep bright crimson and a warm reddish-brown. This brown was often used in the printed transfer outlines. Yellow was the only colored ground used at Battersea. The rose du Barry, royal blue, and turquoise grounds belong to Staffordshire enamels of a later date. Battersea enamels were both painted and printed. Groups of flowers in the Meissen manner were usually painted without a transfer outline, but scenes from paintings after Boucher, Watteau's Cascade and Fêtes Venitiennes and other groups with gentlemen and ladies in eighteenth-century costume and ruins of classical buildings after Panini or Brustolone, usually had a printed outline even though the painting often covered it completely. The scenes are usually in oblong or oval spaces with painted rococo scrolls, shells and masks, or a simple raised decoration of rococo scrolls or diaper trellis as background motifs. The painting is delicate and free.

Ravenet did the finest Battersea painting. His work is distinguished by a flowing line, graceful drapery and fine detail. He is known to have done the following subjects on Battersea enamels: plaques of George II and Frederick, Prince of Wales; a medallion of Prince Charles Edward, disguised as Betty Burke; George III, William Augustus, Duke of Cumberland, Peter the Great, Sir Robert Walpole, Horace Walpole and Admiral Boscawen. Also such religious plaques as The Crucifixion, St. Mary Magdalen, The Holy Family, St. Anthony of Padua and St. James of Compostella, are by Ravenet. He also did a group of mythological subjects including Europa and the Bull, Apollo and Daphne, Venus and Triton, Venus disarming Mars, Venus and Nymph, Perseus and Andromeda, and Paris awarding the apple. Also genre subjects such as The Punch Party, the Fortune Teller, and an interior with a lady and gentleman and a dog. Designs with cupids appear on some boxes and also on the attractive Battersea wine labels. These charming wine labels include tags for Muscat, Lisbon, port, burgundy and the rare old mountain wines. Cupids frolic about the grape trellis, the cider press, or a large barrel. The colorings are delicate and their draperies graceful. These same designs were later copied and used on boxes without the names of the wines.

Chelsea artists are thought to have decorated some Battersea, but the reverse is probably true, since many Chelsea toys and bottles have Battersea enamel lids with the same flower sprays as those used on Battersea.

John Hancock is known for his transfer prints on Bow and Worcester porcelain and some of the same landscapes appear on Battersea and thus may be ascribed to Hancock. Most of the Battersea enamels were inspired by Meissen china while the later Staffordshire enamels took their inspiration from Sèvres and thus have more elaborate painting and colored grounds. The fascinating little bird boxes and those in the shape of human heads and animal heads are thought to have been made at Battersea. They are very similar to the Chelsea porcelain ones. These boxes include some in the shape of swans, ducks' heads, woodcock with a painting of huntsmen and a dog, a dove's head with a print of doves on top, a bullfinch with flowers painted on the lid; a boar's head with a painted scene of a boar and dogs; a dog's head painted with a rose; a pug dog's head painted with a lady caressing a pug dog. Also the heads of Negroes, queens and a head of Neptune with a scene of sea shells and dolphin painted on the lid belong in this group of miniature toy boxes. Battersea is rare and most enamels in shops today called Battersea are Staffordshire, mostly from Bilston or Liverpool, Birmingham or Wednesbury. Enameling may have been carried on in Staffordshire soon after the closing of the Battersea factory, but the earliest mention in *Birmingham and District Directory* is in 1777. In 1781, three enamel box-makers are listed as working at Bilston. Enamelers are also mentioned as working at Birmingham and at Wednesbury until the end of the century. Many of these enamels are as fine as Battersea, but their style, coloring, and subject matter suggest a date from 1760 to 1780. Snuff boxes, patch boxes, and perfume bottles are the same shape as those from Battersea, but instead of white grounds the background is usually deep blue, pink, rose du Barry, green, or yellow. The decoration includes landscapes with figures, ruins or boat scenes, figures in eighteenth-century costume, flowers, fruit and birds. Most of these designs were taken from drawing books including *The Ladies Amusement, or Whole Art of Japanning, Made Easy*. This book was published by Robert Sayer in 1759–60, and includes plates from designs by Pillement as well as ten pages of signed engravings by Robert Hancock, of flowers and birds and of a parrot, currants, and an overturned basket of fruit, a design which is found on both Staffordshire enamel boxes and Worcester porcelain. Other subjects included Chinese pagodas, landscapes, shells, ships, insects and swans and a kingfisher. Other books with similar designs which were used on both enamels and china were issued by Robert Sayer in 1775, 1776 and 1777. One book included the Fortune Telling Woman, Hancock's Tea Party, and The Milkmaids, all scenes which appear on Staffordshire enamel boxes. Rural scenes with cows are often found.

Many times the same scene is found on both a box and an *étui* and often the design varies in details of foreground and background, and the painting and even the coloring are varied. This may suggest that many artists worked on the designs, or perhaps a model was made and copied by apprentices. However, the quality of painting on Staffordshire enamels is often superior even to that on Battersea enamel. These paintings were set against colored backgrounds of pink, deep rose du Barry, dark blue, turquoise-blue, pea-green, lavender-blue, plum-color, brownish-olive, and lemon-yellow, which made them much more colorful than the Battersea set on the white backgrounds.

One interesting article made at Liverpool and also of Staffordshire enamel was the mirror knob or wall peg. The style of using these pegs to fasten a picture or mirror on the wall was much in vogue in the last half of the eighteenth century. These knobs were used in such quantities that it was necessary to manufacture them at little cost. Transfer printed enamels offered a good, yet decorative, solution. Subject matter was of various types. Some of the knobs had simple transfer landscapes with figures or ruins; other had figures of women depicting the four seasons and still another type had pastoral scenes with a peasant and rake. One interesting group of wall pegs shows women and men with hats and hair styles of about 1780. These were taken from books of advertising gotten out for the use of barbers, but while not fine in design, are decorative. These were usually printed and some were hand colored.

From the standpoint of subject matter the most interesting and most valuable knobs are those with the series of portraits of famous Americans taken from the original engravings by Pierre Eugene Du Simitière. Du Simitière made fourteen such sketches from life when in Philadelphia in 1779 and they were executed in Paris by Prévost. Later these engravings were pirated by British publishers and they appear on these enamel mirror knobs as well as on china and pottery. The original series included George Washington, Steuben, John Jay, Laurens, Thompson, H. Gates, Gouverneur Morris, Huntingdon, S. Deane, W. H. Drayton, J. Dickenson, Reed, Benedict Arnold and Girard. Most of these have been found on mirror knobs printed in black or brown transfer on white on an oval shape and banded in a brass or copper mount. Some are also painted in colors over the black transfer. The mounts are interesting in themselves; some are beaded with single or double beading, while others are flat, and still others have borders built up with various levels as a picture frame. Groups of small medallions with the same subject matter as these mirror knobs have been found fastened together with metal leaves and *fleur-de-lys*.

Another series in oval included Dr. Franklin printed in dark purple from an engraving by G. Cooke after the painting by Cochin. Franklin wears spectacles and fur cap. This series also includes Napoleon, Wellington and Lord Nelson and his ship *Vanguard*. The portrait of Nelson and his ship are painted over in crimson, blue, yellow and gray and have the date 1798—a blow to the dealer who sells it as Battersea! Portraits of George III and Queen Charlotte are also found on mirror pegs, as well as actors and scenes from the *Beggar's Opera,* a boy with a flute, a girl with a rake (Rosina), several variations of the classic vase by Guy Green of Liverpool, and American eagles. Five portraits of Washington appear, one in cocked hat and military uniform, printed in dark purple. The portrait of Washington after Du Simitière shows him as an older man and a ribbon scroll fills the space above his head. Metal borders on pegs have designs of laurel, acanthus, beading, roping and fluting.

Boxes with calendars and music form a class apart. Songs and music were printed in black, blue, red, purple or gold in both English and French on these boxes with colored backgrounds. At Bilston some boxes were punched out in relief and painted and often a flower in relief was used in the middle of a bottle or box-lid.

Other quaint boxes were of chintz type. These had printed backgrounds with all-over geometrical line patterns in blue, green, pink or deep yellow and against this ground a floral design or rococo scrolls were painted. Some of the work of the later Staffordshire enamelers is coarse, but quaint and interesting.

Many boxes have the printed transfer design of Britannia holding up the cap of Liberty and crowning the British lion with a wreath while she leans on a scroll inscribed "No. 45" which alludes to the John Wilkes incident, and thus dates the boxes after the incident in 1763. Another box with a print of Britannia and the British lion has the inscription: "Proud of her Geo. III, Britannia rears her head and hopes he will reign many years." This box is also late eighteenth-century Staffordshire enamel. Still other interesting Staffordshire boxes have the portrait of Frederick the Great of Prussia adapted from a painting by Antoine Pesne and engraved by J. G. Wille. The inscription on the ribbon reads "Fridercus Maximus Boruss Rex."

Enamel snuff boxes in the shape of slippers are decorated with sprays of flowers, and little round salt dishes set on three or four legs have medallions of flowers and birds or fruit, or perhaps small scenes set in rococo cartouches. Candlesticks in the form of Greek columns are painted with sprays of flowers and their bases have scenes set in medallions.

However, the biggest supply of Staffordshire enamels on the market today are the little quaint trinket boxes in blue, turquoise, pink, and yellow with a printed border and lettering in black saying: "A Trifle from Liverpool" (or Bath, or Sherborne), or "A Toy from Birmingham." Some of these little boxes are round and others oval and some are no larger than a quarter. Sometimes a verse such as "I love too well, to kiss and tell" is used and other boxes have the inscription, "From a Friend." These are the latest boxes and were probably not worth a dollar when made, and even today, although they are quaint and cute and perhaps even charming, their artistic merit is nil, yet they are fascinating trinkets to collect.

The metal mountings of English eighteenth-century painted enamels are worthy of notice. In the sale of the goods of the bankrupt factory at Battersea in 1756 the newspaper advertisement reads:

"Also a quantity of beautiful enamels, colour'd and uncolour'd, of the new manufactory carried on at York House at Battersea, and never

English Painted Enamels

yet exhibited to public view, consisting of snuff-boxes of all sizes of great variety of Patterns, of square and oval pictures of the Royal Family, History and other pleasing Subjects, very proper ornaments for Cabinets of the Curious, Bottle tickets with chains for all sorts of Liquor, and of different subjects, Watch-cases, Toothpick-cases, Coat & Sleeve Buttons, Crosses, and other Curiosities, mostly mounted in metal, double gilt."

Thus Battersea set the pattern of gilt mountings which was followed by the later makers of enamels, for almost every article has its metal mounting. Some of the mountings are plain, others are chaised or engraved with zig-zag lines or rococo scrolls, while some mounts have scalloped edges. Mounts are applied at openings and at the top and bottom of a box or bottle to strengthen it and protect the enamel edges. Metal is also used in the form of rings or handles on frames of plaques or on box tops or on lids of perfume bottles, while metal chains are used on wine labels. The quality of the metal often suggests the value of the article and where good double gilt has been used, it is usually still in good condition. Sometimes the metal is japanned to imitate tortoise-shell.

In collecting English painted enamels of the eighteenth century one had better start with a reputable dealer and take his word for the quality of the enamel. He may also be able to assure you of getting English and not French enamels. However, the exact place of manufacture cannot always be authenticated, so it is best to judge all pieces from the standpoint of good color, design and workmanship. If these factors are present you have your money's worth.

BIBLIOGRAPHY

Connoisseur, 1932, "New Light on Battersea Enamels," W. B. Honey (two articles).

Catalogue of the Schreiber Collection of English Porcelain, Earthenware, Enamels and Glass, Bernard Rackham, Vol. III.

Battersea Enamels, Egan Mew.

Chapter 16

SILVER WINE LABELS OF THE EIGHTEENTH AND NINETEENTH CENTURIES

A COLLECTION of silver wine labels has both artistic and historical value. Such a collection is not too expensive for the collector of average means and it is a safe investment, for the value of good marked silver never depreciates. England is the best hunting ground, but there is also a quantity of English silver in American shops, and while wine labels are not plentiful there are enough to make collecting them an interesting hobby. However, collecting any article of silver is not for the casual collector, since a knowledge of silver marks takes careful study. Although wine labels are small, they were made by most of the important silversmiths. Their designs and shapes are usually of artistic worth and their workmanship as fine as that of larger pieces of silver.

The first wine labels were made in the period between 1740 and 1760, although an early shield shape by John Holland is dated 1739. Before this date white bottles of Bristol Delft were used, sometimes with the name of the wine painted on in blue. In the middle 1700's Zachariah Barnes of Liverpool made fine labels in Delftware to hang on kegs. But it was not until crystal decanters came into use that silver labels became popular.

The earliest labels were narrow, rectangular and unadorned, except for the name of the wine which included many old types mentioned by Samuel Pepys, but long since gone from use. Among these are Trent, Arrack, Florence, Sack and Wormwood. Early labels also bear such interesting wine names as Mountain, Constantin, rare Methusen, Bene,

146

Silver Wine Labels

Calcavella, Madeira, Tinta, Malmsey, Boal, and Hollands as well as English, Meade and Cowslip. Such names as these are rare and usually indicate an early date. Later the rectangular shape became broader and the ends were often rounded or the corners cut to form an octagon. Feather cutting was the first decoration used and this later developed into a gadroon edge.

Early labels were also made in shield shape and these are found plain or engraved with a grape and leaf design. The crescent shape and a rare kidney shape were also early. Makers of these early labels include John Holland, S. Dell, Henry Bailey, Robert Hennell, Robert Burton, Edward Medlycott, John Harvey, Sandilands and Drinkwater, and Stephen Walsh of Cork, Ireland. On these early labels only the initials of the maker and the lion passant are used. Many early labels are not marked since it was not until 1784 that an Act of Parliament required the marking and gave wine labels the official name of "Bottle Tickets." Sometimes the label was

hung from the bottle by a ring of silver wire instead of a chain. These were attached in various ways, those with hinges being the rarest. Still another means of placing the label on the bottle was a splayed silver hoop. Ring labels are found with crests, and also with plain rectangles. They were made as early as the late eighteenth century by S. Bates of London and later by Phipps & Robinson. One has been found with the rare name Vidonia, a wine from the Canary Islands. The influence of Chippendale

147

design is seen on the earlier labels and later Adam, Hepplewhite, and Sheraton influence is seen in delicate labels with classic vase forms, feathers and engraved crestings.

Later, Hester Bateman (1774–1784) introduced a new type of design which included a shield above the rectangle label. This shield was usually engraved with a family crest or a crest of a regiment. These are very rare. Similar designs were used by W. Cripps, S. Bates and later by Peter and Ann Bateman, so although this type is known as the Bateman type it was also used by other makers. In fact from the very beginning, makers pirated the designs of their competitors and the same makers are known to have repeated their own designs at various periods with intervening years between.

Leaf designs were introduced in the late eighteenth century. These consisted of a single grape leaf in various designs or a group of several leaves, or leaves with grapes. These are the most decorative and most popular type of designs. One of the makers whose leaf forms are especially fine is Edward Edwards, who made a design of one large leaf and two small ones. The Bronté Madeira is dated 1789, while a similar design by the same workman is marked Madeira and dated 1829. Taylor and Perry made some of the finest leaf designs. Leaf designs were also made by the well-known firm of George Unite and by Charles Rawlins in 1823, and by Joseph and Albert Savory in 1840, as well as by many other makers. Wine names on leaf designs include Sauterne, Port, Burgundy, Sherry, Peppermint, Whisky, Medoc, Hock and rare Noyeau, Bucellas and Tinta. The markings on leaf designs are on the top side while other types of labels are usually marked on the back.

A design known as the Boy and Cup was first made in the late eighteenth century and with many variations continued as a popular pattern well into the nineteenth century. One of these Boy and Cup designs was made by Matthew Linwood in 1794 and is thought to be the first die-cut label. A rare one was made by Stephen Walsh of Cork, and others were made by George Unite, T. Phipps and E. Robinson, Charles

Silver Wine Labels

Rawlins, Reilly & Storer, Joseph Willemore, John Robins (who made labels for Windsor Castle), Taylor & Perry, Robert Garrard, and the Batemans.

Another favorite design was the Fox and Grapes which was first made by R. Garrard. A large label of similar design was also made by the well-known maker Paul Storr. The design was also used by S. Howell, Phipps & Robinson, Rawlins & Sumner and others.

Other designs include a lion's head, shells, fruit and flowers, and a few rare labels are in the shape of a clam or conch shell.

In 1773, Matthew Boulton made the first wine labels in Sheffield plate. Other makers of Sheffield plate labels include John Winter & Co., Matthew Linwood, Unite & Hilliare, N. Smith, Watson & Bradbury and James Willmore. Designers of Sheffield plate labels copied all the earlier styles as well as many later designs. They rarely originated a design. Sheffield wine labels seldom have marks; however, when one of good workmanship and design is found it is a welcome addition to any collection. There are a vast quantity of plated labels on the market, many of which are not Sheffield but modern. Old Sheffield labels are usually in poor condition with the silver worn off, showing the copper. The most common type of Sheffield label is rectangular in shape with a reeded or beaded border. This type is not worth collecting, but there are many fine designs in Sheffield plate, including several designs with grapes and leaves and young Bacchus. One such design shows a boy Bacchus astride a wine barrel.

Silver gilt labels were made in various shapes and designs, including lions' heads with grapes and leaves, grapes and masque, the Boy and Cup designs and even extra-large labels with intricate designs of leaves and flowers were made in silver gilt. These labels are rare. Several made by John Reilly and Thomas Robins in 1802 or 1803 have been found as well as some by other well-known makers.

Although labels had often been marked with an initial, it was not until about 1829 that the cut-initial label came into use. Initials were cut into a small rectangle of silver and others were made of the initial outline alone. Some were plain, others had an engraved illuminated design, and still others were embossed with leaves and flowers. Later, the whole name of the wine was given in cut-out silhouette and still later the ugly script names and letters which are still made today came into use. Initial letters, although not an important collector's item are found with many well-known makers' names, including Charles Rawlins, John Tewemlow, Joseph Willmore and George Unite of Birmingham, who made initial labels as late as 1858.

Although no wine labels have been found with American makers' names before the time of Gorham or Tiffany, labels must have been in use in eighteenth-century America. According to newspapers of the time, the wines used in America were those still in favor in England and they were sold in casks, pipes and similar measures which would have required other containers, such as decanters for serving purposes. However, the *New York Commercial Advertiser* of January, 1800, lists "Bristol bottled Porter and Perry." Undoubtedly the labels used at that time were of English make and the reason that we do not find mention of them is that they were considered too unimportant. Indeed, of all the authorities writing on silver, the only references to wine labels are by Sir Charles Jackson, who included labels in his own collection and who lists the following makers of wine labels: William Hamy, John Teare, and Moulong & Gibson, all of Dublin, and Louis de Lisle, John Hardy, Ledsam, Vale & Wheeler, Nathaniel Mills, and Samuel Harwood, all English nineteenth-century makers.

Although I have made no attempt to list all of the makers of eighteenth- and nineteenth-century wine labels, a few additional names may help to show the broad scope of wine-label collecting. To the list of eighteenth-century makers may be added the names of R. T. Tyrell, Thomas Howell, E. Moreley, Samuel Bradley, Samuel Monsey, J. Ebbs, Abraham Tuppy (Dublin), Henry Sardet, Thomas Rush, Robert

LITHOGRAPHS. LEFT TO RIGHT, TOP: Barnet & Doolittle, from "The Grammar of Botany," 1822. *Courtesy The New York Horticultural Society;* P. S. Duval, from "Floras Lexicon—An Interpretation of the Language and Sentiment of Flowers," 1839. BOTTOM: Pendleton, from "Treatise on the Vine," 1830; Childs and Inman, from "The Floral Magazine and Botanical Repository," 1830. Last three, *courtesy the New York Botanical Gardens*

SILHOUETTES. LEFT TO RIGHT, TOP ROW: Girl: "William King"; Woman: "Bache's Patent." BOTTOM ROW: Mrs. Morris, Scotland, 1831: "August Edouart, fecit"; Charles West Thomson: "August Edouart, January 14, 1843." *From the collection of the New York Historical Society*

TRANSFER ENAMEL. LEFT TO RIGHT, TOP: wall peg, John Jay; wall peg, George Washington. MIDDLE ROW: wall peg, W. H. Drayton; enamel box, late 18th c. BOTTOM ROW: wall peg, vase design; Battersea type enamel box with floral decoration on white ground. *Courtesy The Metropolitan Museum of Art*

SILVER WINE LABELS—19TH CENTURY. LEFT TO RIGHT, TOP ROW: lion's head and floral; shell. SECOND ROW: shell; leaf and grapes. THIRD ROW: shell; leaf. FOURTH ROW: crest; leaf. *Courtesy The New York Historical Society.*

Silver Wine Labels

Lowe, Roger Raine, W. Brind, W. Reynolds, Samuel Godbekere and John Stoyte (Dublin).

Additional nineteenth-century makers include: I. Ashley, Smith & Sharp, W. Elliot, John Bridge, W. Kingdom, James Barber and William Whitwell, John Salkeld, Thomas Jenkinson, Joseph Hicks, Rebecca Emms and Edward Barnard, Alexander Edmondstone, Edward Thomason, Alexander Cameron (Dundee), J. Lawrence, W. King, George Purse, McKenzie & Cross, John S. Hunt and R. Gray & Son (Glasgow).

The most important factor in determining the value of a wine label is good design which includes not only the pattern but fine workmanship. A label by a good designer and marked with his name has more value than an unidentified label. Early dated pieces are rare and those with old and unusual wine names are rare. Silver gilt labels are rarer than silver ones.

BIBLIOGRAPHY

Wine, Spirit and Sauce Labels of the Eighteenth and Nineteenth Centuries, Herbert C. Dent.

New York Historical Quarterly, July, 1929, "Silver Wine Labels," Raphael A. Weed.

English Goldsmiths and Their Marks, Sir Charles J. Jackson.

A History of Ancient and Modern Wines, Alexander Henderson, Baldwin, Cradock & Joy, London, 1824.

Chapter 17

PAPIER-MÂCHÉ

THE collector of papier-mâché has a wide range of objects from which to choose. The list runs from furniture and tea trays to snuff boxes, tea caddies, trinkets and boxes. The types and styles of decoration are equally varied, including conventional patterns, naturalistic flowers, and even copies of well-known nineteenth-century paintings. Toward the end of the nineteenth century and in the early twentieth century so much papier-mâché of garish design and poor workmanship was turned out that the industry fell into ill repute. In fact the very name papier-mâché was frowned upon, along with the Victorian ottoman and the antimacassar. Although much inferior papier-mâché was made and is found in the shops today, there are enough pieces of really fine workmanship to justify the enthusiasm of the collector.

The French invented papier-mâché in the early eighteenth century, but it was also made at Birmingham, England, by Henry Clay as early as 1772. The base of papier-mâché was a damp mixture of vegetable matters—paper, hemp, hay and tree bark—which was pressed into sheets upon an iron mold or core. Several such layers were pressed and glued together with glue, flour and resin and dried in an oven. The article was then waterproofed with a mixture of linseed oil and tar, and the shiny varnish coats applied. Between each varnish-coat the surface was smoothed with pumice and chamois. Then the piece was ready for the final decoration which was to give it real interest and value. At first only panels and trays were made. These Henry Clay trays had a decoration of chrysanthemums, bamboo or palms. Their colors were yellows and greens, with blended bronze tints.

152

Papier-Mâché

Models of wood or metal were required for boxes and tea caddies, while furniture, such as tables, was made in sections about a solid core which was cut out and the pieces brought together and finished. Snuff boxes were molded or turned from dried pulp.

The papier-mâché industry in England centers in two cities—Birmingham, where Henry Clay started the industry and where it was later carried on by the well-known firm of Jennens & Bettridge from 1816 to 1864, and Wolverhampton. Although there were other firms producing papier-mâché in Birmingham, Jennens & Bettridge was really the training-school for papier-mâché workers and most men in the industry worked for them at some time. No special characteristics can be attributed to the work of this firm, but no articles of really poor quality were made here.

Jennens & Bettridge stamped their mark on some of their products. The stamp appears as: "Jennens & Bettridge," "Jennens & Bettridge Birmingham," "Jennens & Bettridge—London & Birmingham," "Jennens & Bettridge, Makers to the Queen," "Jennens & Bettridge, Patent Inlaid Gems," "J. H. Bettridge, late Jennens & Bettridge."

Sometimes a crown is shown.

At Wolverhampton, Walton & Co. specialized in making tea trays. They often marked their goods "B. Walton & Co." Other firms who often stamped their goods were Clay & Co., Loveridge, Deans, Deans & Benson, Mapleton, Alderman, and Itlidge.

The decoration of papier-mâché included various motifs, from landscape, flower and geometric motifs, to animals, insects and even portraiture, the latter on snuff boxes of the late eighteenth and early nineteenth centuries. The motifs of design and decoration were influenced greatly by the process of decoration, and this process or method of decoration changed with the various inventions. Thus the decoration of papier-mâché may be classified into various periods which aids somewhat in dating an unmarked article.

The first method of decoration employed was bronze, used with metal powders and alloys. These powders were put on with a swab rather than a brush. The metal powder was sprinkled on the tray or panel and picked or smeared out with various-sized swabs. At that time Trafalgar and Waterloo were recent events and they became subject matter for papier-mâché decoration on trays and pole screens. Later in the century, bronze effects were perfected by Walton & Co. at Wolverhampton and effects of sunlight upon cathedrals and Gothic ruins, including Warwick Castle, Tintern Abbey, Melrose Abbey, Westminster Abbey and the Tower of London, were typical subjects. At this writing a New York dealer has a set of three trays with scenes of the Irish lakes in this later bronze with some foreground painting. One tray is marked, "B. Walton & Co." Gold, which was the most important factor in the decoration of papier-mâché, was used both in powder and leaf form, but no gold paint was ever used. Anyone who has ever tried to apply gold leaf will appreciate the intricate lines of gold in papier-mâché decoration. Gold was used mainly in borders, but also under paint to give brilliancy to a flower, a bird or a butterfly, or under a gem inlay.

The mother-of-pearl inlay which we associate with papier-mâché was not used until 1825, when it was patented by Jennens & Bettridge. Green and pink shell was used for this inlay. It was cut and filed until it had the thinness of paper, then it was put in place with cement. In the best pearl work the pieces were arranged so that they reflected the same color. Roofs of buildings, walls, leaves of trees and centers of flowers were done in pearl work. A level surface is obtained in the best work by coats of transparent varnish and polishing with stone or leather. Nubby pearl work is inferior and of a later date.

In 1847, Jennens & Bettridge took out a patent for gem inlay. Glass beads, gems or real stones were set in a pattern and often the gem was surrounded with gold or silver leaf; then the design was placed in a panel on the box cover, inkstand or writing case and covered with a glass. Although such articles were necessarily fragile, there are some in perfect condition on the market today. The oriental style of decoration is associated with the artist Joseph Booth. This style of papier-mâché decoration included Chinese figures, temples, trees and reproductions of the Willow pattern. Along with the painted decoration was pearl inlay and gold tracery. Tea trays, panels and pole screens especially were decorated in this style.

When we consider the actual painting on papier-mâché it is necessary to mention the artists who worked at the various factories. Most of these men were artists of merit who later made a name for themselves as painters. Certain artists are associated with certain designs. Thus in the realm of naturalistic flower painting, George Neville and Edwin Haselar were well known, especially for the painting of roses. John Breakspear and William Bourne painted verbenas. Thomas Hamson was known for his parrots, while Jackson introduced the lily-of-the-valley design which is often seen on desk sets. David Sargent is remembered for the fern pattern, usually done in brilliant green. The shell pattern and heath and heather are also popular, but were not associated with any one man.

Spiers & Son of Oxford were known for their scenes of Oxford buildings and views.

A border of roses and convolvulus in bronze tones was introduced by Brown about 1850, and is seen on many trays of that time. Later it was used by all workmen at the various factories and called Brown's Border. Even a "liner" must be an able workman and there were men who specialized in lining, just as there were men who did nothing but marbling and wood graining—both later methods of decoration.

A fire screen of papier-mâché, with a view of Oxford, the Martyr's Monument, was exhibited by Spiers & Son in the London Exposition of 1851. Also shown were tables, cabinets, hand screens, albums, writing portfolios, work boxes, card trays and panels, all ornamented with views of Oxford public buildings, gardens, college walks and general views of Oxford and its neighborhood. Other manufacturers of papier-mâché who exhibited articles at the London Exposition were: T. Lane, George C.

Davies, Halbeard & Wellings, Foothorape, Showell & Shenton, I. Sutcliffe, McCallum & Hodson, and Jennens & Bettridge, all of Birmingham; and Jackson & Sons, Charles Frederick Bielfeld, J. Dixon, William Walter Eloure and Henry Clay, all from the vicinity of London.

Because of the size of the flat surface, tea trays, more than any other article, seem to have the finest painting. Of course panels, hand screens and pole screens also offered ample space for painting and thus are attractive items for the collector. Tea trays may often be dated by their edge. The oldest trays had a plain or straight edge, usually nailed on. Gradually edges became curved and turned and were molded by hand into Gothic and Chippendale curves. Many trays had an elaborately painted border, but the center was left undecorated.

Papier-mâché snuff boxes with painted lids offer one of the most fascinating fields of papier-mâché collecting. First, because their subject matter is so varied and their prices are within the range of all purses. Secondly, because very little is known of the artists who decorated these boxes and thus there is a chance of discovering new information, and finally because there is really fine painting on some of these boxes. The boxes were made at Birmingham and Brindley in England and at Brunswick, Germany, and some may have been made in America. Certainly they were decorated there. The earliest boxes had no rim, but later, rims were added and they made a frame or border for the painting. The paintings on these snuff boxes were usually copies of celebrated pictures although there was some original work. Foremost among the English painters of papier-mâché snuff boxes was Samuel Raven. Fortunately for us he signed most of his work and his signature, "S. Raven" is in script on the inside of the lid. Sometimes he also signed the painting on the lid. The signature usually reads: "S. Raven Pinxt. Patronized by H.R.H. The Duke of Sussex and Prince Leopold."

Subjects on snuff boxes by Samuel Raven include: King George IV after Sir Thomas Lawrence; Union Commercial Room, Birmingham Arms of Plane Makers Society; Blind Fiddler, Rent Day, Blind Man's

Papier-Mâché

Buff, The Cut Finger, Village Politicians and Young Bird, after Burnet & Raimbach engravings; The Poacher Detected, after Kid; The Beeswing, Proposal and Congratulations, after Harlow and also after Moses Haughton; Bull Dogs, after A. Cooper, R.A.; Rat-Killing Terrier, after Panel. Landscape scenes include: Moonlight, after Joseph Vernet; Moor Shooting after Philip Reinagle, R.A. Mythological scenes include: Venus, after Titian, and Venus with Doves. Portraits of men and women are seen in Five Senses, after L. Bailly.

Of course there were many other painters who decorated snuff boxes, but the subject matter varied little except in occasional original pieces.

While elaborate French snuff boxes are widely sought after and collected, these humbler boxes of papier-mâché are not especially popular with collectors. Not much is known about them and thus their values have not risen as much as might be expected. They range in price according to the quality of the painting.

In France, snuff boxes of Vernis Martin were decorated with characteristic French genre scenes, landscape and portraits, relying for their effect upon the application of a transparent gold ground over a colored base worked while soft. The foundation color was usually emerald green or lapis blue, while the base of the English and German box is black.

Papier-mâché snuff boxes or patch boxes were made and decorated in almost every country of Europe, and in America as well. However, outside of England and France, the boxes decorated by Georg Siegmund Stobwasser at Brunswick, Germany, are the best known. Stobwasser was an able artist, but he, like Samuel Raven, copied most of his box covers from well known paintings or prints. He owned a factory for the manufacture of papier-mâché and hired a staff of able artists to decorate his snuff boxes. His factory had royal patronage, and his portraits included Mary Queen of Scots, William IV, Maria Foote as Maria Darlington, Napoleon, and Duke Frederick William of Brunswick. He also copied the work of Italian masters and of Rembrandt, Rubens, Teniers, Velasquez, Murillo, Fragonard, David, Lawrence, Wilkie, Westall, and in one instance, a portrait of De Witt Clinton, the work of an American painter. Stobwasser also copied mythological subjects such as Io and Jupiter, Antiope and Jupiter, The Rape of Proserpine and The Judgment of Paris, and some box lids contain paintings of nudes after Van Der Werft. Woody landscapes, The Matterhorn, and Place Jean d'Arc, Rouen, are other types of subject matter for his box covers. There was no factory mark on the earliest Stobwasser snuff boxes, but various marks were used later including: "Stobwasser Fabric," "Stobwasser Fabric—Braunschweig," "Fabrique de Stobwasser a Brunswick," "Stobwassersche Fabrik, Meyer and Wried in Braunschweig," "Stobwasser's Nach folger (Mayer and Wried)," who took over the factory in 1856.

W. Stockmann & Co. also made and decorated papier-mâché snuff boxes in Brunswick from 1811 to 1869. Their goods are marked "W. Stockmann & Co," "Stockmanns Fabrik," "W. St. & Co., Braunschweig" (under a crown), "Herzl Brauns Hof Lackier Fabrik W. Stockmann & Co.," (with crown) or just $\frac{\text{St}}{\text{St,}}$ or "St. St." The title of the picture and the factory number were usually painted inside the box lid. The boxes are large, or table size, measuring three to four inches across. Many papier-mâché snuff boxes were also decorated with prints which were glued on the tops of the boxes. These prints usually depicted portraits of historical characters and scenes from the life of the times.

These boxes were seldom signed and the only marks of identification are the subject matter of the prints which are sometimes labeled. Thus, if one has the interest and patience, it is possible to trace the print maker and establish a date.

A complete list of papier-mâché articles includes trays, fans, hand screens, pole screens, tea caddies, writing cases, blotter covers, ink stands, paper and book racks, vases, jewelry boxes, sewing boxes, snuff boxes, card cases, buttons, drapery holders, tip-top tables, tea tables, chairs, cabinets and other furniture. American snuff boxes of the late eighteenth and nineteenth centuries are chiefly historical and thus worthy of a separate chapter.

In choosing papier-mâché, the collector should select pieces in good condition. The quality of the workmanship and of the painting and decoration determine the value. Geometric scroll patterns are second class. Good pearl work should be matched in color and smooth to the touch. Rough texture of the lacquer ground denotes second-rate quality. The lacquer should also have a high polish. The key to a really fine piece is often the quality and workmanship of the gold work. Aesthetic values alone determine the quality of the painting whether it be landscape, flowers, or portraiture. Study the painting with a magnifying glass. American papier-mâché is inferior to English or Continental, but some furniture was made in New York, and smaller articles were made by many firms all through the nineteenth century.

BIBLIOGRAPHY

English Papier-Mâché, George Dickinson, The Courier Press, London, 1925.

Connoisseur, 1929, Vol. 83, "Samuel Raven," Phillip A. S. Phillips; Vol. 84, "Stobwasser Ware," Phillip A. S. Phillips; Vol. 85, "Stobwasser and Stockman."

Chapter 18

PENNSYLVANIA DUTCH AND OTHER AMERICAN ILLUMINATED MANUSCRIPTS AND CUTWORK. PAINTED AND LITHO-GRAPHED CERTIFICATES

PAPER paintings commemorative of special occasions, drawn and decorated completely by hand, or printed and later decorated by hand, are an interesting form of American folk art. These personal and family records were made throughout the eastern seaboard states and as far west as Ohio. Not only are these primitive pen drawings records of early American life, but the later printed certificates give a record of the old printing presses of the late eighteenth and the first half of the nineteenth century.

Paper paintings are colorful, naive, and decorative. They are harmonious when used with simple American furniture. However such paintings are now scarce and in great demand, so that the prices are high. Also there are fakes on the market. In fact, the characteristics of the artists who make the fakes are well known, and time may come when these twentieth-century pen illuminations will also be collectors' items!

If you are interested in these paper paintings, there are several fields open. Pennsylvania Dutch hand-illuminated items are especially rare and scarce, and one needs a large pocketbook and much patience to secure a good example. Study those in museums and collect with care. There are better opportunities in printed birth and baptismal certificates, and an interesting collection could be made which would include a record of early printing presses of Pennsylvania or of the later Currier & Ives or Kellogg lithographed certificates. There are also opportunities

Illuminated Manuscripts and Cutwork

for those interested in forming collections of cut paper valentines or love letters since these are more plentiful than the illuminated manuscripts.

The source of these forms of early American folk art is European and can be traced directly to the medieval illuminated manuscripts. From this ancient source comes the style of manuscript writing and the illuminated capital letters. From this source also comes the use of geometrical divisions such as circles, squares and rectangles, and the use of pilasters and archways. Interlacing strapwork designs and borders, both geometric and floral designs, including roses, lilies, carnations, pomegranates and grapes may be traced to early religious manuscript illuminations. Angels' heads, double eagles, the cross, the crown and flowers growing from a vase, were also used on old manuscripts. Such imaginative manuscripts as the Fountain of Life in the Bibliotheque Nationale, Paris, which has a decorative tree surrounded by pairs of birds, roosters, peacocks, ducks, heron and deer, are found in naive duplicate form in the *fractur* (as the illuminated manuscripts were called) of the Pennsylvania Dutch. Other designs used in *fractur* were the heart, the tulip, the geometric star and circle, flowers growing from a heart, deer, doves, eagles, the horse, the dog, the American eagle, scarlet tanager, yellow warbler, the lamb, and the butterfly; also candles, the flames of hell, the Pilgrim with his staff, the Devil, and the Ark.

The immediate source for many Pennsylvania paintings was the *Christian A B C Book* made at Ephrata in 1750. This and many other hand-painted illuminated writings and song books of the Ephrata brethren were the inspiration for the teachers of illumination in the Pennsylvania Dutch schools. The *Christian A B C Book* was used as a copy-book for writing, and the exercises made from this pattern book form one type of *fractur* painting. These *Vorschrift* or specimens of a pupil's writing, usually contained a verse from the Bible or a moral precept in Gothic letters, similar quotations in script, and the letters of the alphabet in capitals and lower case, and ended with the numerals from one to ten and occasionally a musical score from a hymn. A *Vorschrift*

161

was usually signed with the pupil's name, place, and date. These *Vorschriften* are written in brown-black ink and decorated in red, green, yellow, orange and blue and sometimes a pinkish-lavender. An unusually decorative one is in brown and deep red with accents of blue. While some *Vorschriften* have no other decoration than the lettering, others have designs which include flowers, angels, birds, vases and flowers and hearts and flowers, as well as a hand-decorated border design. These *Vorschriften* date from about 1750 to 1850, when such teaching was discontinued in the Pennsylvania schools. Rewards of merit, illuminated and hand decorated, were given out by teachers for excellence in reading, writing and singing, and were usually signed by the teacher.

Another class of pen paintings includes the birth, baptismal, confirmation, and wedding certificates. These are divided into several types. First, those which are entirely hand painted and are the rarest and most sought after; second, those partly printed and partly hand decorated; and finally, those that are entirely printed, but hand-colored. This class of illuminated manuscripts is not confined to the region of the Pennsylvania Dutch, but was also used in Vermont, New Hampshire, Massachusetts, Connecticut and Maryland and Virginia. The certificates of Maryland and Virginia and states bordering Pennsylvania show the Pennsylvania Dutch influence in both design and coloring and are also often written in German script. The birth and marriage certificates of Connecticut, New Hampshire, Vermont, and other New England states are written in English and are more realistic in design, including delicate flowers and garlands, representations of figures in nineteenth-century dress who might be the owners of the certificates, and are more delicate in coloring than Pennsylvania Dutch certificates. One Connecticut certificate signed by Eunice Pinny shows an angel, a mother with three children, figures of Faith, Hope, and Charity, and flowers and garlands of leaves. Birth and baptismal certificates have a record of birth, and, in Pennsylvania, a reference to the sign of the Zodiac, the names of the parents, and in the case of baptismal certificates, the names of the clergyman and the witnesses present, as well as the dates and places of birth and baptism.

Illuminated Manuscripts and Cutwork

The usual form of birth and baptismal certificates in Pennsylvania is a five-verse hymn enclosed in panels. The record of birth and baptism is in the center of the certificate with these verses arranged in panels amid decorations of flowers, vines, birds, and angels. Certificates vary in elaborateness of design according to the artist. While many artists are known in connection with these certificates, few examples are signed. The artists included ministers, skilled penmen, and itinerant artists, as well as many amateurs or untaught artists. Families for generations often devoted their lifetimes as decorators of these manuscripts. These same artists decorated book plates, poems, Biblical verses and house blessings, as well as birth and baptismal certificates. Some of these smaller illuminated pieces, which often include rare portraits of Washington, Franklin, Jackson, or a family group such as the portraits of Peter and Rebecca Schneider, painted in 1830, are more difficult to find than the certificates. Here especially the collector needs to beware of twentieth-century fakes.

In fact your chances of finding a signed *fractur* on the market is one in a thousand. However, those interested in collecting printed certificates will find a list of printers helpful since specimens, especially the later ones, are still to be found.

The most common form of printed birth or baptismal certificate has five verses in addition to the hand-written names and place of birth. On one side of the printing is an angel with a bird in one hand and a harp in the other, and on the other side a similar angel with harp and wreath. The spaces below are filled in with birds and baskets or vases of flowers. The space above has an eagle or an angel.

Certificates on this general pattern were made in 1792 by Blumer & Leisenring at Allentown, Pennsylvania, and by G. S. Peters in Harrisburg from about 1825 to 1845, and later by Lutz & Scheffer of Harrisburg and by Johann Ritter in Reading from about 1808 to 1825. At about the same time or earlier, Gottlieb Jungmann and his partners, Benjamin Johnson and Thomas Barton, as well as Jacob Schneider and George D. Gerrish printed baptism certificates at Reading, Pennsylvania. These were decorated with hearts and flowers.

A certificate in the New York Historical Society Collection, printed by Barton & Jungmann in 1790, was decorated by Friederich Speyer in 1798. It has a quaint design of birds, lions, and two men dressed in long robes holding palm leaves and flowers. Another form of printed certificate has panels of birds and flowers on either side of the printing. These were printed around 1785 and one such certificate decorated by Henrich Otto is in the New York Historical Society collection. Other printers of certificates include W. Lepper and E. Stettinius of Hanover, as early as 1798; Kohler of Philadelphia, J. Stöver of Lebanon, Frederick Klebs of Reading, Stark & Lange of Hanover, Johann Herschberger of Chambersburg, and Carl Friederich Egelmann. Egelmann's work is more sophisticated and included realistic engravings of the Baptism, Ascension, and Crucifixion of Christ, as well as the Last Supper. A rare certificate with wood cuts of birds, stars, hearts and deer, was printed by Samuel Bauman at Ephrata in 1805. Joh. L. Hanzsche & J. G. Hanzsche of Baltimore also printed certificates in German in 1836.

Baptismal certificates are not as scarce as marriage certificates. However, although the printed designs of these certificates are interesting, the coloring is often so crude and so carelessly done that any value attached to the certificate is lost. So popular were these certificates, that Nathaniel Currier published a baptismal certificate in German. He also published family registers in 1845, 1850, and 1853, and Currier & Ives published lithographed family registers in 1864, 1873 and 1874 and a family photograph tree in 1871.

A small marriage certificate put out by N. Currier in 1848 is especially interesting. In the center is a lithograph of a man and woman in wedding costume before a minister—and the inscription, "Whom God hath joined, let no man put asunder." At the left are printed requirements for a husband and at the right requirements for a wife. Below are blanks for the names, place and date. In 1857, 1865, 1875, and 1877, Currier & Ives put out similar certificates.

Thirteen In Memoriam certificates were put out by N. Currier and Currier & Ives. The usual lithograph showed a monument with space for a name, a weeping willow and figures of men, women, or children. In 1845, 1846, 1847, and 1849, N. Currier published such prints with St. Paul's Church, N.Y., included. One lithograph also included Cooke's Tomb. Currier & Ives put out In Memoriam lithographs in 1872. These lithographs are not hard to find, for they are not rare or especially valuable, but many of them are interesting, especially those including St. Paul's Church. One of these is signed by J. Schultz, one of the well-known Currier & Ives artists. Such certificates were also made by Kellogg, Foster & Kimmel, and other lithographers of the time, but so little value has been attached to them in the past that many have been destroyed.

Another form of printed and hand-colored *fractur* is the *Haus Segen* or house blessing. These were printed at all the above-named German presses and included a printed prayer for the preservation of the house, usually set within a heart, with flowers and birds as decoration. Verbal labyrinths of the Spiritual Garden, Seven Rules to Wisdom and other texts were also printed and written and decorated by hand. These have been found from the press of Henrich Miller of Philadelphia as early as 1762, from Ephrata in 1788, and from the press of E. Benner at Sumneytown in 1840, as well as many other presses.

Valentines, love letters, patriotic and religious texts were also made in cutwork, an art form which has existed since the earliest times, and was revived on the European continent in the eighteenth century, and thus brought to America. It was not confined to the Pennsylvania Germans, but from the standpoint of design, some of the most interesting American cutwork is from this source. Against backgrounds of black, rose, light and dark blue, orange, brown, and yellow, intricate designs were cut in white or cream paper; silk and cotton were also used as backgrounds and a rare cut-paper design is cut in black paper and set on a buff ground.

Valentines were usually in a design of hearts with flowers growing from their tops and verses written within each heart. Simple cut-work designs are made up of geometric circles, squares, and hearts, while more intricate designs include ferns, vines, flowers, birds, horses, lions, eagles and other animals. Rare cut-paper designs include portraits and sometimes a record of birth is cut in paper.

One of the most interesting designs includes variations of the American eagle with flags, griffin, and inscriptions. One medallion with flowers and birds contains the artist's name, Mary Stringfield. The border has leafage and rosettes. A circular medallion finely cut with birds and foliage surrounded by four large rosettes and a formal lacy border is signed "Hannah Backings." Still another medallion with birds, flowers, and amorous inscriptions has the name Elizabeth Williams. Some of these cutwork medallions were also decorated with painted designs of flowers and birds.

In Germany, religious miniatures were set within a frame of elaborate lacy cutwork, but so far none of these *Spitzenbilder* have been found in Pennsylvania. However the practice of painting over the cut-work was used, and this, too, has its source in Germany, where cutwork was even used for book illustration. Hand-made inks, water color, and tempera were used in Pennsylvania-Dutch color work. These inks seldom fade. The glossy surfaces are tempera. The recipes for making these colors were given in books printed on the German presses in America, and these home-made colors are a means of identifying old specimens of *fractur*. The Ephrata artists used subdued colored inks and water colors, but no tempera. Other artists used glossy tempera as well, and usually used brighter colors.

BIBLIOGRAPHY

Pennsylvania German Illuminated Manuscripts, S. Bornemann.

Bulletin, New York Historical Society, April, 1945, Donald Shelley.

Sale Catalogue, Lorimer Collection.

History of Printing in the United States, Douglas C. McMurtrie.

The First Century of German Printing, Oswald Seidensticker.

Chapter 19

AMERICAN FLOWER LITHOGRAPHS

THE American flower print has been neglected by print collectors. Even those few who specialize in the later flower prints of Currier & Ives have ignored the rich field of the early flower prints of America. These began as book illustrations and were influenced by the European flower prints, especially by Robert Furber's *Twelve Months of Flowers* and *Twelve Months of Fruit*, published in 1730 and 1732. Mark Catesby's *The Natural History of Carolina, Florida and the Bahama Islands*, published in 1731, with many hand-colored engravings, was also probably circulated in America.

The roses of Mary Lawrence published in 1799 and the nineteenth-century works of Redouté, *Les Roses, La Couroune des Roses, Choix des Plus Belle Fleurs* and *Les Mois* probably had a more popular appeal. Other French flower prints included *Souvenirs de van Spaendonck*, published in 1826, and collections of prints by Bessa, Provost and Tessier.

In 1798, in England, Dr. Robert John Thornton issued the first flower prints with landscape backgrounds and when Fanny Palmer did *Landscape, Fruit, and Flowers* for Currier & Ives in 1862, she was undoubtedly influenced by this folio.

While the American field of flower prints is not as fertile as the French or English, it does have an interesting connection with the early American lithographers since almost all early lithographic houses made flower prints in one form or another.

The first and most important item of flower lithography is *The Grammar of Botany*, published in New York in 1822 by J. V. Seaman. It contains 21 lithographic illustrations by Barnet & Doolittle. An

167

interesting note appears in the preface: "The publisher feels a becoming gratification in informing the readers of the work that the beautiful and appropriate drawings, which so highly embellish it, are specimens of American lithography. They are from the pencil of Mr. Stansbury and were executed at the lithographic press of Barnet & Doolittle, of this city."

Historically this connection is valuable and interesting since Barnet & Doolittle was the first lithographic house in America. Isaac Doolittle and William Armand Barnet had studied in Paris and had previously been interested in patents relating to the improvements in steamboats. They worked as lithographers at 23 Lumber Street, New York, in 1821 and 1822. The Mr. Stansbury referred to is Arthur J. Stansbury (1781–1845), who was an artist who also wrote and illustrated children's books, and even preached sermons in New York pulpits. He is best known for the rare *Plan of the Floor of the House of Representatives Showing the Seat of Each Member*, printed by Henry Stone in 1823. In 1828, Rawdon, Clark & Co. printed a series of New York views by Arthur J. Stansbury.

The lithographs in the *Grammar of Botany* are small in scale with fine detail and are hand colored. In the two copies owned by the New York Horticultural Society, the coloring varies. The subjects include: pond lilies, iris, bird of paradise, narcissus, thistle, toadstools, acorns, scabiosa, horse chestnut, mountain pink, the fig, ferns and moss, and even fungus. The flowers are shown dissected with separate sketches of petals, stamens, calyx, anthers, pistil, etc. and also a large view of the complete blossom.

In the next ten years there were quite a few botany books published in America, but most of them were without illustrations or the illustrations were made in England or in some other medium than lithography. The *Familiar Lectures on Botany* by Mrs. Almira H. Lincoln, vice-Principal of Troy Female Academy, published in Hartford, Connecticut in 1829, had ten line and stipple engravings by Illman & Pilbrow after drawings by Miss Lee, but these were not colored. Also *Flora of North America* by Wm. C. Barton, was published in 1821–1822, and contained many colored engravings by such well known engravers as Tanner, Cornelius Tiebout, F. Kearney, F. Shallus, and J. H. Seymour. These prints are hand colored and must have been exceptional at the time they were published, since several pages in the introduction are given over to a discussion of their merits and a comparison with the French botanical prints of the time. Barton's earlier book, *Elements of Botany*, published in Philadelphia in 1803, was also illustrated with numerous engravings by the same artists, but they were not colored.

One of the most interesting and valuable early horticultural books is the *Treatise on the Vine*, published in 1830 by William Robert Prince, the Flushing nurseryman whose forefathers started the nursery in 1730. Of special interest to print collectors is the Pendleton lithograph frontispiece, a large bunch of grapes with leaves. The design and spacing on the page are especially fine and the quality of the lithograph is excellent. The lithograph is in black and white and uncolored, but quite as interesting as most colored lithographs. It is a rare and excellent item for any collection, but of course the whole book is rare and the value of the plate is increased when in the book.

One of the most important early items in American flower lithography was the first and only volume of *The Floral Magazine & Botanical Repository*. This was published by the nursery and seedmen, D. and C. Landreth, of Philadelphia, in 1832. It contained thirty hand-colored lithographs with several pages of explanatory text for each illustration. These lithographs were in detail, but may be considered flower prints, rather than botanical illustrations. The flowers and foliage were grouped in a natural manner, and the arrangement usually resulted in a pleasing design. Flowers included were the hyacinth, passion flower, magnolia, camellia, peony, amaryllis, rhododendron and bignonia. The frontispiece was engraved by J. & W. Watt with a vignette of Landreth's greenhouse by J. B. Longacre (1794–1869), the well-known Philadelphia engraver. The colored lithographs are "from nature on stone by W. Allbright" and were by four well-known early American lithography houses.

The earliest of these, Kennedy & Lucas (1829–1835), started as a looking-glass store at 90 South 3rd Street, Philadelphia. In 1830, they were making lithographs of wagons and locomotives for Thomas Earle's *Treatise on Railroads and Internal Communications*. They also illustrated J. F. Watson's *Annals of Philadelphia* and made technical and sentimental prints and "Camp Meeting," a fine revival print. Their work is considered above average and lithographs by them are valuable in any collection.

Childs & Inman, also of Philadelphia, made about a third of the illustrations in *The Floral Magazine and Botannical Repository*. This company was a pioneer in book illustration and their work is of excellent quality. Cephas G. Childs, an engraver, studied in Europe and started with the Pendletons in Boston in 1829. Henry Inman was a painter. He did most of the lithograph portraits put out by Childs & Inman. The firm also published a view of Mt. Vernon, the Tomb of Washington, and the Capitol at Washington. They also put out theatricals, naval prints, fancy prints, and caricatures, among the latter being the famous caricature of the Trollope Family.

Perhaps the rarest lithographs in the book are those by M. E. D. Brown (1832–1834), of Philadelphia, who also worked for Pendleton, and for N. Currier, for whom he made the famous lithograph of William P. Dewees, M.D., after the Neagle painting.

The last prints in the book are lithographs by J. F. and C. A. Watson of Philadelphia. At this time these lithographers were not listed in Philadelphia as a firm, but later they are known to have illustrated a life of William Henry Harrison and to have made maps.

In 1835, the first volume of the *Horticultural Register and Gardener's Magazine* was published in Boston by Thomas Fessenden with seven lithographs, some colored, by Pendleton's Lithography, Boston.

The plates include Camellia Japonica, Salpiglosis (colored), Cantua Coronopifolia (colored), Gladiolus Cardinalis (colored), Design for a Country seat (black and white), Thillium Pictum (black and white) and Stapelia Irrorata (colored) . The drawing is well executed and some of the plates are colored with distinction. The plates are interesting enough for framing, but of course are more valuable in the book. The same year, 1835, Pendleton did a colored lithograph of a Gladiolus Natalinsis for the first issue of Hovey's Magazine, *The American Gardener's Magazine & Register*. The lithograph was after a drawing by C. M. Hovey. Pendleton's is one of the early American lithography houses, having started business in Boston in 1825. Many other well known lithographers such as N. Currier got their training with Pendleton's, who also had shops in New York and Philadelphia.

In 1836, an interesting little book, *Flora and Thalia or Gems of Flowers and Poetry* by a Lady, was also published in Philadelphia. The illustrations are hand-colored flower lithographs; however, since the first edition of the book came out in England, the plates may be English rather than American. They are not marked or signed. This was one of the first of the sentimental flower books that appeared from then on to the end of the century.

Floras Lexicon: An Interpretation of the Language and Sentiment of Flowers was published in Philadelphia in 1839. The hand-colored lithographs are by J. Ackerman and are from the firm of P. S. Duval. They consist of groups of flowers. The next year, a new edition appeared, and the plates, although the same flowers, were regrouped into a bouquet. The four plates include a wild rose and a vine; a striped tulip, strawberries and jasmine; morning glories, pellagonium and tiger lilies; and lily-of-the-valley and fritillaria.

In 1847 *The Poetical Language of Flowers,* by Thomas Miller, appeared with about twelve Victorian groupings of flowers. Another such book was *The Poetry of Flowers,* 1851; and later editions with a frontispiece and four unsigned hand-colored plates. *The Ladies' Book,* published in New York in 1842, had six hand-colored plates of mixed flowers which are unusually lovely, but the artist's name is not given. This appeared in various editions until 1859 or 1860.

In 1846, a little book, *The Language of Flowers*, with several very poorly colored lithographs, appeared. The introduction starts off: "We love the flowers. Not only do they please the eye and gratify the sense, but to one of a reflective turn of mind, they are the dispensors of instruction."

The Floral Offering, "with ten beautiful bouquets of flowers elegantly colored after nature by J. Ackerman" and published in Philadelphia, has large prints of good quality. In 1859, Mrs. C. M. Badger published her book on wild flowers with large colored groupings of wild flowers. However, no artist or lithographer is given and the prints are not particularly good in grouping or in color.

Of course Godey's Lady's Book should be mentioned among the sentimentals. From its beginning in 1830, there were occasional colored flower lithographs, usually the work of William Ellis Tucker and the lithographer P. S. Duval. In 1843, a lithograph of a moss rose, butterfly and a bug was drawn by A. C. Smith and printed by P. S. Duval. In 1845, a colored lithograph of a vase and fruit appeared, and Godey's Valentine, the frontispiece of February, 1849, by W. E. Tucker, was a decoration of cupids, doves and flowers. Another print in 1848 was a basket of roses, passion flowers, pansies and blue ribbons.

In 1846 *The Monthly Flora or Botanical Magazine* was published in New York for one year. It contained lithographs by Lewis & Brown of 272 Pearl Street. There were twenty-four plates of exotic flowers, twenty-four wild flowers and twelve trees with fruit. Several pages of text accompanied each lithograph. Lewis & Brown, while not pioneer lithographers, were well known for the excellence of their work and these color prints are valuable in any collection.

In 1850 *The Floral Keepsake* appeared with forty-six colored lithographs by Buchanan Lithography of 176 Fulton Street, New York. These included roses, pansies, geranium, digitalis, apple blossom, cactus, veronica, tulips, magnolia, jessamine, china aster, trillium, lilac, carnation, tansy and plates of pineapple and red poppy and coxcomb which are identical with those in the *Monthly Flora Magazine* of 1846 by Lewis & Brown.

In 1846 the first American edition of Thomas Nuttall's three-volume addition to Michaux's *The North American Sylva* was published in America with one hundred and twenty-two hand-colored lithographs from T. Sinclair's Lithography (1839–1889), in Philadelphia. The artists were John T. French, G. Worley, G. West, W. Gambel and E. D. Long, but since they are not listed by Mantel Fielding, they were probably of little consequence. However the prints are interesting, decorative, and well done, and have a close connection with the Redouté & Bessa lithographs in the volumes of Michaux printed in Paris. They include the leaves, fruit and blossoms of such trees as oak, maple, dogwood, laurel, birch, catalpa, tulip tree, buckeye, pine, spruce, and cedars.

The state and national government reports put out between 1840 and 1860 also contain colored lithographs which are worth collecting because they were made by well-known lithographers. *The Natural History of New York,* published in 1843, has colored lithographs by Endicott of New York, who started business in 1828. The prints include oak leaves, poplar leaves, gentian, pickerel weed, silk weed, and the decorative coral root. Endicott lithographs also illustrate a volume devoted to fruits and berries of New York State. R. H. Pease (1813–1869), of Albany, also did some plates in this book. Endicott was one of the most prolific lithographers. The firm did everything from music sheets to horse prints and naval and mail steamers, and did them all well.

The 1853–54 *Report of Explorations and Surveys of Congress* was also illustrated with lithographs by such well-known firms as Akerman of New York, who also did the plates for John B. Newman's *Illustrated Botany,* published in 1846, and other botanical and bird books, P. S. Duval & Co. of Philadelphia, and Sarony, Major & Knapp, New York.

A Handbook of Popular Antiques

American Wild Flowers in Their Native Haunts by Emma C. Embury appeared in 1845. The text was made up of sentimental descriptions and poetry, but the plates are particularly interesting. Each plate is a lithograph of a flower with a landscape background. The flowers are hand colored, but the background is kept in black and white. They are work of the well-known artist, Edwin Whitefield. We do not know what lithographers produced the plates or whether Whitefield may have done them himself. He worked for such well known lithographers as Bufford, Endicott and Lewis & Brown. Whitefield is especially known for his views of American and Canadian cities such as Albany, Troy, Newburgh, Boston, Montreal and Quebec. A collection of Whitefield's sketches is in the Stokes Collection in the New York Public Library. Whitefield also did drawings of flowers from nature for lithographs in the *American Flora 1846–1855* which appeared in four volumes. D. W. Moody, another high-class artist and workman also did some of the plates, and some of the lithography was done by Butler Lithography, Ann Street, New York and by F. & S. Palmer, 43 Ann Street, who also made lithographs from drawings of Fanny Palmer. Each volume of the *American Flora* has from four to six hand-colored lithographs, and flowers including the moss rose, morning glory, iris, anemone, tulip and trillium. The frontispiece is typically Victorian and consists of a wreath of flowers about a sentimental scene.

In 1853 *The Florist and Horticultural Journal,* edited by H. C. Hanson, was published in Philadelphia. It ran monthly issues for several years and each issue had one colored lithograph. Several are by P. S. Duval, the well-known lithographer, others are by L. Lewis and some were "on the stone at the School of Design," while others were by unidentified artists, L. Stroobant and Van Houteano. A drawing of a white camellia is by Mrs. Russell Smith, the wife of the well-known Philadelphia artist and painter of theatrical scenery. The flowers also included are trumpet vine, morning glory, verbena, begonia, coleus, gentian and rhododendron. The prints are good in design and composition and interesting for framing.

The interest in the flower print was so great in mid-Victorian days that lithographers began to turn out separate prints in both small and large folio size. The first Currier & Ives flower print that was dated came out in 1846. It was a small print called The Bouquet, signed N. Currier, 1846. In the following ten years that N. Currier was alone in business, he put out about a dozen other flower prints, including The Flower Vase in 1848, Flowers, a small undated print with roses, bluebells, fuchsia, petunias and a humming bird, many rose prints including moss roses, The Hundred-Leaf Rose, signed by J. Schutz, and a Water Lily (10.5 by 14.12 inches). Any of these prints is interesting if found in good condition, since they are early. The J. Schutz print is especially interesting as is any signed Currier & Ives. Schutz also did views for Currier & Ives including City Hall, and the first appearance of Jenny Lind at Castle Garden, which is one of the rarest of New York views.

The titles of Currier & Ives flower prints are interesting for their Victorian sentimentality. Besides the flower vase, flower basket and flower stand, there is the Floral Group, Floral Gift, Floral Offering, Floral Treasure, and Floral Tribute; the Bouquet of Roses, Choice Bouquet, Ladies Bouquet; then there are the many prints of moss roses, enough to form a collection in themselves. The Easter group is also interesting. There is Font at Easter, Easter Flowers, the many Easter Crosses, including the small flower-covered cross with a black background. Many sentimental prints also include bouquets or vases of flowers. There are also many fruit prints that are combined arrangements of fruit and flowers. Perhaps the most interesting of these is the set of four, Spring Flowers, Autumn Fruit, Summer Flowers and Summer Fruits. Each is a still-life group of fruits and flowers in a basket. Perhaps the finest of these flower still-life pieces are those drawn by F. F. Palmer.

Mrs. Frances Flora Bond Palmer did many fine prints for Currier &

Ives. Her work as a landscape artist has been well recognized, but little attention is given to the fine fruit and flower prints she did. In fact, excepting J. Schutz and perhaps one or two others, they are the only fruit and flower Currier & Ives prints that are signed. That Fanny Palmer did many flower prints that are not signed is also certain, and both her brother and sister were artists and also worked on the prints. Also, many of the other flower prints which are not signed may have been by well-known artists. The following signed fruit and flower prints by F. F. Palmer are interesting and rare:

706, The Season of Blossoms, 1865 771, Garden Orchard and Vine, 1867

735, American Prize Fruit, 1862 730, American Autumn Fruits, 1865

749, Fruit and Flower Piece, 1863 776, Landscape, Fruit and Flowers, 1862

all marked "F.F. Palmer, Del., C.&.I."

The last-named print is perhaps the best known of the flower and fruit prints. It is usually sought by collectors because there is a view of the Hudson in the background. However as a still-life composition, it is especially pleasing. On a table on a terrace is a bouquet of roses, tulips, iris, Easter lilies, pansies, geranium and fuchsia in a white Parian ware vase. On the table are fruits and berries in a basket and in a green cauli-flower-leaf dish. A humming bird plays about a trumpet vine on a trellis at the left and in the distance the sailboats on the Hudson can be seen. This is a large print and a copy in good color and good condition is well worth the price it brings.

Perhaps the Currier & Ives are the most interesting of these late American flower prints, but anyone collecting flower prints and interested in the lithographers as well should include examples of prints from the other firms working at the same time. These prints are not as available as the Currier & Ives, partly because they did not make as many prints and also because they have been ignored for many years. James S. Baillie who one time worked as a colorer for N. Currier later set up his own lithography. He also had a shop and sold picture frames. From 1843 to 1850 he issued a large number of prints including flower prints and sentimentals. Kimmel & Forster issued prints in 1865–66 and did flower prints as well as sporting, liquor, and Civil War prints. One interesting print is of gray squirrels and purple grapes and brown grape leaves. The print is low in tone and the coloring is almost a wash so that the texture of the lithograph is shown. Benjamin W. Thayer was a lithographer in Boston from 1840 to 1851. Several flower prints from his lithography have been found. Haskell & Allen also of Boston copied Currier & Ives in 1872 and also put out fruit and flower prints of their own design.

The Kelloggs of Hartford, Connecticut, who did a business almost as extensive as that of Currier & Ives also included flower prints, and from the fact that they are numbered "Flowers No. I," etc., they probably put out quite a number. In a Kellogg advertisement of 1830, among other types of prints, botanical prints are mentioned.

Bufford was another large firm that operated both in New York and Boston from 1835 at least to 1876. Even as late as 1876, their catalogue included Moss Roses, Sea Mosses, Fruit Gems and vases and baskets of flowers. These late prints were undoubtedly chromos, but probably were the same in subject matter as earlier hand-colored prints.

The early trade list of Endicott, New York, also included such prints as Moss Rose, Rose, Bouquet of Flowers and Fruit Piece.

Sarony & Major, New York, put out a print called The Flower Vase and their print, Charles, has an interesting Victorian vase of flowers similar to the vases used in Currier & Ives prints. Although I have not seen other flower prints by this firm there is no question but that they made others.

In 1854 Wm. Sharp & Son, Boston, well known for their flower prints, book illustrations, views and portraits, put out a series of water lily prints. Each print fifteen by twenty-one inches showed one, two or three red and white Victoria Regia water lilies. The prints are not hand colored but chromo lithography. Prior to this date, in 1847, Sharp's lithography did the color prints in the *Transactions of the Massachusetts Horticultural Society, Vol. I, No. I, July, 1847.* The drawings were done by Mr. Sharp.

Also it is certain that Pendleton, Sinclair, and other lithographers who illustrated botanical books, later issued separate flower lithographs. Why collectors interested in flowers or those who collected from the standpoint of American lithography have neglected this field seems strange. Of course this chapter has only called to the attention of print collectors the rich field of American flower lithography and not made any attempt to be a check list or even to have covered all the firms and artists involved. There is more material to be found in libraries, and, from the collector's standpoint, in print shops and old second-hand book stores.

BIBLIOGRAPHY

America on Stone, Harry T. Peters.

Currier & Ives, Harry T. Peters, Vol. I and II, Doubleday, Doran & Co., Garden City, N. Y.

Currier & Ives: A Manual for Collectors, Jane Cooper Bland, Doubleday, Doran & Co.

American Graphic Art, F. Weitenkampf, The Macmillan Co., New York.

Chapter 20

AMERICAN CUT SILHOUETTES

IN the first half of the nineteenth century, before photography became popular, the silhouette was the customary form of portraiture and the cut silhouette was the most popular because it was the cheapest and easiest to obtain. Today, from the collector's viewpoint, cut silhouettes are also the easiest to obtain. Although signed or really fine silhouettes bring a good price and are not plentiful, charming heads, sometimes in their original frames, are to be found. Silhouette artists worked in and near the large cities in New England; New York, Philadelphia, Charleston, and New Orleans, were also centers for silhouette artists. Originally these towns were the markets where silhouettes were to be found, but with the migration of families from place to place and the exchange between dealers, today silhouettes are to be found wherever there is a good antique shop.

Cut silhouettes are of two types. First those cut by machines of various types and finished by hand, and second silhouettes cut by hand with scissors or knife. Machine-cut silhouettes were called hollow-cuts. A sheet of paper was fastened to the frame of the machine, which looked like an artist's easel and stood between the artist and the subject who was seated on a chair, so that his profile shadow was cast on the paper. The artist traced the shadow which was reduced by a pantograph or "monkey." Then he blocked the profile and cut it out with knife or scissors. The remaining hollow-cut was mounted on a black ground of silk, velvet, or paper. Sometimes accessories such as frills, buttons, collars or hair are sketched in or painted by hand.

One of the best-known hollow-cut artists was Charles Willson Peale of Philadelphia, 1741–1826. Peale was also known as a sculptor, portrait painter and a miniaturist. Washington was profiled on Peale's machine in 1794. Silhouettes cut by Peale have regular, rounded, flowing line contours, and a rounding bust line. They were usually mounted on black ribbed silk. Peale used three different stamps which were impressed on the white paper below the profile. They are "Museum," "Peale's Museum," with a spread eagle above, and the rarer mark, "Peale." Of course some Peale silhouettes are not marked at all. Occasionally Peale silhouettes are found with the hair touched up with  India ink. Peale often furnished frames and the "Museum" mark on these is a means of identification of the silhouettes.

Another of the finest and best-known hollow-cutters was William Bache. Bache was an Englishman who came to Philadelphia in 1793 or 1794 and worked in and out of Philadelphia until 1812, when he moved to Western Pennsylvania and met with an accident that necessitated the amputation of his right arm. Bache cut profiles of George and Martha Washington, Thomas Jefferson, and other well-known people. He left an album of duplicates which contains nearly two thousand profiles. They

include cut and paste type, hollow cuts and painted profiles. Painted details are delicate and of refined workmanship and the white paint has a bluish tint. When marked, Bache's silhouettes are stamped "Bache Patent" in an oval with rosettes in each corner and three roses in the center. His women often have delicate frilled collars and hand-painted ringlets. Other well-known hollow cut profilists of the early nineteenth century were William M. S. Doyle of Boston, who worked with a partner named Bowen. Doyle also painted miniatures and cut with scissors. His profiles are signed in his own writing.

Henry Williams painted miniatures and cut silhouettes in Boston in 1813. He did not sign his scissors-cut profiles, but his hollow-cuts are stamped "Williams." His silhouettes are often finished with fine detail of hair and lacy frills.

Todd also made hollow-cut silhouettes in the early nineteenth century. His scrapbook containing about 2,000 profiles is in the Boston Athenaeum. His profiles are recognized by their style. A forelock of hair hangs over the forehead and ruffs, ties, hats, and other accessories are included in the cutting. Todd's bust line is a simple curve. His men are more attractive than his women. William King also belongs to this early group. King's women are especially charming. While King cut many profiles there are few available. The mark is an impressed "King" or "W. King" in a rectangle.

Other artists who worked primarily in the hollow-cut were Moses Chapman, Augustus Day of Philadelphia, whose stamp was "Day's Patent," with crossed brushes in the center; H. Page; William Chamberlain of New London, New Hampshire; Everet Howard; E. P. Jones; J. Brown; R. Letton; John Thompson; and Joye & Seager.

Scissored profiles were taken full length as well as bust length. Among the best known scissors-cut artists were Augustin Edouart, William Henry Brown, William James or "Master" Hubard, Master Hanks, Samuel Metford, Philip Lord, and M. A. Honeywell. The earliest of these is Master Hubard who arrived in New York in 1824. He travelled along the eastern seaboard cutting silhouettes in connection with exhibitions of his "Papyrotamia" or collection of silhouettes, and the musical wonder, the "Panharmonicum." His profiles included many American celebraties such as De Witt Clinton and Martin Van Buren. They are characterized by a scooping bust curve and usually stamped in ink or impressed "Cut with Scissors by Master Hubard without Drawing or Machine," or "Taken at the Hubard Gallery," or "Taken at the Hubard Gallery, 109 Strand, New York." Sometimes he touched his silhouettes with bronze. These are rare, especially the full-length portraits which also have a hand-painted foreground. Hubard later studied with Gilbert

Stuart and Sully, became a portrait painter and settled in Baltimore. A catalogue of Hubard's Gallery of Silhouettes was published in New York in 1825. It included many street scenes, animals, the famous Epsom Races, portraits of mounted riders, children with dogs, flowers and plants as well as subjects taken from the Elgin Marbles, scenes from Dr. Syntax, and caricatures.

Master Hanks or Hankes was also an infant prodigy. His work is not as fine however as that of Master Hubard, although his gilding is better. His busts have a deep rounding curve under the arm. His women usually have elaborate hair-dos. The full length profiles and the ungilded busts are the rarest items. His profiles are marked "Gallery of Cuttings, Cut by Master Hanks with Common Scissors." Another prodigy whose work will not however compare with that of Hubard or Hanks is M. A. Honeywell, the girl without arms, who cut with the mouth in 1809. The signature is "Cut Without hands by M. A. Honeywell," or "Cut with the Mouth." Gilded profiles by Honeywell are very rare. Another prodigy, Master Sanders K. G. Nellis, cut with his feet in 1836.

In 1806, Martin Griffing rode a horse from house to house cutting silhouettes. The Rev. Joseph Stewart also worked at this date in Hartford, Connecticut. And, in 1811, an advertisement of Cotter appeared in the Providence, R. I., paper. Profiles were also made by a long list of amateurs from Major André and Nelly Custis, to George Perkins who in 1850 made copies of William Henry Brown silhouettes.

Catherine Hill and Mrs. Catlin who worked in Philadelphia in 1835, and the many Pennsylvania Dutch primitives cut with cutwork frames or painted costumes and framework may be added to the list. These latter are interesting for the painted detail rather than for the cutting. Many really fine silhouettes were also made by amateurs and remain unidentified since they are unsigned.

The two most interesting silhouettists, not only because of the quality of their work, but also because its subject matter included so many well-known persons, and because of the added background interest, are

AMERICAN HISTORICAL SNUFF BOXES. A. Washington on horseback, painted. B. memorial of Washington's death, engraving by Thomas Clarke. C. Martin Van Buren, printed. D. General Andrew Jackson, printed. E. Park Place, New York. F. Andrew Jackson, Daniel Webster, Henry Clay and Martin Van Buren. Painted and bronze decoration. E—*Collection of the Museum of the City of New York;* all others—*Collection of Samson Selig*

UPPER LEFT AND RIGHT: English tôle bread tray and tea pot, late 18th c. LOWER RIGHT: Painted tôle chestnut urn, France, late 18th c. All three in the *collection of the Cooper Union Museum.* LOWER LEFT: Pennsylvania tôleware coffee pot, 19th c. *Courtesy Metropolitan Museum of Art*

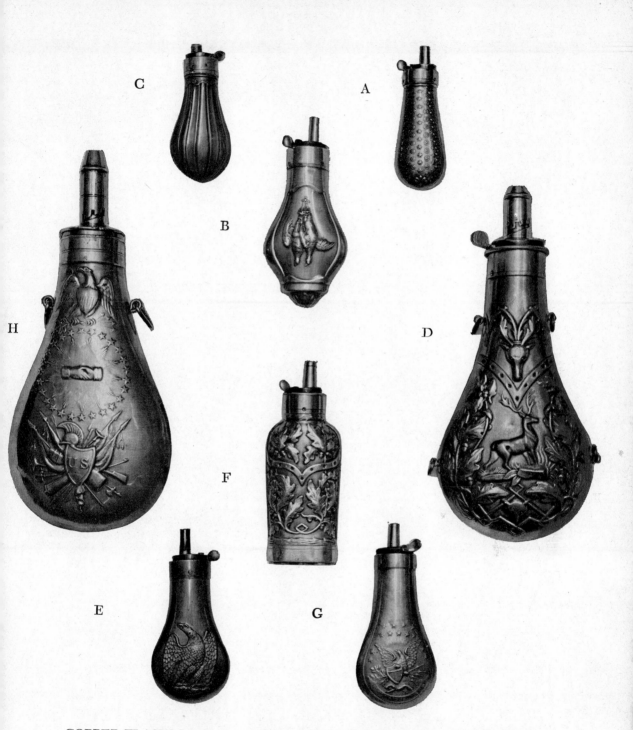

COPPER FLASKS I. A. Star and moon design. B. Dead game design. C. Fluted
design. D. Deer-and-oak-leaf design. E. Colt pistol flask. F. Rectangular flask,
oak-leaf design. G. Colt pistol flask, eagle design. H. Friendship flask. *Courtesy
Robert Abels*

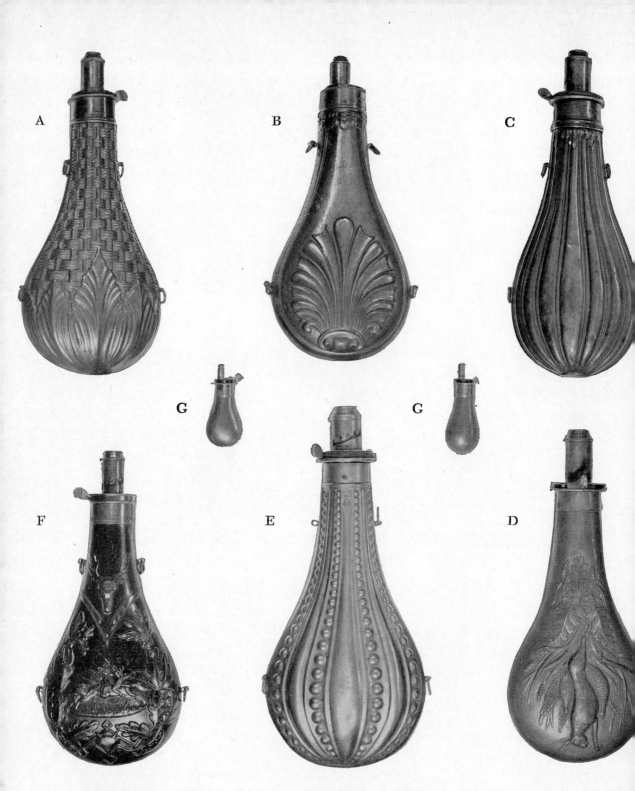

COPPER FLASKS II.   A. Basketweave design, Jas. Dixon & Sons. B. Shell pattern, Hawksley, H-R-16-B-2. C. Fluted pattern, Jas. Dixon & Sons. D. Dead game pattern, Jas. Dixon & Sons. Rare Detail. E. Beaded pattern. Hawksley H-R-16-B-2. F. Plainsman's flask, Indian on horseback, American Flask & Cap Co. G. Two miniature pistol flasks, Jas. Dixon & Sons. *Courtesy Raymond L. J. Riling, Philadelphia*

American Cut Silhouettes

August Edouart, the Frenchman, and William Henry Brown, the artist from Charleston, S. C. Brown cut with scissors usually in full-length profile and used touches of gilding and white paint. His figures are often set against lithograph backgrounds made by the Kelloggs of Hartford. He also cut ships, fire engines and railroad trains. In 1824 Brown cut a silhouette of Lafayette, and in 1832 he was at Salem, Massachusetts cutting silhouettes of such well-known New Englanders as Dr. Prince of the First Church. He cut groups of figures and sometimes whole families. In 1846 he published a *Portrait Gallery of Distinguished American Citizens* which contained silhouette portraits against Kellogg's lithographed backgrounds. The twenty-six portraits included Jackson, Harrison, Calhoun, Clay, Tyler, Randolph, Van Buren, Webster, John Quincy Adams, De Witt Clinton and others, and today the book is as rare as are original Brown silhouettes. In 1931, a reissue of six hundred copies of the book was published by G. A. Baker of New York.

On the profiles in the book, details of dress and hair are put in with white chalk. The attitudes of the men are characteristic; however the hands are usually in one of three positions: in the pockets, crossed at the back, or holding a cane. Thomas Hart Benton holds his magnifying glass and several portraits have one hand extended at the front. The figures all face to the right. Brown has cut character and individuality into his likenesses. The lithographed backgrounds are also especially interesting. It is too bad to whet your appetite for a Brown silhouette, for they are so rare that there are few even in museum collections.

In 1839, Augustin Edouart, who had already achieved fame in France and England, came to America. In the *New York Mirror* of September 28, 1839, the following announcement appeared: "The apartments of Monsieur Edouart in Broadway nearly opposite the Apollo Gallery are well worth a visit." From this notice it would appear that Edouart had been here some time; in fact profiles dated February, 1839 are in the catalogue. From New York, Edouart went to Saratoga, Boston, Philadelphia, and to almost every city of any size in the Eastern and

Southern States. Edouart kept books of duplicates with the sitter's name, date, place, and even autograph. A few years ago some of these books were found and this together with a New York sale of these duplicates added interest in Edouart silhouettes. Whether Edouart is the greatest silhouettist is a debatable question, but the minute details and the care which he took in signing his silhouettes and preserving his records have

increased the knowledge about Edouart and have brought to light many interesting silhouettes taken by him.

Edouart cut the full figure in profile. Not all, but many silhouettes (and these are the most interesting), were placed against a background of sepia wash or a lithograph. These lithographs were by Unkles & Klason of Cork, Ireland, and were long enough to serve as a setting for an entire family. However he often cut them and used part as background for one silhouette. The background most often seen contains a fireplace, a painting on the wall, a table with cloth cover, a window, and a piano. Another background includes bookcases, a table with pen and inkwells, and a window with a church in the distance. Still other backgrounds depicted a ballroom, or a scene at the waterfront. The draperies and the carpet design in all the lithographs are similar, and when Edouart made a rare sepia wash as a background the details were similar to those in the lithographs. That he made some backgrounds while the sitter waited, is shown by the unfinished bits left where the tacks held the paper on the board. Edouart signed his silhouettes "Augn Edouart, fecit," with the year, and sometimes the month and day. In his catalogue was a description of the sitter and his business or profession. Thus we can trace many otherwise unidentified silhouettes. Edouart did not touch up his profiles with gilt or paint, but he often penciled in details of clothing and hair. The cut-out collar is a characteristic of his work. His figures have a suaveness and elegance. Indeed he is the society painter rather than a portrayer of rugged characteristics or individual character. There is a good supply of Edouart silhouettes on the market today.

There are many fine silhouettes which are not signed and which cannot be identified. For these reasons, it is well to learn to judge a silhouette aside from its label. Good silhouettes are characterized by a flowing contour line which indicates authority and sureness in the cutter. An acquaintance with costumes and hair styles of both men and women in the different eras will aid in dating a silhouette.

BIBLIOGRAPHY

A Catalogue of Silhouettes by August Edouart, Arthur S. Vernay.
Ancestors in Silhouette by August Edouart, Mrs. F. Nevill Jackson.
Shades of Our Ancestors, Alice Van Leer Carrick.
Brown's Portrait Gallery.
Articles in *The Magazine Antiques.*

Chapter 21

AMERICAN HISTORICAL SNUFF BOXES

AMERICAN historical snuff boxes offer a fascinating field for the collector, especially for those who enjoy historical connotations in their antiques without too much insistence on pure art. Beginning with Washington in the late eighteenth century, snuff-box history extends into the nineteenth century, down through Grant's administration.

Materials of American snuff boxes are as varied as subject matter. The earliest snuff boxes were of wood or tin or pewter, many being made in the form of shoes or slippers with sliding tops.

Some metal boxes are painted. These boxes are of thin iron or tin about three inches long, with octagonal corners and a hinged lid. The portrait of Com. Thompson, U.S.N. (1786–1832), is the decoration on one of these interesting metal boxes. This type of box is scarce and therefore valuable. One oval pewter box has a relief portrait of Commodore Decatur and the year 1812. Stephen Decatur in the frigate *United States* won a battle over the British frigate *Macedonia* on October 25, 1812. This battle between the *United States* and the *Macedonia* was painted by T. Birch and engraved by Tanner. Several different views of this battle were used on snuff boxes.

Round horn boxes three by one and one-half inches deep, have carvings in relief of famous battles, well-known scenes, and figures from fiction or history of the times. The work closely resembles the relief designs on gutta-percha daguerreotype cases, and many are of similar composition, but some are of pressed horn and took inspiration from the famous pressed-horn boxes made by Obrisset in the early part of the eighteenth century. Some composition boxes even copy the Obrisset rose

186

design. The Revolutionary War and the War of 1812 are depicted on these boxes. One box has a relief showing the sinking of the British ship *Serapis* by the *Bonhomme Richard* under the American Admiral, John Paul Jones. A nineteenth-century pressed composition box has an anchor in relief in the center of its cover with the inscription "U.S.N." and "Don't Give Up The Ship," which were the dying words of Captain James Lawrence in the battle between the U.S. frigate *Chesapeake* and the British frigate *Shannon*.

Another type of American historical snuff box was made of turned wood. These were commemorative boxes and were made from the wood of famous buildings and ships. The lids of these boxes had a metal plaque or coin which referred to the event commemorated. Such a box is the turned and polished oak-box with the gold shield and inscription "Taken from the U.S. Frigate *Constitution*, presented to J. G. Farlee, by Mrs. A. A. Brownell." Quite a number of these boxes are in existence and are not only valuable for their historical significance, but for the beauty of the wood and the workmanship.

However, by far the largest group of American snuff boxes are those of papier-mâché. Some of these have horn linings and some are lacquer on a wooden rather than papier-mâché base, but all are enough alike in appearance to be classed together. The black lacquer or papier-mâché snuff boxes often had painted portraits or scenes, but many had printed or engraved covers. Often the subject matter of a painted cover is the same as that on a printed cover. While there were many more boxes made with printed covers than with painted ones, at the present time the printed covers are more difficult to find. They may be hidden away and forgotten in attics and storerooms, or since they were so common and so little thought of, they may have been destroyed.

For some unknown reason these boxes have been left unnoticed for years, and even the few persons who have collected them have not been interested in where they were made or who decorated or made them.

In the last half of the eighteenth century, when snuff-taking reached the average man, there was a demand for snuff boxes in large quantities at popular prices and for boxes which were light to carry, yet of good wearing quality. Papier-mâché met these requirements. It was machine made, light in weight, and kept the snuff cool and moist. Papier-mâché does not crack or warp with ordinary care. Furthermore, it is an excellent background for painted or applied-print decoration since it takes paint and varnish and holds paste. The papier-mâché snuff boxes of the late eighteenth and nineteenth centuries were usually round, but some were rectangular. Pocket boxes were from two inches to three and one-half inches in diameter, but some as large as four inches were made for table use. The largest known center for the manufacture of papier-mâché snuff boxes was Birmingham, England, where a group of artists, including the well-known painter of genre subjects, Samuel Raven, were kept busy painting snuff boxes. America got her supply as early as 1764, according to an article in the *Boston Gazette* of September 27 of that year, which reads: "Imported from Bristol and London by William Jackson, Brazenhead, painted and paper snuff boxes." No doubt the subject matter of these boxes was the same as that used by Raven—portraits, hunting scenes, and genre scenes copied from well-known paintings of the day. Snuff-box covers were printed in France, England and America.

Just who were the print makers of many of these boxes is not known, but we do know that some of the snuff-box prints were designed and engraved in America by well-known American print makers including Samuel Maverick, Thomas Clarke and James Smillie.

The boxes with scenes and portraits relating to Washington are perhaps the most interesting of the early boxes. And the most valuable of these boxes, because it is signed, is the box with the print showing a memorial monument to Washington. The print shows an obelisk under a weeping willow. On the obelisk is an oval portrait of Washington of the Stuart type with cherubim above and laurel wreaths below and the inscription, "G. Washington" and "There is Rest in Heaven." At the side of the monument is a figure of a man and two figures of women, one depicting Hope resting on an anchor, with one hand pointing heavenward. In the margin of the print is the signature "Thomas Clarke Sculpt. Newbury Street, Boston. This print is similar to a larger print on a brick-work background signed "T. Clarke Sculpt. 1801 Boston." A smaller print with the same subject matter and same borders was also made at this time. These two later prints have the figures at the left of the obelisk, while in the small snuff-box print, the figures are at the right. This smaller print is 3.4 inches in diameter which is snuff-box size, and on this smaller print and on the print on the snuff box in the Selig collection, the decorative borders are omitted. But there is a triple circular frame and the outer circle is broad and black. Thomas Clarke was an English engraver who was first heard of in America in about 1797. He made plates for the *American Universal Magazine* in Philadelphia and illustrations for *Telemachus,* published by David Longworth of New York, and also worked in Boston, but disappeared from view soon after 1800.

Several other printed snuff-box covers with Washington subjects were also made. They may have been earlier than 1800, or they may have been made at a later date than the memorial box. I think they were made before. They are not signed and so far I have been unable to identify the engravers. There are at least two portraits of Washington, one taken from the engraving of Washington at twenty-five years by J. De Mare and the other taken from a portrait of Washington by Gilbert Stuart. This latter box has a decorative border of acanthus leaves which is the same as the border found on several other portrait boxes. There is no evidence to point to Gilbert Stuart himself as a maker of snuff-box designs, but his father owned a snuff factory in Narragansett, R. I., and, according to Stuart's own words, he was born in a "snuff-mill." He was an inveterate snuff-taker and owned many boxes. He owned one snuff box with an engraving on the cover and the title, "Com. Perry Capturing the Whole of the British Fleet on Lake Erie, September 10, 1813."

Prints of Mt. Vernon were used on snuff boxes and a small rectangular box with a print of Washington leaving New York in 1783 and probably printed near this date, was owned by Franklin's son and eventually inherited by Mrs. Bache of Philadelphia, the grand-daughter of Franklin. Although I have no direct evidence, I believe that boxes with this subject were printed soon after the event. Whether it was taken from an American or English print, I do not know, but enough snuff-box covers were made by American designers and enough were actually engraved in America to lead me to believe that many more unidentified boxes could be traced to American engravers of Philadelphia, New York, or Boston. Among designs after Stuart is the portrait of Isaac Hull, commodore of the *Constitution,* which occurs on the top of one box, and on the bottom of the same is a yellow print of the battle between the *Constitution* and the *Guerriere,* adapted from the painting by Thomas Birch. Boxes with historical scenes on both top and bottom are doubly valuable.

An adaptation of a David Edwin (1776–1841, Philadelphia) engraving from the Stuart painting of Commodore William Bainbridge is on one papier-mâché snuff box, and on another a print by the same engraver of Stephen Decatur after Stuart. These engravings were originally made for the *Analectic Magazine* and appear in issues of the year 1813; the same is true of a Leney engraving of a West painting of Robert Fulton. Leney came from London to the United States in 1805 and made bank notes and engraved Bible illustrations. The prints on these boxes of 1812 were reduced and whether they were re-engraved by the original engravers or by someone else is not known. The prints on the portrait boxes, however, all have borders, which do not appear in the magazine prints.

There are several prints of Lafayette from both portraits and sculpture. Lafayette's visit to America in 1824 and 1825 was commemorated by at least four different prints on snuff-box covers. The most interesting one is Landing of General Lafayette at Castle Garden, New York, 16th

American Historical Snuff Boxes

August, 1824, showing the round fort at Castle Garden and in the foreground the smoke of cannon firing the salute, as on the Clews earthenware. Outside a laurel-leaf border in small letters is printed "Entered accord. to act of Congress the 27th day of October 1824 by Samuel Maverick of the State of New York." Samuel Maverick, one of the best-known American printers and engravers, printed another view of the same scene, but this small, round one was produced expressly for use on snuff boxes. Another print of the same scene was made by Charles Rollinson. It has a similar inscription, is 3.2 inches in diameter and has an oak-leaf border.

Other prominent engravers put out American historical scenes that were re-engraved for snuff boxes. Decatur's victory of the *United States* over the *Macedonia* from a painting by T. Birch was printed by Benjamin Tanner, who also did a print of the launching of the steam frigate *Fulton* in 1815 from a drawing by John James Barralet (1747–1815, Philadelphia). Other Lake Erie scenes were done by Sully & Kearney and engraved by Murray, Draper, Fairman & Co., and a Thomas Birch painting of Perry's victory was reproduced by A. Larson. A print on the cover of one papier-mâché snuff box has Battle of Lake Erie, September 10, 1813 on the top, and on the bottom a print of Commodore Perry's report to W. Jones, then Secretary of the Navy. Several print-covered snuff boxes also commemorate the Battle of New Orleans, and portraits of naval and army heroes of the War of 1812 include Commodore Decatur, General Alexander Macomb, Jacob Jones, Commodore Perry, Captain Lawrence, and Commodore Thompson and Captain Isaac Chauncey. Several boxes celebrate the end of the war of 1812. One box has a print of an allegorical group inscribed *"La Paix fait unit l'Angleterre a l'Amerique."* Probably this box was made in France. Another box has a cover engraving with two figures and a shield with the inscription, "Glory to the American Arms," and on the bottom "America shows to the world the trophy of her victories."

Another group of later printed snuff-box covers shows portraits of the Presidents. These were of two types. One series was printed in black

Taking of Macedon Ship English frigat, faving fought daring feven and ten minutes By the Americain Frigat the united Stat's

on cream, yellow, or green paper; another series had bronzed backgrounds and the print was hand-colored. The latter are usually found in better condition than the plain uncolored prints and were probably more highly prized by their original owners.

Among those portraits of the Presidents are several of Andrew Jackson. One box has a yellow steel print top and shows Jackson as a young man with the inscription "Seventh President of the United

States." Another box had a painting of Jackson and was at one time the property of Lewis McLane, Secretary of the Treasury during Jackson's administration. Another papier-mâché box has an engraving of Henry Clay from the painting by W. J. Hubard. A box with a print cover on a gold ground is inscribed, "James K. Polk, Tenth President of the United States," and there are also several boxes that have engravings of Zachary Taylor. One box has a bronzed print with the inscription, "Old Rough & Ready. The Hero of the War with Mexico, Genl. Zachy. Taylor."

Among the bronze background prints are portraits of Martin Van Buren, William H. Harrison, James K. Polk and Zachary Taylor. These bronzed background prints were probably not later than the plain prints, but were an attempt to make the print appear as a painted portrait. A box with a green print cover shows General Harrison notified of nomination for President while plowing, and a bronze background print has the inscription, "Harrison obtains a cession of 51,000,000 acres of land from Indians."

In the collection of Samson Selig is also a box with a cover portrait of Henry Clay. It was presented by Clay to Dr. Thomas Sheeler of Conewango, New York, and was specially painted by order of Clay. The inscription reads "H. Clay."

Other well-known Americans whose portraits may be found on printed or painted papier-mâché snuff boxes are Benjamin Franklin (in fur cap and glasses—French inscription "Benjamin Franklin, *Né a Boston dans la Nle. Angleterre le 17 Janvier 1706*") ; General Alex. Macomb of the War of 1812, after the portrait by Sully (yellow background) ; Jacob Jones, Esq., of the United States Navy, from Rembrandt Peale portrait; Major General Brown, U.S. Army (1821) ; Washington Irving; Daniel Webster; and later on, oblong boxes and portraits of General U. S. Grant and Admiral Farragut were painted in oils.

Among the most interesting pictures found in snuff-box prints are the scenes of American cities, especially New York. Many of these were cut from the series of New York views brought out by G. Melksham Bourne in 1831 after the drawings by Thomas Burton, and were engraved by Stephen H. Gimber of New York, and H. Fosette and James Smillie.

James Smillie came to Quebec, Canada from England in 1823. From 1827 to 1829 he returned to study drawing and engraving in Edinburgh, Scotland and in 1829 he came to New York. At first he got a job as a jewelry engraver, but by 1831 he had established himself as an engraver of paintings and was connected with the firm of Hatch & Smillie and had the commission to do many of the Bourne series of New York views. He also did a series of engravings for the *New York Mirror* after paintings by Weir, and a series of Rural Cemeteries of America from his own sketches. Later he worked almost exclusively for the National Bank Note Co. making vignettes for bank notes and stamps. Among the stamps engraved by James Smillie were the first pictorial colored stamps of the 1868 series. He engraved the Surrender of Burgoyne stamp, The Landing of Columbus, and the Declaration of Independence after Trumbull. Smillie's interest for us lies in the fact that while in Canada he made a snuff-box cover engraving as a pot boiler.

Just how many of the Bourne series, which was the largest series of New York views ever made, were cut for use on snuff-box covers is not known. However, I have identified several black and cream engravings of the series on papier-mâché boxes, including the Junction of Broadway and the Bowery from plate VIII. This plate was both drawn and engraved by Smillie. Park Place, New York, from number IV in the series, is printed and hand-colored on a box in the Museum of the City of New York; and St. Thomas Church, Broadway, from number VI of the series, is in the collection of the New York Historical Society. Also the view of New York from Weehawken was used.

The borders on these snuff-box prints are interesting in themselves. Some are lines of varying widths, others are wreaths of laurel or oak leaves, or a classic border of acanthus leaves. Sometimes the artist who made the border signed his initials. The same acanthus border was used on a Lafayette portrait box and on a box with a portrait of Washington Irving.

There are no identifying marks on any of these snuff boxes. They were machine made; there is seldom any workmanship to value and the prints are on poor-quality paper. The paintings are mediocre and their value is in their quaintness as seen on the early painted tin boxes. Otherwise the value is in the subject matter, and since American historical subjects are in great demand now, the values are quite high.

Aside from subject matter, a snuff box should be judged by its condition. Broken corners and chipped lacquer or torn and worn prints are not to be desired. However one seldom finds a snuff box in perfect condition. If you are collecting snuff boxes of famous Americans, the condition is secondary to the documentary proof of the original owner. If you are interested in the miniature scenes rather than the boxes, patient search may be rewarded. The New York Public Library owns a small print of the Landing of Lafayette at Castle Garden by Samuel Maverick which was intended for use on a snuff box. These prints usually came on large sheets or broadsides and were sold to the dealer who cut and pasted them on the papier-mâché snuff box. However, many prints such as the Bourne series, which was not originally intended for use on snuff boxes, were cut down and used. A comparison between the snuff-box print and the folio print will show that in some cases parts of trees, figures and buildings have been left out.

BIBLIOGRAPHY

The Magazine Antiques, November, 1945, "American Engravings on Papier-Mâché Snuff Boxes," Katharine M. McClinton.

Chapter 22

TINWARE: TÔLE, PAINTED TIN, PIERCED AND BLOCKED TIN, STENCILED WARE

PAINTED tin is the general classification for a large group of articles which includes the more sophisticated tôle, or painted tin or pewter of Wales and Holland, Tôle Peinte of France, and the simpler American products. For the collector there is a variety of articles from tea pots, coffee pots, boxes of all sizes, candlesticks and cookie cutters, to the stately chestnut urns and tea caddies of Welsh and Dutch makers.

Tinware was first japanned (painted) in an effort to imitate the lacquered wares of China and Japan, the japanning process having been found to be an easier means to the same end. In England japanning was started in Pontypool, Wales, by Thomas Allgood and John Hanbury about 1660, but the industry did not flourish before 1700 and ended there in 1822. They used opaque paint mixed with varnish and applied with a brush. Allgood's varnish was a product of soft coal that could be mixed with the pigments or used as a transparent finishing coat. Articles are of various types of construction and design and consist of tea trays, trinket trays, waiters, bread trays, tea pots, coffee urns, candlesticks, snuffers, cannisters, tea caddies, etc. The earliest have pierced border patterns and surface decoration and the well-known tortoise-shell ground. These date to the first half of the eighteenth century. The more elaborate pieces such as coffee urns, chestnut urns and tea pots, belong to the end of the eighteenth century. The first designs were of seaweed and butterflies, scenes and Chinese flowers. This ware was also made at Bristol by J. Bartlett & Sons who specialized in bowls and cannisters with Chinese designs on a green ground. The industry also spread to Usk

196

Tinware

where it was carried on, using brown and crimson grounds, by members
of the same Allgood family from 1761 until 1822. An all-over meandering pattern is typical of Usk wares. Japan ware was also made at Bilston,
Birmingham, and Wolverhampton. Much of the ware was made in
Holland, at Ziest and Hoorn, and sent to Wales to be decorated. Iron,
tin, copper and pewter were also japanned in France as early as 1744, by
Simon Etienne Martin and others. The designs were usually in black
and gold, with Chinese or Japanese designs mingled with rococo decorations. Even silver and Sheffield was japanned.

The eighteenth-century wares of Pontypool and Usk are easily
identified by their forms and by the use of other metals in the handles,
finials and feet of the various articles. The shapes are usually classic, undoubtedly influenced by Adam and his school. The chestnut jars were
distinctive pieces. They were urn-shaped or boat-shaped and had pineapple or acorn tops. On New Year's Day they were filled with hot chestnuts, and the rest of the time served as mantel decoration. Coffee urns
were made in the shape of urns and cylinders and usually had their own
trays, while candlesticks were in the form of Corinthian columns. From
the middle of the eighteenth century, bases, lid terminals, handles, and
shapes followed the current styles in silver. Lions' feet were used, and
lead or brass lions' heads with rings served for handles, and acorn finials
topped the urns, and the tea and coffee pots. Background colors were
black, brown, blue-green, mustard, cream, red and black, and red mottled. The designs included Chinese and Japanese motifs, grape designs,
leaves and wreaths, a rose and leaf border, acorn border and plain gold
and silver borders. Classic columns often divided the design into panels
which were filled with portraits, landscapes, and figures. Typical designs
of Usk manufacture were stars, stripes, intersecting circles, decorated
loops, scroll and cornflowers and leafy tendrils. An all-over sprig design
was popular at Pontypool as well as the favorite tortoise-shell background pieces.

Tinware was imported from England to America as early as 1737.

In 1738, Paul Revere imported japanned tea caddies, trays, bread baskets, candlesticks and other articles from Pontypool. Also, from the fact that Revere entered into so many different types of business, and had a nephew, Philip Rose, who was a decorator of tin, it seems possible that some tinware was made and decorated at the Revere shop. For many years pierced lace edge trays have been known as "Revere" trays. Designs of a shepherdess and rococo ornament with flowers are more typical of French work. The background of French tôle is usually a velvety blue, cream or rose du Barry. In the time of Louis XV these were made at a factory called *Du Petit Dunquerque.*

The japanning of metals was not only an industry, but also a vocation for ladies of leisure. So great was the interest that two books giving details of the methods employed were published in England. In 1688, John Stalker published *A Tretise of Japanning and Varnishing.* This includes full directions for gilding silver, copper, brass, and Princess metal. Another book, *The Method of Learning to Draw in Perspective* included "A new and curious method of japanning . . . to make black or gilt Japan-ware as beautiful and light as any brought from the East Indies." In this book, printed by J. Peele in 1732, "from the mss. of the great Mr. Boyle," the colors used are of interest because they may be of some help in identifying the old pieces: "The Whites are Ceruse or Flesh-white. Yellows are Yellow-oker, English-pink and Dutch-pink. Reds are Vermilion, Red-Lead and Lake; Blues are blue Bisé and Indigo. Blacks are Lamp-black and Ivory or Bone-black. Greens are Vertigrease ground, or Verditer and Dutch-pink ground together. Browns are Fullers-earth and Spanish-brown. Purples may be made between red and blue, till you see them mixed to your Mind."

The author suggests taking designs from china, or using coats-of-arms. Just how much of the japanned metal in the shops today is the work of amateurs who followed these directions is not known, but it is something to think about.

COMPOSITION DAGUERREOTYPE CASES. TOP: Washington crossing the
Delaware, after Emanuel Leutze. BOTTOM, LEFT TO RIGHT: musicians, A. Schaefer,
die maker; the fortune teller, after silver piece by J. Angell. *Courtesy The New
York Historical Society*

ENGLISH TEA CADDIES. FIRST ROW: Fruitwood apples and pear, Sheffield escutcheons. SECOND ROW, LEFT TO RIGHT: Sheraton type, satinwood and mahogany; Sheraton type, satinwood; burl walnut, ivory escutcheon; THIRD ROW: Oval, satinwood and amboyna; tortoise shell; Sheraton type, mahogany and satinwood. FOURTH ROW: Hepplewhite type; Sheraton type, inlay of ivory; Hepplewhite type, vase inlay on satinwood. *Courtesy J. E. Treleaven—Needham's Antiques*

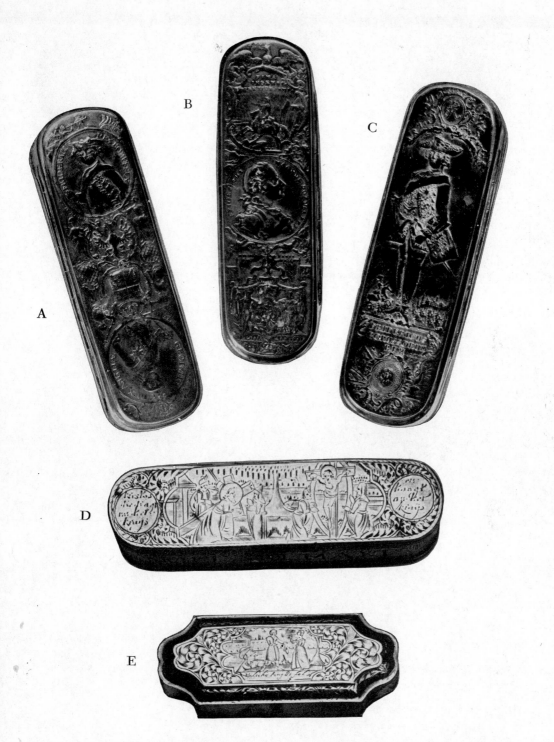

A. B. and C.: 18th c. German brass and copper tobacco boxes, with portraits of Frederick the Great and scenes of his battles. *Courtesy The Metropolitan Museum of Art*. D. Dutch tobacco box, scenes of Crucifixion, early 18th c. E. The Gossips, 18th c. Dutch tobacco box. *Courtesy The New York Historical Society*

LITHOPHANES FROM BERLIN ROYAL PORCELAIN MANUFACTORY.
LEFT TO RIGHT, TOP ROW: Peasant Woman. Mark: "K.P.M."; The Woodsman, after a painting by Thomas Barker. Mark: "K.P.M." BOTTOM ROW: Magdalene, after a painting by Guido Reni; Going to Church. *Courtesy The Metropolitan Museum of Art*

Tinware

Perhaps Mrs. Sarah Morehead read these books, for in the *Boston Evening Post* of 1748 she advertises "Japanning lessons and painting on glass." However she may have studied with John Waghorne since he "had the Honour to teach several Ladies of the First Quality in England" and put his advertisement for teaching japanning in the *Boston Gazette* of 1740 and 1741.

At about this same time the first tinsmith started business in America although blocked tin and japanned ware continued to be imported from England. Blocked tin resembles pewter and was made by early pewterers. It was cast rather than rolled and stamped. It was never made in mass quantities but was sturdy and inexpensive. It was sold from house to house by peddlers. As early as 1758, block tin cream pots were advertised for sale in the *Boston Gazette*. In the *New York Commercial Advertiser* of 1800, block tin from London is advertised and in 1838, Boardman & Hart were selling block tin in New York. In 1847, Reed & Barton bought the blocked-tin shop of Nathan Lawrence in Baltimore. The stock consisted of tea ware, castor frames, lamps, pitchers and candlesticks.

In 1740, at Berlin, Connecticut, William and Edward Pattison started in making tin for the people of the village. It was first made in their own home and sold locally, but the business grew until peddlers were employed to travel through the country. At first they peddled on foot with their wares in large tin boxes, but later carts and horses carried the goods as far west as Ohio. The Pattisons themselves are not known to have painted this ware, but it was hand wrought and hammered, and some was decorated and may have been blocked or pierced. Articles made by the Pattisons include coffee pots, sugar boxes, bread baskets, flour boxes, graters, gill cups, pepper boxes, tumblers, kettles, pans, pitchers, candle boxes, candlesticks, chandeliers, pierced lanterns, egg coppers, hot water urns, and Harts and rounds. Typical designs were conventional flower motifs and geometric patterns. Simple brush strokes served as flower and leaf forms and often the design was in gay colors upon a white band. Simple tin lamps and candlesticks and round and rectangular light sconces were also included in early tinware.

As early as 1798, Zachariah Stevens set up a tin shop in Stevens Plains, Maine. Articles were made of sheet tin and decorated by Stevens and members of his family who were associated with him in the business. The articles included tin boxes, bread trays, tea pots, tea caddies and cake boxes. The decorations were usually floral motifs, roses, rosebuds, grapes, cherries and other fruit and the backgrounds were cream, sulphur-yellow, blue-green, red and vermilion. Some of the pieces were made presents for members of the family and these have initials which aid in identifying the work. Hattie, Sally and Maria Francis are known to have decorated much of Stevens' tinware. They used the typical floral and berry and leaf designs, but often we find conventional patterns in "Connecticut fashion." Designs were put on the body of the piece, and borders of flowers and leaves and scrolls or ribbons marked the tops and bottoms of boxes, tea pots, or tray borders. Colors used included rose pink, prussian blue, orange, chrome yellow, vermilion, and white lead.

Butler tinware made at Brandy Hill, Greenville, New York, from about 1824 to 1850, is of particular interest because much of it is marked and can thus be definitely identified. It was decorated by Aaron Butler and his daughters Ann, Marilla and Minerva, with hearts, flowers in wreaths or sprays, peacock-feather patterns, and fruit designs. Ann Butler signed her pieces "Ann Butler" or "B," within a heart with wreaths or sprays of flowers, dotted outlines, and often white borders with drapery or fringe or tassels. Tulips, roses and birds, forget-me-nots and strawberries and stars were also used. Minerva Butler often signed her full name but sometimes only the initials "M.B." On Butler tinware the highlights are white, the shadows red and leaves are yellow-green with black veins.

Pennsylvania Dutch tinware was of two types: painted and unpainted, the latter being plain or punched. Among the plain unpainted

Tinware

tin items are wall sconces, tin candlesticks both low and tall, chandeliers, match boxes and mirrored comb cases. Fluted tin pudding molds have panels with geometric markings, and, on the bottom, an indented design of flowers, birds, or corn. Of especial interest are the tin cookie cutters made by itinerant tinsmiths who traveled from house to house. Cookie cutters were most used at Christmas and for this reason many of the designs such as stars, Santa Claus, Christmas trees, angels, sheep, camels

and the Holy Family relate to the Christmas theme. Other cutter designs are a wooden shoe, a cat, hen, pig, swan, duck, dog, man, woman, Uncle Sam, Indian Chief, William Penn, mounted rider, preacher, Mennonite woman, Amish child; or later, a baseball player. Tulips, trees and leaves, hearts, parrots, eagles, geometric designs and fruits form another class. Cookie cutters were also made in the shape of such household articles as bottles, shoes, hats, pipes, axes, wheelbarrows, pistols, guns and daggers.

Punched or pierced tin is not as easy to find as painted tin. Tin mirror frames and small cupboards were made of punched tin. Especially interesting, however, are the coffee pots. These were usually made in three sections on a base and the handle and spout were in separate sections while the dome-shaped lid had a separate tin or brass knob. The punched design included a large floral motif, usually a vase with several flowers and leaves, stars, and borders of conventional flowers and leaves. Peacocks and tulips were also favorite motifs. The name of the maker often appears punched in the handle. Known marks are "W. Slade," "J. Ketterer" and "M. Uebele."

Painted Pennsylvania Dutch tinware is distinctive in color and decoration and decidedly different from other painted tinware. Plain paint is used without the lacquer base and thus the surface is dull. The background colors include black, brown-black, bronze, red, yellow, cream, blue and green.

Pennsylvania Dutch tinsmiths were highly skilled, for the shapes are fine in contour and workmanship. The articles included trays, coffee pots, tea pots, tea caddies, boxes, snuffer trays, nutmeg graters and pepper and salt shakers. The finest pieces from the collector's standpoint are the painted trays. Flat trays had plain and Chippendale curved edges while deeper bread trays had plain curved edges. Perhaps the finest tray design is the peacock with its red head and neck, and blue and gold body, perched upon a spray of flowers such as dahlias, dogwood, or primroses. Gold-stenciled conventional borders or brush comets complete the tray decoration. Sometimes an exotic bird or peacock is perched on an urn and sometimes fuchsias are a part of the floral decoration. Other trays have chrysanthemum, rose, or love-apple motifs. While the design is usually in the center of the tray, some trays have floral borders and plain centers.

The coffee pot was another important painted tin piece. These usually had a black, brown, or bronze ground with a bright design of flowers and leaves or fruits such as apples, pomegranates, or plums. Some designs are geometric. A design of fruit and leaves on a red ground is rare and hard to find.

Stenciling was begun in 1817 and some of the old workmen were employed up to 1850. The stenciling was usually in bronze on a black background. Many commercial pieces such as sugar, coffee, spice and flour bins for stores were of this stenciled type. Also bronze spice boxes in sets.

Painted tea pots are scarce, but tea caddies decorated with fruit or tulips, and trunk boxes with rounded tops and brass or iron handles are more plentiful.

Much of the old tin has been repainted lately so the collector must beware of new work.

In all types of painted tinware the rarest background colors are cream, yellow, blue and greens, with black and brown the most common and easiest to find. While shapes are important, design and coloring and the condition of the decoration are of utmost importance in forming a collection. English tôle chestnut urns and trays and hot water urns are rare and expensive but American painted and unpainted pieces in various states of preservation may be seen at all antique shows. The commoner stenciled wares, especially grocery-store spice and flour bins which are decorative and useful, may occasionally be found in junk shops.

BIBLIOGRAPHY

Connoisseur, Vol. 73.

The Magazine Antiques, Articles by Esther Stevens Brazer, March 1936, July 1937, June and September 1939, July 1945.

Pennsylvania Dutch Stuff, Earl F. Robacker, University of Pennsylvania Press, Philadelphia, 1944.

Guide to the Collections of Pontypool & Usk Japan, Humphrey Milford, London.

Chapter 23

DUTCH AND GERMAN
TOBACCO BOXES

For those interested in collecting with historical sidelights, the brass and copper tobacco boxes of Holland and Germany offer a fertile field. There is beauty of material and workmanship, and in the Dutch boxes especially, a certain quaint humor and an interpretation of the everyday interests of the average man of the era. While the German boxes relate to the glory of war, the Dutch boxes give the story of the quiet, peaceful life and the interests of the Dutch sailor, small merchant or housewife.

Thus, on the tobacco boxes of each nation the character of the nation is revealed—the Dutch, a home-loving, peaceful nation, use simple subject matter related to everyday life; the Germans, a military nation, glory in depicting their victories and scenes of warfare.

The Dutch boxes are made of copper or brass or a combination of the two materials. They are from four to six inches in length and two to three inches wide, according to shape, and are about one and one-half inches in height. In shape the boxes are oval, circular, rectangular, with simple curved ends or oval curved ends, or of book shape. Some few of the boxes date from the seventeenth century, but most of them were made in the eighteenth century. Dutch brass tobacco boxes were made from about 1635 to 1794, principally at Amsterdam. They were also copied later for tourist trade. Although a few rare boxes are signed, they are undoubtedly in museums and are not available for the collector today.

The Dutch boxes were usually engraved. Most oval boxes have borders of floral scrolls usually quite crude in workmanship, alternating with raised rope-like borders, and the scenes or inscriptions are placed within ovals, circles, or cartouche-shaped spaces. Sometimes the workmanship is so crude and the inscriptions are such colloquial Dutch that there is no question that they were made for the sailors, farmers, and others of the bourgeoisie. Yet these very limitations give them an interest.

In subject matter some of the scenes refer to Biblical subjects such as the Crucifixion, the Resurrection, Adam and Eve, Queen Esther, or the saints of the Catholic church. Of this latter class is an oval engraved and hatched box with etched leaf borders and rope margins, from the Metropolitan Museum Collection. On the top is an incised representation of the Virgin and Child in eighteenth-century dress and the inscription:

"Come Pilgrims with joy, this Virgin worship; then shall she hear your prayer before you shall return. She is the Advocate for us all; therefore visit Her at Kevelaar." Kevelear is a town in Rhenish Prussia which has been a place for yearly pilgrimages to the Virgin since 1642. On the reverse side of this box is a crude incised portrait of St. Anthony of Padua holding the infant Christ. Another oval box has a decoration of both religious and secular interest. On the top in a circle is an incised picture of Elijah being fed by the ravens, and on either side stand two puppets in eighteenth-century Dutch costume. The borders consist of a peculiar overlapping pointed leaf form, and incised lines. The circle on the reverse of the box has a naked angel and a tree form and perhaps refers to the scene of Mt. Horeb. It is flanked by the puppets of a man and woman similar to those on the box top.

One of the finest boxes with religious scenes is an oblong box with a combination of brass and copper. On its top is a scene, inlaid in copper on brass, of the Crucifixion, and in smaller circles the inscription, "Jesus Christ carries the cross. And hangs on the cross." The bottom of the box shows the Entombment and Resurrection and the inscriptions in circles at either end: "There arises from his tomb," "Makes known to Mary in the Garden."

On the side of the box is the archaic Dutch inscription *"noyt vool makt"*—never perfect. The combination of brass and copper and the simplicity of the design make this box especially interesting, while the archaic Dutch inscriptions point to the seventeenth century as to date.

Scenes of the bear pit show one of the interests of the people, while tavern scenes, scenes of ships departing, and everyday scenes of a man and woman or a family in a cart, or a street scene, are the simple subject matter of other boxes. One box has the inscription "Oh my beautiful mistress," while another, showing a man and woman and servant in a cart, has the inscription, "Is it not fine to have a cart and horses in this world?" A scene of a departing traveler and a ship has the quaint inscription, "I am sailing like a hero to faraway lands; were it not for money I should prefer to remain quietly here." This is undoubtedly a sailor's box.

Another sailor's box of brass has a scene in the countryside and on the reverse, a scene with ships. The borders are typical incised-leaf scrolls and the inscriptions read "I kiss my beloved on the land and by the sea." An amusing rectangular box with crude leaf borders on its copper sides and a figure of a court jester on the brass top and bottom says in the Dutch inscription: "My name is 'Razor' but behold my brother clown!" The Wine Dealer's Riot at Amsterdam in 1748 is also shown on a box, and another popular subject was the Planting of the May-Tree.

Another lovely box of this genre type is in the Metropolitan Museum Collection. It is a rectangular box with ogival curved ends and has lined rims, chased and engraved borders of leaves, and has inlaid brass sides with leaf scrolls and a panel of inlaid brass, with scenes of two women and a man on one side, and a man and woman and priest in the panel on the reverse side. The inscription reads "A deceptive tongue is vicious. It brings nobody anything." A brass oval box with incised line and crude leaf borders has a top and bottom panel of tavern scenes. Two figures are seated at a table, and the inscriptions read, "By the wine cup one can be merry" and "A glass of beer is our pleasure." This drinking or tavern scene and the scenes of the sailor and his sweetheart were some of the most popular, and thus many boxes of this type are found.

The story of the Scotchman, John Law, and the Mississippi Bubble is told on another oval brass box. The usual curved borders with lined margins and incised scrolls make a setting for the top and bottom panels. On the top is the figure of Heer Johan Louw and in his hand a paper which reads "Financier." On the reverse another portrait of John Law with a cartoon story showing a windmill and the inscription *"Kloop met molen"* (I walk with the windmills, or I am crazy). The inscription "buying on the margin" and, in his hand, a paper that says  "Financier" are other bits that tell the story. At the bottom is the inscription, "Wind is the beginning and Wind the end."

John Law lived in Holland for some time and probably when he launched his great financial scheme many Hollanders were taken in. He died in 1729, so the box dates within a few years of that date. This box was inspired by the copper engraving by Schenk.

A brass book-shaped box has incised panels of a man and woman and the inscriptions, *"Goett Begin—Goett bekage"* (Good beginning is a good end). An oblong box with rounded ends and a bevelled margin has copper sides with crude hunting scenes and leaves, and scenes on the top and bottom panel of a man presenting a flower and a box to a woman. At the ends in borders are the quaint inscriptions, "There is the rose, my sugar box" and on the reverse—"Here is my troth, O sweet Miss." Another class of oval brass boxes has molded and corded edges, engraved floral borders, and the tops and bottoms have crests or monograms. The box shown has the shields of the seven provinces of the United Netherlands and the head of the lion of Holland. On the bottom is the same lion in a circle between two roundels, each with a popinjay and flowers. The spaces are filled with acanthus scrolls and the side borders have

the overlapping leaf pattern. The crests and the workmanship date this box in the seventeenth century.

Oblong brass boxes with a perpetual calendar top and bottom are rare and were made and carried as early as the middle of the sixteenth century. The top of the Dutch eighteenth-century box shown has a crude bust of Julius Caesar in an oval and the date 45 B.C. In the opposite oval

is the bust of Pope Gregory XIII with the erroneous date 1482. It should be 1582, the date of the promulgation of the Gregorian calendar. Above the calendar is the date 1497, and below, the inscription, "The Perpetual Almanac." On the side is the inscription "Straight Ahead." These calendar boxes were also made in the eighteenth century in Germany.

In the collection of the New York Historical Society are several rare and valuable Dutch boxes. One oval brass box with roped edges and renaissance floral borders has a pierced and engraved design on its top and bottom. The scene on the top is a medieval boar hunt—three men with spears and bows and arrows, several dogs and a boar. The background is foliated. On the bottom of the box is a scene of cupids in the clouds shooting arrows at a group of men and women below. The background is red velvet and behind the pierced design on the inside of the top is a renaissance arabesque design and two window openings. This box dates from the seventeenth century. Whether this was for snuff in combination with tobacco or whether this box was a large snuff box is not certain. In general design and construction it is similar to the other Dutch tobacco boxes, but the workmanship is superior.

Another all-brass, but rectangular tobacco box also dates from the seventeenth century. It is also pierced brass, but against a brass background, and the workmanship is cruder than that of the first box. On its top and bottom surfaces the story of the prodigal son is told with figures against a background of tropical foliage, and on a center plaque inscriptions recite the story: "An unthinking son squanders his father's money. But he returns with tears on his cheeks and God changes his heart. He is again invited and received."

Subject matter on other boxes of the seventeenth century include Venus and Amor, the Emblem of Amsterdam, Faith, Hope and Charity and portraits of Hus and Luther. Other seventeenth-century boxes told the story of the murder of the brothers Jan and Cornelis de Witt in 1672. One such box was engraved by Romein de Hooghe (1645–1708). Johannes Bernardus Barckhuyzen, who was an engraver at the mint in Amsterdam in the eighteenth century also engraved prints by J. Smit and S. van Esveldt for tobacco-box covers.

A rectangular copper box of a later date has its top and bottom divided into medallions. The center medallions have the pictured story of Queen Esther and King Ahasuerus on one side and Judith and Holofernes on the reverse, and in spaces at either end, the inscriptions tell the story. The background spaces are filled with foliage scrolls.

Brass and copper tobacco boxes were made in Germany between

about 1750 and 1780, at Iserlohn, an ancient metal-manufacturing town in Westphalia and at Elberfeld, a center of metal manufactures near Düsseldorf. These boxes were of the same materials as the Dutch boxes, but they were usually embossed rather than engraved and were almost always oblong in shape with curved ends. They were made of a twelve-inch strip of copper joined to form the sides of the box, and the tops and bottoms were brass with the embossed designs. One box dated 1755 has scenes of the earthquake at Lisbon, Spain. It was made by Johann Giese of Iserlohn. Another rare box has a portrait of Stadtholder William V. It was made by Johan Henricus Hamer of Iserlohn in 1777. Except for a few such boxes the decoration referred to the Silesian or Seven Years' War and to the battle triumphs of Frederick the Great, King of Prussia, against the French, Austrians, and Russians. Portraits and battle scenes together with rococo decorations cover the tops and bottoms of the boxes. Among the sieges and battles illustrated are Crefeld, Minden, Zorndorf, Rosbach, Lissa, Warburg, Prague, Fryberg, Lowositz, Reichenberg, Kesseldorf and Heldberg.

Some boxes are also found with scenes of the Russo-Turkish Wars and the battle scenes of Tschesmé, Kugel, Bennern, Foksham and Baratagh. Portraits, besides that of Frederick the Great, include those of Ferdinand of Brunswick, George II, and George III, Marshall Daum, the Princess of Orange, Maria Theresa and Frances of Lorraine.

The battle scenes are similar, and without the inscription, one could not be distinguished from the other. The pattern followed on almost all of the boxes was of a large battle scene in the center space with an inscription below, and medallion portraits in circles at either end; or perhaps the center space may be taken by the portraits in medallions and the battle scenes may be in small spaces at the ends, or crests and coats of arms may replace the battle scene. On the remainder of the surface are rocaille decorations.

It is interesting to note that the design of these boxes follows closely in both subject matter and decoration the design on glassware

Dutch and German Tobacco Boxes

made in Nüremburg, Silesia and Bohemia throughout the eighteenth century. Battle scenes, medallion portraits of Frederick the Great, with the inscription "vivat Fredericus Borussorum," hunting scenes, scenes of ladies and gentlemen at a tea or dinner party, and the rococo embellishments are almost the same on both glassware and tobacco boxes. The inference is that the inspiration came from the glassware since many of the old goblets and covered glasses date early in the eighteenth century while the boxes were not made before the middle of the century.

The workmanship of the German boxes varies. Some designs must have been put on the covers by careless workmen since the same design is often found with its edges overlapping the top cover, and on some the lettering is so near the edge that the tops of the letters are cut off. The embossing on other boxes is not rounded or clear cut. However we do know the designers of the German boxes, for the majority of the boxes were signed with the artist's name or initials and often the place of manufacture. The signatures to look for are: "J. H. Hamer, fecit," Iserlohn, who is listed in the *German Kunstler Lexikon, Thieme Becker,* as working in 1760. Johann Heinrich Giese engraver of Iserlohn in 1756. He signs his boxes "John Henry Giese," "Giese," "Johan Hendrich Giese," or "Joh. Henr. Giese—Iserlohn." "J. Henry Becher," or "J. Henrich Becker f." was also from Iserlohn.

Another artist signed *"Jadma"* or *"Jakm"* and still another signature found is "Keppelman" who is Johan Adolph Keppelman. It is possible that *Jakm* or *Jadma* is an abbreviation of Keppleman since both workers came from Iserlohn. Still another signature found, but not identified is $\frac{\text{H \& W}}{\text{D \& H}}$ Elberfeld and the date usually found with these initials is 1759. It is difficult to value the artists since the designs are so similar and it is thus really the workmanship that gives a box its value. The full-length portraits of Frederick are striking. One box signed *"Jakm"* has such a portrait with the royal seal in a cartouche above and "Fredericus Borussorum Rex" and the artist's signature below, with the crest and battle flags and rocaille decorations at the bottom. On the reverse of this box are three medallions. The center oval has a scene of the battle of Torgau and the inscription, "Complete victory of the Prussians over the Austrians at Torgau." The left medallion has the figure of Marschal Daum on horseback, and the right medallion shows Frederick the Great on horseback. This side of the box is also signed *"Jakm."*

Another box has medallion portraits of George III of England and Frederick the Great with joined royal coats-of-arms of England and Germany and the reverse of this box has battle scenes of Prague and Lowositz, and at one end, a portrait of Frederick in an oval and the Spread Eagle crowned with "F.R." on its body. The inscription reads: "Your name is good enough to conquer them all. Already the whole world knows of your War progress. You begin with conquering." This side of the box is signed "J.H. Hamer, F."

Another signed box, rectangular, with brass top and bottom and copper sides, has a profile bust of Frederick the Great in the center medallion. In a cartouche at the top is the portrait of Frederick on horseback before an army encampment, and the inscription in Latin, "Mighty in Fame, Mightier in Arms." The lower cartouche has the royal arms of Prussia with the motto, "For glory and Fatherland." The box is signed beneath the medallion portrait, "John. Hen. Giese Fecit, Iserlohn." On the bottom of the box is the three-quarter medallion portrait of Ferdinand, Duke of Brunswick, in hat and uniform with cane. In a cartouche below is the White Horse of Hanover and in the cartouche above, a scene of the battle of Minden and the Latin inscription, "Victory of the Allies, Rout of the French at Minden, August 1st, 1759." The box is also signed on this side. This box has no border, but the identical design at the Metropolitan Museum of Art has a scalloped border and is about one-eighth inch larger to take the border.

An unusual and interesting box commemorates the end of the Seven Years' War. The top of the box has three full-length portraits of Frederick the Great, Peter III, and Frederick Adolphus with a small circular table and a paper with the word "Pax." The German inscription at the top reads "Perpetual peace between Russia, Prussia and Sweden." To the left, on a scroll below the figure of a woman blowing a trumpet, is the inscription, "Thus everything alternates after war and the shedding of blood. Let us enjoy the Mercy of Heaven and the pleasure of Peace." At the right, on a banner, under a seated figure with a wreath and a banner with the word "Friede" is the inscription, "Heaven grant that the example of these three may soon be followed by all warring parties." The bottom of this box has a beautiful design of three rococo cartouches with the Imperial and Royal Shields of Russia, Prussia, and Sweden. Both top and bottom of this box are signed, "J.H. Hamer, fecit, Iserlohn."

Undoubtedly some of these boxes were made for Dutch trade since they have inscriptions in Dutch rather than German; however, since they are signed by the German artists and often with the place of manufacture, they are surely of German rather than Dutch make. One box with a Dutch inscription has views of Hanover and Brunswick and center medallions of Ferdinand and Carol. The Dutch inscription reads, "They are in dread of our heroes and fly outside danger. No wonder, for fear is worse than death." On the bottom of the box is a naval scene in a cartouche and to the side figures of Liberty and Harmony and Latin inscriptions: "By ships was the country saved." "Through harmony small things grow great." "O golden Liberty."

Other boxes show scenes of Amsterdam, and one box, said to have been taken from a Hessian prisoner of war, has a view of Leyden. This box is in the collection of the Museum of the City of New York.

Dutch inscriptions are used on a box showing a large scene of the battle of Crefeld within rococo decorations and with the signature *"Jakm."* The Dutch inscription reads, "Over the Rhine is Prince Ferdinand gone. And over Clermont a victory won." The reverse of this box has a scene of the battle of Minden and medallion portraits of Prince Ferdinand and Marshal Contades at either end. The Dutch inscription reads, "Thus can Prince Ferdinand make Contades faint-hearted. At

Minden where he had him at advantage. There he attacked the French on every side, until in a short time they thought it best to fly." This side is signed *"Jadkma."*

There is still another type of subject matter used on German tobacco boxes. These subjects relate to the life of the times, but to court life or that of the upper classes, rather than to the sailor or farmer class, as is the case with the Dutch boxes. Scenes of boar and deer hunting with dogs and mounted riders and forest backgrounds, set within rocaille decorations, are especially interesting. One box has a tea party scene on one side, and a hunting scene on the reverse. The hunting scene is signed, "Giese, Fecit" and has the inscription in German, "The countryman loves but his field, and the miner his metals. So is there nothing in the world for me that can take the place of hunting."

Another box with a fine hunting scene has a German inscription, "Riding to hunt and catching much. Be the quarry ever so swift, nothing has yet escaped me. Whatever falls to my lot, I slay." The bottom of the box has medallions of Europe, Africa, Asia and America, a ship scene and a smoking party, and the Shields of the United Netherlands. The Dutch quatrain reads: "I navigate as a hero to far-lying coasts. Were it not for the gold much sooner would I rest and remain on land and keep my comfort and drink a glass of wine and smoke a pipe of tobacco." This side of the box is signed "J.H. Hamer." An almost identical design on another box, but on copper instead of brass, is signed "Giese." The reverse of this box has rococo decorations and an unusual scene of a balcony and figures with bales of cargo. The Dutch inscription reads:

> *Money, money, that's the thing;*
> *Money's the highest blessing.*
> *By money is everything from afar procured.*
> *By money am I wont to bring to the land,*
> *All that in the Congo grows and all that Sumatra plants.*

The little smoking party shown in a cartouche on each of these boxes

Dutch and German Tobacco Boxes

is especially interesting in view of the fact that Frederick William II of Prussia had a smoking club in 1740 and set the style for such clubs and gatherings. At a time when smoking was thus at its height of popularity, the brass tobacco box must have been in great demand.

These brass tobacco boxes are not plentiful, but they are comparatively inexpensive. However they are so useful and decorative that they are sought by the average buyer as cigarette boxes, so if you discover a box, buy it on the spot.

BIBLIOGRAPHY

Het Huis Ond & Nieuw, Vol 9. pp. 151, 179—"Onde Tabaks doozen," A. O. von Kerkwijk.

Catalogue, City Art Gallery, Manchester, England.

Metropolitan Museum Collection.

Chapter 24

AMERICAN NINETEENTH-CENTURY
POWDER FLASKS

Brass, copper, and zinc powder flasks of the nineteenth century are
absorbing items for the present-day collector. Not only are they
an interesting accessory for the gun collector, but their subject
matter, which includes patriotic insignia, is correlated with the interests
of the historian, for the story of the use and manufacture of metal flasks
begins at the close of the War of 1812 and continues through the Civil
War.

There are several collectors who have large collections which include all the important types of flasks and the different designs, but
generally the antique public is not aware of these powder flasks. However, one department store had a collection among a large stock of brass
bric-a-brac. They were selling the flasks to be mounted as lamp bases.
In such shops the prices are low, but a dealer who knows these flasks,
particularly one who deals in military antiquities, asks a good price. The
values on flasks are mounting.

Although powder containers in flask form were used in some countries along with the earlier powder horn, they were often of unusual or
precious material such as tortoise shell, carved ivory, mother-of-pearl
and silver or hand-painted metal, and each flask was one of a kind. Quantity manufacture of powder flasks did not come until after 1800 abroad
and about 1830 in the United States, when the die-stamped metal flask
replaced the flask of precious materials or hand-engraved brass. While
the flasks with the die-stamped designs gained the greatest popularity,
there were also simple cylinder flasks made without designs. For example

216

there is the simple small angular flask stamped "Robbins and Lawrence, Windsor, Vt., 1849" that was made for the Revolving-Hammer Pistol.

Die-stamped metal flasks were made in both England and America with similar designs. English flasks were made for the American market and American manufacturers copied the designs of English flasks. For example many scenes with dead game were made in both England and America, but the English designs were frequently of more detailed pattern.

The majority of the die-stamped flasks were made of brass or copper or a combination of the two metals, although some were made of zinc and pewter; they were rarely made of silver or Sheffield. Originally the brass and copper flasks were finished with a lacquer (in shades varying from pinkish-brown to black) which has worn off the majority of the old flasks. These flasks were made in several sizes from ¾" x 1¾" to 4⅞" x 10¼", the small pistol flask holding two ounces of powder, and the sixteen-ounce flasks for larger sporting arms and fowling pieces. Flask nozzles were made to match the bore of the gun muzzle or cylinder chamber. The "sloping spout" has always indicated use in connection with Colt's Navy Pistol and is known therefore as the Navy spout. The number of cord rings varies from two to four, while pocket flasks have no cord rings. Rings are both round and triangular in shape, but triangular rings were nearly always used with military flasks. In shape, flasks vary from bottle or flask shape with long necks, to rectangular shapes with short necks, and oval flasks with no hips. The curves vary and no two flasks of different design have the same form or measurements. This variation in form is interesting in itself.

Flasks may be classified into three general divisions: pocket pistol, military, and sporting flasks. The "contract" military flasks date after 1830. Although the Army had flasks made at a number of the National arsenals as early as 1826 and adopted them soon afterward, the Navy did not order any "contract" flasks made until 1842, but manufactured metal flasks at various Navy Yards around this date. In the correspondence of the Navy we find the following references to the powder flask: "24th Feb. 1842: The Commissioners have it in contemplation to introduce a substitute for the powder horn, which will be more convenient and economical than the horn now used in the service, and they desire you to have six copper flasks made and sent to this office, of the shape shown in the enclosed diagram with a thumb spring at the top large enough to hold one pound of priming powder, with a statement of their cost."

The correspondence about the flasks continues for several letters on March 1 and 2, 1842. All-copper and copper flasks with brass tops are discussed, and the all-copper flask chosen. Then there is a letter to stop all further work on powder horns and "substitute a copper flask, in place of the horn," and finally an order for five hundred copper flasks.

On December 18, 1844, the Navy ordered copper powder flasks from George Stimson and on August 18, 1845, 1,200 copper powder flasks were ordered from George Adams. Navy flasks were also made by N. P. Ames. A Navy flask by Ames, marked 1843, was made before the flasks by Adams and Stimson. The Navy flask, as the collector knows it, is a copper flask with a plain, non-adjustable brass top and has a design of an anchor and the letters "U.S.N." The Navy flask is eight inches by four and one-half inches in size and holds sixteen ounces of powder. Adams Navy flasks have been found with 1845, 1846, 1847 and 1848 year marks, and Stimson flasks were made in 1850, as well as those for the 1844 order described above.

Army flasks include the rare "Public Property" flask which is copper with a brass nozzle and four cord rings. On one side are the words, "Public Property" and a bugle, and on the reverse side only a bugle. A plain copper flask with a bugle is made by Baker and marked with his name. There are numerous varieties of flasks with an eagle and bugle. The one marked "Dingee 1832" has a bugle, eagle, and "U.S." The flask of 1833 has a bugle, eagle, "U.S." and one set of cord rings and is marked "R. Dingee." Another flask has only the eagle and bugle and no maker's name.

American Powder Flasks

Variations of a patriotic design including a cannon, flags, eagles, an anchor and crossed pistols and rifles, were made by several makers. One of these with a cannon, shield, flags and crossed rifles and pistols above is marked "Colt's Patent," and dates about 1850. A large Colt flask with cannon, flags, crossed rifles, and pistols below is marked "Colt's patent" on the ribbon at the bottom and also on the cap. These large flasks with cannon were made for old model holster pistols. Still another flask has

a design of cannon and flags, with an eagle perched on the cannon and a double row of stars with crossed pistols on one side. This is copper with a brass top, and is marked "American Flask Co." on the cap. It has four cord rings. This flask is made in several sizes for both rifle and pistol and is often unmarked.

A rare cannon and anchor copper flask with brass top is marked, "Colts Patent—K.K. 37." The design is on one side only. It was made for the "Dragoons" and K.K. 37 is company marking. Small flasks both with and without decoration were made to go with Colt revolvers as the Colt advertisement says: "A powder flask of lacquered copper with a measuring neck to throw the proper powder charge for the arm it was cased with." Cases with Colt revolvers were often made up in London and these included a powder flask made at Sheffield for Colt instead of a regular Colt flask. These were plain without design and bag-shaped, one marked for Colt's Pocket Pistol, or for Colt's Navy Pistol. The small Colt flask with the eagle was made for old model pocket pistols. In 1839, cylinder flasks came with Colt revolvers and were known as Patterson chargers.

There are at least sixteen variations of the eagle pistol flasks. First, there is a standing eagle holding a flask and revolver in his talons. These are found with slight variations of pattern and in several sizes, and some are marked "Colt" and some are unmarked. The flask with the standing eagle in a panel is unmarked. A flask with eagle and shield and stars and "E Pluribus Unum" on a ribbon below is marked "Colt," but the same design is also found unmarked. In the *Civil War, 1864* catalogue of Schuyler, Hartley, and Graham, a powder flask with eagle, stars, and "E Pluribus Unum" is illustrated and the name of the agent, William Greener of Birmingham, England, is given. A similar eagle design is marked "Remington's Ilion, N.Y." on a ribbon. Another flask made in three different sizes shows a cartouche of leaves and flowers surrounding an eagle with laurel leaves in its talons. A variation shows an eagle with arrows in the other talon. An eagle on a hummock is marked "Colt." Colt flasks were made between 1855 and 1865 and were marked both "Colt" and "Colt's Patent" and it is presumed that they were made by an outside contractor. An eagle standing on waves is marked "G. & J.W. Hawksley," Sheffield, England. Other variations are also found.

One of the most interesting flasks is the Peace or Friendship flask. It shows a pair of clasped hands within a circle or oval of stars and an eagle and shield above, and a crest with "U.S.," flags, cannon, guns and liberty cap below. This flask was first made in the 1830's and continued to be made by various makers for over forty years. The earliest dated

American Powder Flasks

Peace flasks were made by R. Dingee and dated 1833. They are of copper, with two triangular rings and the hands are in a circle of stars. Ames made Peace flasks in 1834, 1837, 1838, and flasks with this design up to 1850 have been found. The hands are enclosed within a circle of stars. They are marked "N.P. Ames" and the date. J. Batty made Peace flasks in 1847, 1850, and as late as 1857. Some were copper and the 1850 Batty flask was brass with triangular cord rings. The hands are in an oval of stars. The number of stars varies on these flasks and this is thought by some to indicate the date.

The larger flasks were used in the West, and any large flask could be termed a "Plains Rifle Flask." These flasks made by the American Flask and Cap Co. have a design of oak leaves which encloses a moose, or a hunter and dog, or two dogs, or an Indian rider charging at a buffalo. Above the scene is a seven-star chevron and a moose head; also there is a small dog or fox head below the scene. These are large flasks eight inches by four and one-half inches and have four round cord rings. They are usually stamped "American Flask & Cap Co." on the cap.

Flasks with various other hunting scenes are enclosed within arabesques of flowers and leaves. The costume of the hunter will be an aid in dating such a flask,—one with a tall hat being of an early date, and the design English in origin. A hunter and dog are enclosed within a circle of birds on a flask marked "patent," with no maker's name. Many of these scenes or those with a single dog or hare were made in zinc. Running deer and dogs in a panel with another dog in a panel above are shown on a copper flask which is unmarked. A design of three ducks in the marsh grass within a cartouche is marked "American Flask & Cap Co." Another duck design is marked "James Dixon." The Bear in Tree flask was made by American Flask & Cap Co., while a design of three horses' heads was made by G. & J.W. Hawksley of Sheffield, England. A design of an Indian, tree and deer is marked "Batty 1853." The Highlander design was made by American Flask and Cap Co. as was the Centennial Exposition's flask dated 1776.

Flasks with dead game were popular both in England and America. One of the loveliest of these designs is marked "James Dixon & Sons." It is copper, seven and one-half inches by three and one-half inches, has four rings and a design of a hanging group, woodcock, pheasant and rabbit tied above with a bowknot. This is English, but the same design was made both in England and America without the bowknot. A design of a hanging rabbit, birds, and wheat with leaves above is also fine English workmanship. Another fine flask has two birds hung within a panel on the flask which is shaped like a perfume bottle. There is no mark. Flasks of this design were exhibited by James Dixon and Sons at the 1851 Exposition in London. They are described as "powder and pistol flasks ornamented with silver. . . . The very delicate-coloured bronze is the result of an oxide which is made to adhere artificially to the copper; it is brushed with rouge-powder, which materially improves its appearance." Two dead-game designs were exhibited, one within an oval of arabesque strapwork and the other a large design of a rabbit and birds hanging from a hook. A design of a trumpet-vine with leaves and flowers is on another flask and still another illustrated in the catalogue of the London Exposition has a leaf border. Several plain flasks are also shown, one rectangular in shape.

A flask in the shape of a gun stock is marked "Frary, Benham Co." Another gun-stock shaped flask has a masonic symbol and is marked "American Flask and Cap Co." These flasks were late and were made between 1860 and 1870.

Large Overland flasks with brass tops and four cord rings are an addition to any collection. These are found with a shell design and a beaded fluting design, both made by Hawksley, and a plain fluted design with a leaf top made by Dixon, as well as a fine basket weave with a leaf bottom which was also probably made by Dixon although not marked. The earliest flasks were made by Sykes in England for the English sportsman. Captain Lacy writing in *The Modern Shooter* in 1846 says in effect that the Sykes patent powder flask is best.

American Powder Flasks

Some of the rarest flasks are also English, such as the flask with the two marriage scenes marked "James Dixon." Other rare flasks were marked "Massachusetts Arms Company, Chicopee Falls"; one is marked "Pistol" with the Massachusetts Arms mark in a circle on the other side, the other with banners and a hand holding a pistol and marked "Massachusetts Arms Co., Chicopee Falls" on both sides, while a third has the trade mark on one side and an eagle on the other side. Another rare flask is marked "Linsays Young America" on the brass top. It is a flask for a double-barreled pocket percussion pistol and has a design of an eagle with "E Pluribus Unum" and crossed pistols. The small moon and star flask is also rare, as is the Indian Hunter with the standing elk and tree borders which is marked, "J. Batty, Springfield."

Powder flasks were used much later than most collectors realize. When the first flasks were made we know that the Army and Navy were still continuing to use the antiquated powder horn. Also long after cartridges were made, many people still continued to use the powder flask. Several catalogues and price lists give us the designs, sizes, and prices of flasks. The price list of flasks sold by E.K. Tryon, Jr. & Co. of Philadelphia in 1871 includes the following:

Colt's 2 oz. common spring	$1.75 per doz.
2 oz. Eagle & Stars and E Pluribus Unum	2.00 per doz.
4 oz. Shell	2.75 per doz.
4 oz. wreaths, dogs & birds, Navy charger	3.50 per doz.
8 oz. Wreath and deer	3.00 per doz.
8 oz. Wreath and deer pat. inside spring	5.00 per doz.
10 oz. shell	5.00 per doz.
12 oz. fluted common spring	6.00 per doz.

Then, under common powder flasks, medium, various size shell designs are listed; under fine, shell, fluted, bead, dead game and dog and tree designs are listed. This catalogue is owned by Ray Riling of Philadelphia, Pennsylvania. In the Landauer Collection of the New York

A Handbook of Popular Antiques

Historical Society is the 1881 catalogue of John P. Moore's Sons, 302 Broadway, New York. Flasks listed for sale include "heavy copper wreath pattern, dead game, shell, fluted, plain, Dixon's assorted patterns, and flasks by G. & J.W. Hawksley." Prices range from $2.50 to $20.50 a dozen to the trade and sizes range from eight ounces to sixteen ounces.

In 1889, The Ideal Tool Co. advertised "plain brass nickeled powder flasks." The last patent for a metal powder flask was taken out by D. Wright of St. Louis under date of December 29, 1891.

A collection of metal powder flasks could cover the whole American field, including popular designs and makers' names, or one may limit his collection to the Army and Navy flasks or patriotic flasks. One might also choose hunting flasks to form a specialized collection while others might collect with the idea of adding to historical data. Flasks could also be collected in relation to the guns with which they were used and their part in the history of firearms, or for the industrial history connected with the mechanical improvements and patents relating to the manufacture of the flasks and firearms.

BIBLIOGRAPHY

Collection of Flasks and Books of Ray Riling, Philadelphia, Pa.

Collection of Powder Flasks of Robert Abels.

Collection of Powder Flasks of Philip J. Medicus.

Hobbies Magazine: January, 1941, Wilbur F.S. Quick; April, 1941, Wilbur F.S. Quick; October, 1943, Waverly P. Lewis; January, 1944, Waverly P. Lewis.

Chapter 25

LITHOPHANES

At the present time, there are sufficient lithophanes on the market and the prices are low enough to make their collection of special interest to the amateur collector. To date, the interest in lithophanes is not widespread.

A lithophane is a transparent porcelain panel or sheet usually in the biscuit or unglazed state. The shaded design is formed by variations in the thickness of the paste, so that a shaded effect not unlike a mezzotint is obtained when the plaque is held before a strong light. The design was first hand-modeled in paste, then a wax relief or plaster-of-paris die or mold was made from which many copies could be produced. These white biscuit plaques were invented in 1828, in Berlin, but the idea of making transparencies in porcelain is attributed to M. le Baron de Bourgoing in France in 1827. However lithophanes were not manufactured until some years later as indicated by the designs.

Lithophanes were made to hang in windows against the light. They were also mounted in lamp shades and used as screens in candle stands of wrought iron, wood or gilded iron. Lithophanes are made entirely in white, or white with colored frames, and some are painted in naturalistic colors. Lithophanes were made in Berlin, Meissen, Holland, France, Denmark and England. The Berlin Royal Porcelain Manufactory, which claims their invention by a man named Pott, exhibited "lithophanie" in the Crystal Palace in London in 1851.

The subject matter of the lithophanes that are on the market today is consistent with the years of their greatest popularity, between 1834 and 1858. Subjects are taken from well-known paintings of Victorian artists and of the Italian masters popular in the era, and also from genre paintings and engravings, and landscapes and scenes of European cities.

Lithophanes at the Metropolitan Museum of Art in New York City are of German manufacture and include Magdalene, after a painting by Guido Reni; Going to Church, a portrait of a woman in peasant bonnet against a background of Gothic church architecture, marked "131"; a View of Dresden, marked "118"; a Harbor Scene at Sunset, marked "26"; a man in a peasant costume, marked "K.P.M. 183 S" from the painting The Woodsman, by Thomas Barker; and a woman in peasant costume, marked "K.P.M. 184 S."

In the Berlin Exposition, in 1844, sixty-eight different lithophanes were exhibited. These included Views of Naples, Worcester Cathedral, the Vatican, Raphael's Madonna of the Chair, and a view of Unter den Linden. Other German lithophane subjects include scenes from popular novels such as the dining-room scene from Scott's *Quentin Durward*, marked "998 N"; scenes from Faust; Jews in Exile with the German inscription, *"In Den Wassern zu Babylon zitzen wir und weineten";* a Shepherd and a dog; a boat scene of a man and a girl, marked "K.P.M. 107 N"; a peasant woman with a child in a wicker basket against a mountain landscape, marked "K.P.M. 355." The Shepherd with his dog and a flock of sheep and hunting scenes were popular subjects on German lithophanes. Still other lithophanes were of nudes with drapery and clouds being carried by cupids, and other emblematic designs.

Lithophane scenes are often found in the bottoms of German beer mugs. These usually show love scenes or drinking scenes. Still other German subjects include genre scenes of children and dogs such as The Pretender, which shows a dog and a boy with his father's hat down over his face. This plaque is marked "K.P.M." in the bottom corner.

A lampshade with metal frame at the Museum of the City of New York contains lithophanes with the following subjects: Bastion Falls, Kauterskill Glenn, marked "K.P.M."; Children and a Doll; Children playing with a powder puff at a dressing table; group of children outside a cottage; mother and child; women on horseback in the mountains. These are all of Berlin manufacture but must have been made for the English or American market. They were made in great quantities at Berlin between 1834 and 1851. Other scenes included the following, all marked "K.P.M.": Staten Island, Harbor of New York; The Niagara Falls; Organ Grinder and Monkey; Boy Writing on the Wall; Lovers at a Rustic Gate.

Sometimes the marks are on the front and sometimes they are on the reverse of the plaque. Other marks from the Royal Manufactory in Berlin are "B.P.M." which stands for Berlin Porzellan Manufactur, and "P.P.M.," Prenssische Porzellan Manufactur. "K.P.M.," although a mark similar to that used on Meissen, refers to "Königlichen Preussische Manufactur" or "Königlichen Porzellan Manufactur" at Berlin, rather than to the Meissen factory, although they were made later at Meissen. "E.G.Z." is also a German mark. German lithophanes are usually marked with letters for numerals, or both, and lithophanes without marks are not of German manufacture. Some German lithophanes are glazed, while others are unglazed and have the effect of bisque and are often called Parian by dealers.

Lithophanes were also made at various factories in France. Some are white and others are colored. The subject matter, while similar to that on German lithophanes, has a tendency toward the genre. Colored French lithophanes have such subjects as a cobbler's family outside his cottage; a school master with boys and a visiting mother, and the Young Photographer which shows boys playing with a camera. There are woodland scenes with dogs, children, and two beggars, while others depict a man, child and cat by a fireplace, and a cottage dooryard showing a girl with a dog and birds in cages. These lithophanes are four and one-half inches by five and one-quarter inches and are in light pastel colors with their raised borders painted black. While they are of French manufacture, they have no identifying marks. However, one French factory which made lithophanes was located at Rubelles and the lithophanes here were made

A Handbook of Popular Antiques

in one or more colors and were usually marked "A.d.T." with a serial number, or "Rubelles." These marks are given in William Chaffers' *Marks and Monograms on Pottery and Porcelain*. Chaffers also states that the manufacture of lithophanes ceased at Rubelles in 1858. Subjects of lithophanes from the Rubelles factory include a Windmill and Sailboat marked "A.d. T. 81" with an "S" on the reverse side; An Eastern Mosque, with a lake and palm trees and figures in a boat, marked "A.d.T. 85," "S" on reverse; A castle scene by moonlight, marked "A.d. T. 299," "S" on reverse side; Lovers in ruins of a Gothic Church, marked "A. d. T. 289," "S" on reverse side; Figures in a Romanesque Church with tombs, marked "A. d. T. 332"; A Revolutionary Battle Scene by moonlight showing a fallen soldier and one with bayonet and a burning town and cannon in the distance, marked "A. d. T. 61." These plaques vary in thickness and in workmanship of the details of the pictures. Although they are generally four inches by six inches, their exact proportions vary. Sometimes the frame is raised, but often the frame is low and on the same level with the lowest surface of the porcelain. This latter arrangement makes the lithophane more fragile.

Lithophanes were manufactured in England from Nantgarw porcelain prepared at Bristol and made at the South Wales Pottery, Llanelly, and may have the mark "S.W. P." At one time they were used extensively in England, but outside of lamps or frames, few have survived.

Along with the majority of other Victorian minor arts, lithophanes do not have much art value. They represent genre and sentimental subject matter characteristic of Victorian art, and a process of manufacture no longer in existence. For these reasons, and for their quaint charm when in good condition, they are desirable.

BIBLIOGRAPHY

Antique Collector, Vol. 81937, "Lithophanes," Francis Buckley.

The Magazine Antiques, Vol. 29, p. 146.

A Guide to the Collections of Welsh Porcelain, Isaac J. Williams, Humphrey Milford, London, 1931.

Chapter 26

COMPOSITION DAGUERREOTYPE CASES

FROM the standpoint of subject matter, the composition daguerreotype case is one of the interesting collector's items of mid-Victorian minor art. These cases were also the first plastic products made in America. Their covers are examples of the work of the best-known die makers of Victorian days. The shellac composition was similar to that used today in phonograph records, checkers, poker chips and electric light sockets.

· The first daguerreotype cases were made of paper pressed in a mold in the same manner as papier-mâché. The paper was then painted and varnished to imitate leather. William Shew, a daguerreotype artist of Boston, made these cases as early as 1844 with geometric, arabesque, and rose designs. In 1846–1847, Gordon & Stadley of Boston made a few scenic designs and a head of Washington. Other designs on paper cases included the Eagle and Flag, Birds and Vase, Urn, Lyre, Beehive, and various floral and conventional designs which were afterward used on composition cases. Paper cases were made at Scovill Manufactory before composition cases became popular.

Composition daguerreotype cases were first patented in 1854 and continued to be made as late as 1880. Samuel Peck of New Haven, Connecticut, who had operated daguerreoan rooms from 1846 to 1851, was the first to patent the plastic case. Peck's patent reads: "Improvement in manufacture of Daguerreotype cases. Pat. Oct. 3, 1854. The boxes are made of a composition of shellac and sawdust or fibrous material with a suitable coloring matter, passed between hot rollers and when plastic, pressed into molds.

"Claim: Covering the surfaces of the composition with thin plates of burnished metal or paper previous to its being pressed in the die. The coating thus made gives the advantage of surfaces to paste the lining to and also a very neat metallic ornament at small additional cost."

Although this patent is listed as an improvement, it is the first plastic case patent recorded. In August, 1855, Halvor Halvorson assigned his patent, which included the use of gilded paper to strengthen the plastic, to Horace Barnes. However, Peck includes the Halvorson patent in his cases and thus must have purchased it as some time from Halvorson or from Horace Barnes. From 1857, S. Peck & Company became a subsidiary of Scovill Manufacturing Company, although a part of the S. Peck output was taken over by E. Anthony of New York who also advertised cases of their own manufacture. However, cases with Anthony's name have not been found.

In May, 1854, Anthony did take out a patent for the improvement of the embossed velvet cushion. In the *New England Business Directory* of 1856, daguerreotype-case manufacturers listed in addition to S. Peck of New Haven were Scovill Manufacturing Company of Waterbury, Connecticut; Holmes, Booth and Haydens of Waterbury, Connecticut, and A. P. Critchlow & Company of Northampton, Massachusetts. One of the best-known and most prolific of all case manufacturers was Littlefield, Parsons who made Union cases controlled by patents taken out in 1856 and 1857. Another well-known maker was Wadams & Company, who controlled the Kinsley and Parker hinge patented in 1858. The Florence Manufacturing Company of Florence, Massachusetts, made cases of Florence composition in 1866, and one is in the collection of Warren F. Kaynor, Waterbury, Connecticut.

Since many other firms are listed in directories as case makers, and cases have not been found with their names, it seems probable that they made paper cases or that they assembled the plastic cases but did not actually manufacture the plastic composition tops and bottoms. However, J. F. Masher of Philadelphia, who in 1853 invented the stereoscope which was used in some leather or paper cases, later, in February, 1857,

Composition Daguerreotype Cases

took out a patent for ornamenting daguerreotype cases. Paper with a coating of a compound of water, potash and gelatine, was used to make an imitation tortoise-shell wood or marble case. Just who manufactured these cases or if they ever were made in wholesale amounts is not known.

Scovill Manufacturing Co. furnished most of the oreide brass mats, that surrounded the picture and served as a frame. These were die stamped and often hand chased. Designs varied from geometric patterns, arabesques and flower and leaf borders to drums, eagles, and other patriotic emblems. Holmes, Booth, & Haydens of Waterbury, Conn. also made three brass mats. Among their designs are mats with flags and cannon in the corners.

I. A. Martine & Company and E. Anthony and Company, both of New York, were manufacturers of the silk and stamped velvet cushions and linings for the front of daguerreotype cases. E. Anthony advertising in the *Daguerreian Journal,* November 1, 1850, includes the following in his advertisement:

"Cases of own manufacture of every style and quality. Papier-Mâché or Pearl Inlaid. Turkey Morocco, Snap cases. Cases manufactured to suit the taste of any customer. Name embossed on cushion. Case makers supplied with leather, silk, velvet, hooks, etc."

Cushions are usually of red velvet; occasionally gold or blue velvet was used. The embossed designs range from conventional medallions, vases of flowers, musical instruments, or a single flower, to the name and address of the daguerreotypist. In themselves these embossed mats would form a quaint collection.

The smallest plastic cases were small, locket-size round cases made to hold two portraits. These were two inches by two inches and had screw-on tops. They were made in red, green and tan-colored composition, as well as the more common brown and black. These small cases have not been found with a maker's name. Oval and square cases with hinges are found in two by two-inch, two and one-half by three-inch, and three and one-half by four-inch sizes. While many of these small cases have conventional designs on their covers, they are also found with figures, patriotic scenes and animals. The most common size case is a rectangle five by six inches. Octagonal and hexagonal cases with angled and curved sides are found in five by six inches. The largest cases are seven by nine inches, while long, narrow cases made for four portraits were made in three by five-inch, three and three-quarters by six and one-quarter-inch, and two and one-half by four-inch sizes.

Many cases are signed with the names of the die sinkers, and from these signatures I have compiled a list which includes some of the best-known die sinkers of New York, during the late 1850's, and down to 1880. Several of these die sinkers were engravers as well. With the exception of dies which were made by Samuel Peck himself, and some made by H. W. Hayden, the other die sinkers were located in New York. Directories as early as 1841–42 list Frederick P. Goll, Jr., engraver and die sinker, at 112 Fulton Street, New York. In 1844–5 Frederick P. Goll and Frederick C. Key are listed, and since Key's name disappears after 1846–1847, any dies impressed with his name, such as the cannon design, were in the shop of F. C. Key and Sons, of Philadelphia, who are listed as die sinkers and engravers in *American Engravers on Steel and Copper* by Stauffer. This is undoubtedly the same firm. F. Goll remains in the New York Directory down through 1858. In 1849, F. Seiler is listed at 57 Gold Street, and in 1850, Seiler & Rupp and F. B. Smith & Hartman are listed. From 1857–8 to 1873, the name of Anthony Schaefer, die sinker at 83 Duane Street, appears in *Wilson's Business Directory,* and in 1859–60, A. Henning & Eymann are listed at 29 North William Street, New York.

These die makers do not seem to have confined their work exclusively to any one manufacturer, since we find their names on the cases of various makers. The trade of die sinker is considered so low that die sinkers have gone without mention; in fact they are rarely allowed to sign their names. Now, however, perhaps their day has come, for surely the name of the die sinker increases the value and is an aid in dating a plastic daguerreotype case. In the Landauer Collection at the New York

Composition Daguerreotype Cases

Historical Society, there are several die makers' trade cards, including one of Fred B. Smith, 122½ Fulton Street, New York, which reads, "Metal and General Die Sinker; Dies & seals for jewelers, silversmiths, military ornaments, army and navy medals struck in gold, silver and composition." In the correspondence between the New York and New Haven shops of S. Peck & Company, between 1877 and 1880, is the note "Washington Monument box top, involving two weeks' work for Smith, the die sinker."* This case top design was registered August 28, 1877. The cases include the name "Smith" in the die. From a study of the directories we find that dies of F. Goll, Key, and F. Seiler are the earliest, and those by Smith and Hartman antedate the Smith dies. Also, there was a J. Smith who is not listed and may have been employed solely by S. Peck. Some of the old dies have been preserved in perfect condition. Others, even when still in use, failed to register certain small details because of foreign material that damaged the die, especially the die sinker's name, which is often missing or illegible. The design of Washington's head appears both with and without surrounding stars due to defects made by foreign material in the star part of the die.

In 1877, the demand for composition cases was so great that we find the following note in the S. Peck correspondence: "Do not let the dies rest an hour of the twenty-four, not even a minute."

Designs for composition daguerreotype cases include scenes from American history, sentimental compositions, mythological, religious, political, fraternal and patriotic scenes and designs. Various trades are represented and scenes from the popular fiction of the day, landscape, flowers, shells, and conventional designs. Most scenes and designs are surrounded by borders of rococo scrolls, flowers, leaves and arabesques. All are in high, characteristic baroque relief. The designs are taken from pattern books of the era and are the same as those found on book covers, furniture carvings and various articles of bric-a-brac. Subject matter was seldom original with the die makers, but was taken from drawings, en-

* Courtesy Scovill Manufacturing Company.

gravings, and paintings, which were popular during mid-Victorian days. Many of the designs were also used on plastic album covers, collar boxes, and for plastic clock fronts.

The following is a classified check list of designs on gutta-percha daguerreotype cases of American manufacture which I have seen:

HISTORICAL

By Peck and Halverson: Capture of Major Andre (After painting by Asher B. Durand) F. Goll, die maker. Landing of Columbus (From painting by J. Vanderlyn in Rotunda of Capitol at Washington, D. C.), Pat. Nov. 1st, 1877, F. B. Smith & Hartman, die makers. Washington Monument, Richmond, Va. (Aug. 28, 1877), Smith, die maker. Geo. Washington Profile, F. Goll, Diemaker—Inscription—"First in War, First in Peace and First in hearts of Countrymen" (Border of stars, flags and laurel). Medallic Profile of Washington (After bust by Houdon).

By Littlefield, Parsons & Co.: Washington Crossing the Delaware (After painting by Emanuel Leutze), F. B. Smith & Hartman, die makers. Monument—Havana, Cuba. *Monitor* with "cheesebox turret" flying American flag. Fort at right flying American flag. Ft. Sumter with flag and sailing vessel. Gen. Marion inviting British Officer to Dinner (Based on painting by John B. White). Liberty (by the Ocean) symbolical composition. Sir Henry Havelock (British General) (Marked in die). Shield, Flags and Cannon with laurel wreath below. Shield and Eagle, Inscription "The Union—Constitution." Eagle and Scroll with "Constitution and the Laws" (olive branch behind scroll). Star-shaped shield, "Union"—stars in background. Conventional design shield, cannon and cannon balls, flags, rifles, and liberty cap. Eagle on Waves, Flag and Cannon. Cleopatra.

By Wadams Mfg. Co.: Benedict Arnold's Escape, Charter Oak.

By Scovill Mfg. Co.: Crossed Cannon, Key, die maker, Genuine Union case improved. Fine gilt and burnished hinge. Crossed Cannon, pyramids of cannon balls, liberty cap and anchor—border of flags, shield and laurel.

234

Composition Daguerreotype Cases

Unmarked: Head of Julius Caesar, border of Shells and "C" scrolls.

LODGES

By Scovill Mfg. Co.: Odd Fellows.
Unmarked: Masonic.

SENTIMENTAL AND GENRE SUBJECTS

By Littlefield, Parsons & Co.: The Faithful Hound, from painting by Johann Gellert (Mother, child and dog). Chess Players. Three Musicians at Piano, A. Schaefer—die maker (before 1873). Children Playing with Toys. Farm-Summer (after Currier & Ives), Haying, Boy with butterfly net. Lady with Curls and Fichu holding girl, cat and spaniel.

By A. P. Critchlow & Co.: Woman Kneeling Embracing Child, dog lying at left. Friar Asleep Against Tree Trunk, church in background.

By Samuel Peck: The Blind Beggar. Going to Market. The Tight Cork (title in die). Calmady Children after painting by Sir Thomas Lawrence, H. W. Hayden, die maker. County Dance.

By Wadams Mfg. Co.: The Elopement.

By Kinsley & Parker: The Elopement. Country Home Scene, Man and woman by brook, boy running.

By Scovill Mfg. Co.: Pacing Horse six and one-half by three inches. Yacht Design eight and one-half by five and three-quarter inches.

RELIGIOUS SUBJECTS

By Samuel Peck: Rebecca at the Well. Pope Leo, J. Smith, die maker. Pope Pius. Angel. Harp and Columns (Memorial) Open Bible on altar—Matt. 69—"Our Father Who art in Heaven, etc." Cross, Acorn Border.

By Littlefield, Parsons & Co.: Angel.

By A. P. Critchlow & Co.: Church Window.

By Holmes, Booth & Haydens: The Vision of Ezekiel (inscription in die).

Unmarked: The Holy Family, Henning & Eymann, die makers (1859–60, New York Directory). Star and Cross.

MYTHOLOGICAL SUBJECTS

By Samuel Peck & Co.: Voyage of Cytherea.

Unmarked: Europa and The Bull. Morning (Angel flying to right scattering roses).

FICTION

By Littlefield, Parsons & Co.: Lady and Falcon. Marriage of John Alden and Priscilla. Lady Diana Mannering. Red Riding Hood. Paul and Virginia.

By A. P. Critchlow: Bobby Shaftoe. The Fortune Teller, Cavalier and Gypsy group with dog. Story from Sir Roger de Coverley by Addison and Steele. Figure in background is portrait of Addison. From silver piece by J. Angell, Strand, London, exhibited in New York Crystal Palace, 1853.

By Samuel Peck & Co.: Maude Muller with hay fork. Fairy Head in Rose.

By Holmes, Booth & Haydens: Highland Hunter. The Young Pretender.

By Wadams Mfg. Co.: Una, Spenser's Faerie Queene.

TRADE AND OCCUPATIONS

By Littlefield, Parsons & Co.: Fireman. Agriculture, farm scenes around cartouche, ladder, rooster and hens, wheat, etc. Cartouche, and firemen's activities—ladder, hose, etc. Beehive and Plow. The Kill (Hunter and fallen deer).

By Scovill Mfg. Co.: Wheat and Plow.

By Samuel Peck & Co.: Agriculture.

ANIMALS AND CHILDREN

By Littlefield, Parsons & Co.: Children with Butterfly Net, Deer and Cupids. Two Birds and Nest. Boy with Flag and Gun. Boy and Girl at Stile. Girl Under Tree.

By Samuel Peck & Co.: Two Deer, Smith (die maker).

By Scovill Mfg. Co.: Boy by Haystack playing with Rabbit.

By A. P. Critchlow: Chasing Butterflies.

Unmarked: Children and Lambs, F. Seiler, die maker.

FRUIT AND FLOWERS

By Littlefield, Parsons & Co.: Urn with flowers suspended by chains. Basket of Flowers (large). Basket of Flowers (small). Vase and Columns. Strawberry.

By Holmes, Booth & Haydens: Fruit Basket. Grapes. Vase of Fruit.

By Samuel Peck & Co.: Fruit. Bunch of Mixed Flowers. Adv.— "Genuine Union Case improved Fine Gilt and Burnished Hinge."

By Scovill Mfg. Co.: Acorns: Lilies and Grapes. Urn with Fruit and Vegetables. Grape Vine.

MISCELLANEOUS

By Littlefield, Parsons & Co.: Shell. Beehive and Garden Tools. Chain and Buckles. Trefoil cutwork design backed by silk or velvet. Geometric designs with centers painted gold.

By Samuel Peck & Co.: Fountain. Belt and Buckle. Geometric designs with centers painted gold.

By A. P. Critchlow: Beehive. Beehive and Garden Tools (variation).

By Scovill Mfg. Co.: Cameo Inset Heads in plastic and lava.

In addition there are at least a hundred different geometric and conventional designs of various makers. Of a collection of six hundred cases owned by Warren F. Kaynor of Waterbury, Connecticut, the majority are by S. Peck, Littlefield, Parsons, or A. P. Critchlow.

REFERENCES

Collection of Warren F. Kaynor.

Collection of Oscar T. Barck of Brooklyn.

Collection of The New York Historical Society.

Chapter 27

EIGHTEENTH-CENTURY ENGLISH
TEA CADDIES

TEA caddies, or tea chests as they were first called, have, so far, been neglected by the American collector. For this reason, tea caddies are available today although fine examples are expensive. However, a beautiful inlaid tea caddy is well worth its price, for usually the finest materials and the most expert workmanship were put into the making of these small chests.

In the late seventeenth century in England, tea was an expensive item available only for the use of the upper classes. The tea supply was kept under lock and key and small ornate boxes or tea chests which held one compartment for black tea and one for green tea were used to store the household supply. These boxes were brought to the table and the hostess who kept the key unlocked the box, and mixed the tea herself. The design of these tea caddies follows the furniture styles of the eighteenth century and a knowledge of these styles, their general characteristics, the woods, and designs used and the methods of decoration in each period is necessary for the collector to have an intelligent approach to such a collection.

In Queen Anne's reign tea chests were made of shagreen, an untanned leather of horse or ass, or shark's skin, dyed black or green. Some few chests were also made of mahogany. However, these early tea chests are rarely found, and it is not until the Chippendale period that we have much definite information or the chance of finding any chests described. Of course tea chests of the Chippendale period are rare. I know of one large collection of several hundred tea chests and it includes only one

English Tea Caddies

of the Chippendale period. However, designs of tea chests are included in Chippendale's *Gentleman and Cabinet-Maker's Director,* published in 1754. In this volume two plates of tea chests are shown which set the style for tea chests of the period made by Chippendale or by less well-known cabinet makers.

Tea chests of this period, and until late in the century, were made of the finest materials and by the best workmen. The Chippendale tea chest is usually of mahogany with applied metal mounts in the French manner, or with carving. It is casket-shaped and usually has scrolled corners and feet and a *bombé* front. Of the designs shown in the *Director,* all but one have this general shape, although the metal decoration varies from only a handle and feet of metal, to complete corners and applied scrolls of metal work on the corners and bottom edge. The keyhole has a gilt metal escutcheon. The box, with straight sides and no feet, has a pattern of applied wood carving in geometric design. Another chest illustrated has an applied carved Chinese fretwork design. Carving is also used in borders and horizontal bands. Some chests have silver mountings and silver claw-and-ball feet as well as interior fittings of silver.

The tea caddy of Chippendale design in the Metropolitan Museum has feet, handle, and escutcheon of silver. It is simpler and more dignified in form than the designs in the Chippendale Director. Motifs of decoration to look for in the Chippendale period are shells, acanthus leaves, "C" and "S" scrolls, lion heads and claw-and-ball feet, fretwork in Chinese design and Gothic tracery designs.

The name tea caddy as well as tea chest is used in Hepplewhite's *Guide,* which was published in 1788. While mahogany was still a popular wood, satinwood, harewood, maple, burl walnut, rosewood and fruit woods are now used. In the *Guide,* six designs are shown and the "ornaments may be inlaid with various colored woods or painted and varnished." Two of these Hepplewhite designs have curved *bombé* fronts. The rectangular caddies shown all have casket tops and one has bracket feet, while the others have a wooden plinth instead of feet. The designs include delicate strings of husks, classical vases, paterae, and flower and acanthus-leaf scrolls with a human figure. The only metal used on these caddy designs is on the handle, and the escutcheon is of ivory. These chests mark a transition between Chippendale and Hepplewhite, since the majority of the inlaid chests have no feet, and are rectangular, square, or oval, although they may be rectangular or hexagonal with chamfered corners.

Another plate of tea-caddy drawings in the *Director* includes one rectangular caddy with two inside divisions, and one oval and one square caddy, each with only one inside compartment. These are elaborately decorated with panels and borders of delicate floral design. Caddies similar to these designs are found today, but usually the more decoration and inlay, the higher the price. Oval caddies of painted wood with flowers, allegorical or mythological scenes and vases and festoons of flowers are beautiful when well painted, and they usually were done by an artist of considerable ability. Although this painting is in the style of Angelica Kauffman, it is doubtful if she herself ever painted a tea caddy. Motifs of decoration to look for on caddies of the Hepplewhite era are: pendant husks, floral swags, paterae, acanthus leaves, rosettes, ribbons, ears of wheat, Prince of Wales feathers, and classic architectural details. Rare Hepplewhite design tea caddies have an inlay of three Prince of Wales feathers or marqueterie designs in green and other colored woods, with borders of satinwood or panels of wood veneer, with the split-wood grain forming the pattern. Veneer was usually applied to a structure of deal or mahogany.

Sheraton tea caddies were usually made of satinwood or rosewood with an inlay of geometric designs, crossed diagonal lines, laurel, bowknots, classic urns, lyres, fans, paterae, stars, conch shells, wreaths of flowers, honeysuckle and waterleaf designs and baskets or bouquets of flowers. The escutcheon on these caddies is usually of bone or ivory and the handle brass. These tea caddies in the latter part of the eighteenth century were influenced by Adam and the designs of the painters Pergolesi and Angelica Kauffman. Some caddies had insets of small miniatures under glass or Wedgwood plaques, and some caddies were painted with floral decorations. Motifs of design due to Adam influence include festooned husks, honeysuckle, Grecian urns, wreaths of flowers, egg-and-dart moldings, palmette and pineapple, men's heads, lion heads, griffin and human figures.

Tea caddies at this time were also made of ivory inlaid with lines of silver, ebony, or tortoise shell. They had silver finials on the lids and a silver shield for the owner's name or crest. Various shades of tortoise shell, from golden tan to green, were also used for caddies. These had lines of ivory or silver. In 1803, Lord Nelson gave Lady Hamilton a tortoise-shell tea caddy with silver lines and ivory knobs and a silver plate with an inscription bearing both their names. This tea caddy is now owned by an American collector, and caddies similar to this are found in the shops today.

Late eighteenth-century tea caddies were often made in fruit wood modeled in the form of apples, pears, plums or melons. These were sometimes left in the natural wood and polished, but often they were painted in naturalistic fruit colors. Fine red apples and green pears are especially decorative. Tea caddies were also made of Tunbridge Ware with geometric designs or landscapes set in a mosaic-like pattern of whitewood, yellow barberry or nutmeg, oak, purplewood, zebra, ebony, lignum-vitae, Brazil orange and other woods upon a mahogany base.

Small medallions of engravings transferred on wood were also set into tea caddies. Later tea caddies were also covered with rolled paper work in various designs—white, colored, or gilt. Straw work designs in geometric pattern and scenes also were used on late eighteenth-century tea caddies. These types of boxes were often the work of amateurs, while the earlier inlaid wood boxes were made by trained craftsmen. Later still mother-of-pearl on papier-mâché and tôle were used for tea caddies. The large casket-shaped wooden caddies, veneered with maple, amboyna or rosewood, with three interior compartments and a Sheffield handle and bone escutcheon, belong to the nineteenth century.

A study of the woods used in tea caddies is one of the interesting angles of collecting. The woods most commonly used for the construction or background of eighteenth-century tea caddies are mahogany, rosewood, satinwood, amboyna, sycamore and harewood. Chippendale preferred the dark mahogany, and tea caddies of the Chippendale period are of darker wood than those of the succeeding periods. Light-brown mahogany and other light woods were used in the most decorative boxes of the eighteenth century. The wood is often a key, or at least an aid in placing a tea caddy in a certain period or date. Wood was usually used in veneer form, and fine-grained pieces were chosen. Often the veneer was placed diagonally to get an effect of pattern. For inlay, the more exotic woods were used, including coromandel. Purplewood with a coarse open grain becomes purple when cut, but gradually fades after polishing. Olivewood is smooth and fine grained, and has a golden-yellow tone when polished. Kingwood was used for cross bandings. It is purplish-brown in color. Macassar ebony is dark with long black graining. For wine red the cabinet makers had amaranth, although cherry, coralwood, red mahogany and yew, which gave a lighter red, were used more often. Olive, lemonwood, sandalwood and acacia gave yellow tones, and walnut was both gray and brown. Green came from young twigs of oak, from lignum-vitae and from green ebony and calembour, while rosewood and palisander gave the autumn shades, and lemon and holly were used for contrast. Fruit woods such as pear were stained to produce various delicate colors. Other woods used were light barberry and holly, sycamore, box and citron. It is not easy to identify all of these woods since many have changed color with the years. In identifying wood, a knowledge of the grain is important.

A few words should be said about the interiors of tea caddies. They were lined with tin or lead foil which, however, is now usually missing or in bad condition. Often the top of a caddy is lined with velvet. The interior has one, two, or three divisions, depending upon the size of the box, and often there are slits in the wood for the silver caddy spoons. The section for the tea usually had a wooden cover of the same wood as the exterior of the box and a knob of ivory or silver. Often, however, the cover had an inlaid design as well. Boxes have also been found with sterling silver covers, while some boxes had silver, pewter, glass or china cannisters enclosed within the tea caddy.

At a recent auction in New York City of a small collection of eighteenth-century English tea caddies, those of turned fruit wood in apple, pear, or gourd shapes brought higher prices than either a Sheraton caddy of satinwood and tulipwood, with inlaid harewood urn and shell paterae, or an inlaid mahogany caddy, or a sycamore caddy with shell panel; while an oval satinwood caddy inlaid with a marqueterie basket of flowers and a square caddy of lacewood inlaid with a shell in an oval panel were also neglected. There were several reasons for this: the quality of the workmanship of the inlaid caddies, the shell inlay on sycamore being the best in execution, and the scarcity of the fruit caddies, plus the fact that a collector of fruit shapes was also in attendance.

There are no makers' names or marks of identification on these cabinet makers' tea caddies. The collector must be the judge of the value of a piece. First of all, his judgment must include the recognition of fine workmanship, whatever the material. A knowledge of the designs used and a taste for good design will also be an aid in judging the value of a tea caddy. Precious materials such as silver, ivory, tortoise shell or fine wood also determine the value of a tea caddy. Good proportions and a pleasing shape—rounds and ovals are rarer—as well as good condition are also facts determining the value of the caddy.

BIBLIOGRAPHY

The Dictionary of English Furniture, by Percy Macquoid and Ralph Edwards, Charles Scribner's Sons, New York.

Apollo Magazine, Vol. 23, 1936; Vol. 37, 1943.

The Magazine Antiques—see Cumulative Index.

Old English Furniture and Its Surroundings, Mac Ivor Percival, William Heinemann, London, 1920.

INDEX